An OP

The Building of t

John Pinder is a Visiting Professo

and Chairman of the Federal Trust in London. He was the Director of the Policy Studies Institute from 1964 to 1985. He has given courses in five European countries and speaks five European languages. His books include *Britain and the Common Market* (1961), *The Economics of Europe* (1971), *Federal Union: The Pioneers* (with Richard Mayne, 1990), and *The European Community and Eastern Europe* (1991).

OPUS General Editors

OPUS books provide concise, original, and authoritative introductions to a wide range of subjects in the humanities and sciences. They are written by experts for the general reader as well as for students.

The Building of the European Union

John Pinder

THIRD EDITION

Oxford New York
OXFORD UNIVERSITY PRESS
1998

Oxford University Press, Great Clarendon Street, Oxford OX2 6DP
Oxford New York
Athens Auckland Bangkok Bogotá Buenos Aires Calcutta
Cape Town Chennai Dar es Salaam Delhi Florence Hong Kong Istanbul
Karachi Kuala Lumpur Madrid Melbourne Mexico City Mumbai
Nairobi Paris São Paulo Singapore Taipei Tokyo Toronto Warsaw
and associated companies in Berlin Ibadan

Oxford is a registered trade mark of Oxford University Press

First Published as European Community *1991*

Second edition first published as an Oxford University Press paperback 1995

Third edition published as The Building of the European Union *1998*

British Library Cataloguing in Publication Data
Data available

Library of Congress Cataloging in Publication Data
Data available

ISBN 0–19–289315–7

1 3 5 7 9 10 8 6 4 2

Typeset in Times 10/12pt
by Stephen Wright-Bouvier of the Rainwater Consultancy, Faringdon, Oxfordshire
Printed in Great Britain by
Cox & Wyman, Reading, Berkshire

Contents

Acknowledgements

This book is the product of over four decades of reflection about the European Community and now the European Union: why and how it has developed since its foundation. My view has been influenced during this period by the critique of sovereignty, leading to the idea of federal union, which was evolved in Britain in the decade up to World War Two and of which Altiero Spinelli was the foremost post-war exponent, and by the example of Jean Monnet, who showed how union could be approached through a series of substantial steps.

I also owe much to countless other people from many countries who have helped me to acquire knowledge and generate ideas about the subject. Among the bodies that have provided a context for this I am particularly indebted to the Federal Trust in London and the College of Europe in Bruges. For comments on various chapters of the book I am grateful to Geoffrey Denton, David Coombes, Richard Corbett, Nigel Haigh, Robert Hine, Christopher Johnson, Guillaume McLaughlin, Edmund Neville-Rolfe, Simon Nuttall, Michael Shackleton, and Dennis Swann, and on the whole text to John Palmer and Pauline Pinder. The responsibility for any remaining errors and, for better or worse, for the ideas behind the book is entirely my own.

Foreword

The aim of this book is to explain how the European Community has become the European Union of today, from the laying of its first foundation in 1950. It tries to show how and why the powers, policies and institutions have developed through the subsequent half-century. The first edition was written at the end of its first four decades, and much can still be learnt from that experience. But much too can be learnt from the great changes which have occurred since.

In 1990 the Soviet Union still existed, Germany was in the process of unification, the Maastricht Treaty was still on the drawing-board, Mrs Thatcher was Prime Minister of the United Kingdom, and Jacques Delors President of the European Commission. Since then, the Maastricht Treaty has established the European Union, strengthening the powers and institutions of the Community and setting up the flanking 'pillars' for co-operation on internal and external security and foreign policy. The single market has been largely completed. The euro has been adopted as the single currency by most of the member states. Austria, Finland, and Sweden have joined and negotiations are in train for the accession of the Czech Republic, Estonia, Hungary, Poland, Slovenia, and Cyprus. There have been major agricultural and budgetary reforms. The Amsterdam Treaty, if and when it is ratified, brings further institutional reform.

These and many other events have made it necessary to produce a radically revised book. It also has a new title that better reflects the new reality, while retaining the essential significance of the old one. The Union is seen as the result of a process which has built many federal elements into a structure where the intergovernmental principle remains strong. The future of the Union, in particular the relationship between the federal and the intergovernmental principles, is far from certain. But on this point the reader should be warned. The Union is in my view more likely than not to develop farther in a federal direction; and should do so.

May 1998 JOHN PINDER

Abbreviations

Note

With the revisions of the treaties at Maastricht and Amsterdam, the numbering of the articles has become unduly complicated. The Amsterdam Treaty therefore provides for a logical renumbering. If and when this Treaty enters into force, the reader may for some years ahead be using old or new copies of the treaty texts. So where this book refers to specific articles of the European Union Treaty (EUT) or the European Community Treaty (ECT), the pre-Amsterdam number is given first, then the post-Amsterdam number is given after an oblique stroke. Thus Article A EUT, which becomes Article 1, is written Article A/1 EUT, while Article 157 ECT, which becomes Article 213, is written Article 157/213 ECT. Likewise Title IIIa ECT, which becomes Title IV, is written Title IIIa/IV ECT. Where there is no change, only the one number is given. While not very convenient, this seems to be the least inconvenient formula. Such is life in the EC/EU.

ACP	African, Caribbean, Pacific countries
BSE	Bovine Spongiform Encephalitis
CFC	chlorofluorocarbon
CFSP	common foreign and security policy
CIS	Commonwealth of Independent States
CO_2	carbon dioxide
Comecon	Council for Mutual Economic Assistance
Coreper	Committee of Permanent Representatives
CSCE	Conference on Security and Co-operation in Europe
EAGGF	European Agricultural Guidance and Guarantee Fund
EC	European Community
ECB	European Central Bank
ECSC	European Coal and Steel Community
ECT	European Community Treaty
ecu	European currency unit (equals £0.7, $1.1 in May 1998)
EDF	European Development Fund

EEA	European Economic Area
EEC	European Economic Community
Efta	European Free Trade Association
EMI	European Monetary Institute
EMS	European Monetary System
Emu	economic and monetary union
EPC	European Political Co-operation
ERM	Exchange Rate Mechanism
ESCB	European System of Central Banks
Euratom	European Atomic Energy Community
Gatt	General Agreement on Tariffs and Trade
GDP	gross domestic product
GNP	gross national product
GSP	Generalized System of Preferences
IGC	Intergovernmental Conference
IT	information technology
Maastricht Treaty	*see* TEU
MCA	monetary compensatory amount
MFA	Multi-Fibre Arrangement
mfn	most-favoured nation
Nato	North Atlantic Treaty Organization
NCE	non-compulsory expenditure
OECD	Organization for Economic Co-operation and Development
OEEC	Organization for European Economic Co-operation
PHARE	Poland and Hungary: aid for economic reconstruction (extended to other Central and East European countries)
SEA	Single European Act
Single Act	*see* SEA
TACIS	Technical Assistance to the Commonwealth of Independent States
TEU	Treaty on European Union
VAT	value-added tax
WTO	World Trade Organization

Introduction

The European Union is in 1998 on the threshold of great changes. The euro is to become the single currency for most of the member states. Negotiations for the accession of six new states have begun and membership, which already covers almost all of Western Europe, will before long extend to most of Central and Eastern Europe too. The Union's institutions will be reformed. Its powers may reach beyond the economy and the environment into the fields of foreign policy and defence.

The Union, and the Community which preceded and is part of it, has never been easy to understand. It escapes the conventional categories of international relations and federal state. It stands between the two, pulled in one direction by the power of the nation-state and in the other by integrative forces.

The nation-state has had its charismatic champions, most notably President de Gaulle and subsequently Prime Minister Thatcher. It is also protected by a multitude of lesser defenders occupying positions of power in politics, the administration, and the economy of the member states. Its role in the inter-state system is rationalized by academics of the realist and neo-realist schools.

The integrative forces have included economic interests apt to gain from the larger market and political interests seeking security and influence for the member states. From the founding initiative of Jean Monnet up to the period of Helmut Kohl and Jacques Delors, there has also been the impulsion of federalists, who have sought to establish a system of European democratic government as a framework for peace and prosperity. Following the example of Monnet, they have worked to put in place successive elements of federal powers and institutions to deal with particular problems, allying themselves to this end with specific economic and political interests. The neofunctionalists went some way towards explaining the process. The concluding chapter of this book tries to show in what ways they fell short and how a more complete explanation may be devised.

While the member states retain much of their power, the integrative forces have changed the political map of Europe and continue to do so. The aim of this book is to show where the Union now stands between conventional international relations and federal system, and how the dialectic of nation-state and integrative forces has brought it to that point.

1 Creating the Community and the Union: Nation-State and Federal Idea

The European Community, which remains the central element in the European Union, is a remarkable innovation in relations among states. Its institutions are more powerful than those of conventional international organizations, and offer more scope for development. Much of their specific character was determined in a few weeks in the summer of 1950, when representatives of the six founder members, France, the German Federal Republic, Italy, Belgium, the Netherlands, and Luxembourg, agreed on the outline of the Treaty to establish the European Coal and Steel Community. The initiative had been taken by Robert Schuman, the French foreign minister, who explained the gist of his proposal with these words:

> . . . the French Government proposes to take action immediately on one limited but decisive point . . . to place Franco-German production of coal and steel under a common High Authority, within the framework of an organisation open to the participation of the other countries of Europe . . . The solidarity in production thus established will make it plain that any war between France and Germany becomes not merely unthinkable, but materially impossible . . . this proposal will build the first concrete foundation of a European federation which is indispensable to the preservation of peace . . .[1]

World War Two, national sovereignty, the federal idea

World War Two was a catastrophe that discredited the previous international order and, for many Europeans, the basic element in that order: the absolutely sovereign nation-state. In the Europe of such states, France and Germany had been at war three times in less than a century, twice at the centre of terrible world wars. Autarky and protection, fragmenting Europe's economy, had caused economic malaise and political antagonism. Fascist glorification of the nation-state had been revealed as a monstrosity; and many felt that insistence on its sovereignty, even without fascist excess, distorted and ossified the political perspective.

This critique pointed towards the limitation of national sovereignty. It was accepted by many people of the anti-fascist resistance, in Germany and Italy as well as the occupied countries. While the idea of limiting sovereignty in a united Europe was widespread, some influential figures were more precise. They envisaged a federal constitution for Europe, giving powers over trade, money, security, and related taxation, to a federal parliament, government, and court, leaving all other powers to be exercised by the institutions of the member states.[2]

Such ideas evoked a ready echo from those Europeans who asked themselves why the war had occurred and what could be done to ensure a better future; and they were encouraged by Winston Churchill who, in a speech in Zurich in September 1946, suggested that France should lead Germany into a United States of Europe. Not everybody noticed that he was reticent about the part that Britain should play in such a union; and many, impressed by the magnanimous vision of the wartime leader with his immense prestige, did not realize how hard it would be to accomplish. For despite the popularity of the federal idea in Continental countries, the structures of the states were gathering strength again and were to prove resistant to radical federal reform.

Some of this resistance stemmed from the principle of national sovereignty as a basic political value. General de Gaulle was to be the most powerful and eloquent exponent of this view; and Mrs Thatcher was a subsequent protagonist. But most of the resisters were more pragmatic. Many bureaucrats, central bankers, and politicians would allow that sovereignty could in principle be shared on the right terms and at the right time: but the right terms were not on offer and the right time would be later.

Two main strategies were devised to overcome the reluctance of governments. One, promoted by the Italian federalist leader, Altiero Spinelli, was to mobilize popular support for a constituent assembly, in which the people's representatives would draw up a European constitution. But this idea bore little fruit until, with the direct elections to the European Parliament in 1979, Spinelli persuaded the people's newly elected representatives to design and approve a Draft Treaty to constitute a European Union. The other strategy, devised by Jean Monnet, was to identify a 'limited but decisive point', as Schuman's declaration put it, on which governments could be persuaded to agree and which, without going the whole way, would mark a significant step towards federation. With this idea, Monnet was to secure an early and spectacular success.

Founding the Community: the ECSC

Monnet's 'limited but decisive point' was the need for a new structure to contain the resurgent heavy industries of the Ruhr, the traditional economic basis for Germany's military might, which had been laid low as a result of the war. It was clear by 1950 that industry in West Germany must develop if Germans were to pay their way in the world and help the West in its rivalry with the Soviet Union, and that this required the revival of German steel production. Of the western Allies then responsible for West Germany, the United States and Britain were increasingly insistent on this. France, through history and geography more sensitive to the potential danger of German power, insisted that the Ruhr's heavy industries should be kept under control. But France lacked the means to restrain the Americans and British; and there were Frenchmen in key positions who realized that the perpetuation of an international Ruhr authority such as had been set up in 1948 to exert control over the Germans, apart from being unacceptable to the two Allies, would be an unstable arrangement, apt to be overturned by Germany at the first opportunity. Hence the idea of a common structure to govern the coal and steel industries, not only of the Ruhr but also of

France and other European countries.

This idea was not the invention of Monnet alone. Officials in the French foreign ministry were also working on it.[3] But they would surely have created a conventional international organization, governed by committees of ministers, whereas Monnet was determined that the new institutions should have a political life independent of the existing governments: that they should be 'the first concrete foundation of a European federation'.

It is the theme of this book that the concept of European institutions which go beyond a conventional system of intergovernmental co-operation, however imperfectly realized, has given the Community, and now the Union, its special character: its stability, capacity for achievement, and promise for the future. It is of course possible to argue that the Community is, on the contrary, essentially an intergovernmental organization to secure free trade and economic co-operation, and that the rest is frills and rhetoric. This book sets out a case for seeing it as more than that.

Monnet, from his vantage point as head of the French *Commissariat du Plan*, persuaded Schuman to adopt the more radical project; and he did it at the moment when the French government was most apt to accept, because a solution to the problem of German steel could no longer be delayed. Monnet's solution had the merit of meeting not only the French national interest in the control of German steel but also a wider interest in the development of European political institutions. The proposal was immediately welcomed by the governments of West Germany, Italy, Belgium, the Netherlands, and Luxembourg; and it was enthusiastically received by the wide sectors of opinion in those countries and in France that could be called broadly federalist, in the sense of supporting steps towards a federal end, even if not all would be precise in defining this. The project also received strong and steady support from the United States.

Support for the federal idea had mushroomed in Britain too in 1939 and the first half of 1940, culminating with the Churchill government's proposal for union with France.[4] But after the fall of France in June 1940, with Nazi domination of the Continent, British interest in European union ebbed. For more than a decade after the war, British governments wanted to confine their relationship with the Continent to no more than a loose association. They were not ready to accept the federal implications of Monnet's proposal. So the six founder members negotiated the Treaty establishing the European Coal and Steel Community (ECSC) without Britain or the other West European countries that took the same view.

As chairman of the intergovernmental conference that drew up the ECSC Treaty, Monnet was well placed to ensure that his basic idea was followed through. The High Authority was to be the executive responsible for policy relating to the coal and steel industries in the member countries, and its decisions were to apply directly to the economic agents in each country, without requiring the approval of its government. The policies envisaged in the Treaty bore the mark of French planning ideas. Investment in the two industries was to be influenced by the High Authority, though not subject to much control. Prices and production could be regulated, but only if there were crises of shortage or over-production. Policies for training, housing, and redeployment were to cater for workers' needs. Competition was at the same time to be stimulated by rules on price transparency, as well as by anti-trust laws on American lines.

Monnet insisted on the principle of the High Authority's independence from the member states' governments because his experience as an international civil servant had convinced him that it would be hamstrung if they controlled it too directly. But that raised the question of the High Authority's accountability. Monnet, in his inaugural speech as the first President of the High Authority in August 1952, was to explain the Treaty's answer like this. The High Authority was to be responsible to an Assembly (now called the European Parliament), which would eventually be directly elected, and which had the power to dismiss it. There was recourse to the European Court of Justice in cases that concerned the High Authority's acts. In short, the powers defined by the Treaty would be exercised by institutions with federal characteristics, sovereign within the limits of their competences. The policy of the High

Authority and those of the member states would be 'harmonized' by a Council of ministers, voting by majority 'save in exceptional cases'. Monnet ensured that the federal elements in the Community would be clearly explained by employing Spinelli's help in drafting the speech.[5]

Monnet's idea was that the European federation would be built over the years on this 'first concrete foundation' as new sectors of activity were brought within the scope of the pre-federal institutions; and the establishment of the European Economic Community and Euratom in 1958 lent remarkable support to this view. But he does not appear to have foreseen how much the Council would come to dominate the politics of the Community, as the political structures of member states came to assert themselves against the realization of the federal idea. This reaction led to a long-drawn-out conflict within the Community, which began with a major assault by General de Gaulle as President of France and continued up to the 1990s, with Britain succeeding de Gaulle as champion of national sovereignty. But first, there was to be an early rehearsal in the political battle over the project for a European Defence Community.

The failure of the Defence Community

In June 1950, a few days after the conference to draw up the ECSC Treaty had begun, the Communist North Korean regime invaded South Korea. This, following the coup in Czechoslovakia and the Berlin blockade which had demonstrated Stalin's will to build up Soviet power in Central Europe, convinced the Americans that the defence of Western Europe required a military contribution from West Germany. As they began to press for this, France was again confronted by the question that had arisen when German steel production was to be expanded: how to square French security with a revival of German power.

Monnet was among those who found the same answer to the issue of defence as he had to that of steel: to pool the resources of France, West Germany, and other European democracies in a

European Defence Community (EDC). The French proposal for a European army quickly secured the support of the governments of France's five ECSC partners and the six countries began to draw up an EDC Treaty. But this time the project 'touched on the core of national sovereignty', as Monnet was to put it, concluding that 'Now, the federation of Europe would have to become an immediate objective'.[6] The six governments did not at first appear to recognize the implications of this for their states, and negotiated about defence integration without paying much attention to the political structure to which the integrated forces were to be responsible. But this issue did not escape the notice of Spinelli, who had given much thought to the problem of integrating nation-states in a European federation. He persuaded the Italian government that federal institutions would be required to control a European army and the Italian government persuaded its five partners that such institutions must be envisaged.[7] They invited the newly established ECSC Assembly, slightly adapted for the purpose, to design a Treaty for a European Political Community. The result was a quasi-federal constitution to complement the EDC Treaty, which was itself ratified by West Germany and the Benelux countries (Belgium, the Netherlands, and Luxembourg), with the Italian parliament waiting on French ratification.

Here, however, the project ran up against the defence of national sovereignty, stronger in France than in the other five countries. Stalinist Communists and nationalist Gaullists were root-and-branch opponents; and they were joined by enough doubters from the centre parties to create, by 1954, a parliamentary majority against the EDC Treaty, which was accordingly abandoned by the Assemblée Nationale in August of that year. Many of these doubters had supported the proposal in principle, but feared that Germany would come to dominate the Community in the absence of British participation. But the British were, like the Gaullists, determined to preserve their national sovereignty. So the EDC project failed; and many doubted whether the federal idea could recover from this apparently decisive defeat.

The Treaties of Rome

Despite this setback, the federalist forces regained the initiative within a matter of months, returning to the economic field where national sovereignty seemed less directly threatened. The Benelux countries put forward a proposal for a common market to cover the whole of trade, not just one sector like the ECSC. This appealed to economic liberals and the more dynamic businesspeople, particularly in Germany and the Netherlands; and to many it promised a European economy big enough to accommodate the scale and specialization required for contemporary technologies, and thus to compete with the United States, then still the world's unchallenged economic superpower. Monnet, continuing his sectoral approach, was meanwhile developing a scheme for an Atomic Energy Community, responding to one of the recurrent phases of European worry about energy supplies. This project was more popular in France, and the two together were taken up by the governments of the six ECSC countries at the Messina conference in June 1955, less than a year after the failure of the EDC. Again with strong American support, and against Britain's sceptical aloofness, the Six negotiated the two Treaties of Rome, signed in that city in March 1957, establishing the European Economic Community (EEC) and the European Atomic Energy Community (Euratom), which entered into force on 1 January 1958.

The EEC's institutions were modelled on those of the ECSC. It shared from the outset the same Parliamentary Assembly and Court of Justice. The significant difference lay, however, in the relationship between the EEC's executive and its ministerial Council. Instead of High Authority, the new executive was called the Commission; and this reflected a weakening of the federalist impulse and a strengthening of the ministers representing member states' governments over against the independent European executive. With de Gaulle as President of France from June 1958, this reaction was accentuated, and when the institutions of the three Communities were fully merged into one set of Community institutions in 1965, the merged executive was likewise called the Commission.

It was the scope of the powers which these institutions exercised that made the EEC a radical new departure. The creation of a common market for all goods and services was a project of great political and economic significance. The economies of the six member states had been separated by tariffs, quotas, and non-tariff barriers. The EEC Treaty set the aim of abolishing all these barriers on trade between them. The non-tariff barriers comprised a host of laws, regulations, and official practices that impeded trade, and their complexity made their removal difficult to ensure. The Treaty set the objective of removing them but left the methods to be settled later; and this remained largely undone until the 1980s, when the single market programme was set in train. But the tariff had been the great historic instrument of protection; and quantitative restrictions on imports, or quotas, had also been rife in the post-war period. The removal of all tariffs and quotas from the trade among member states was a truly radical project; and here the Treaty was decisive, setting out in detail a programme for eliminating them progressively over a transitional period of 12–15 years. On imports from outside the Community, the member states' existing tariffs, above average for France and Italy, below for Germany and Benelux, were to be aligned on a common external tariff, itself generally at the average level, over the same transitional period.

While this customs union was the backbone of the EEC Treaty, the Treaty also provided for many of the other common economic policies to be expected in a federal system. Apart from the removal of non-tariff distortions to trade, there was provision for the free movement of workers, enterprises, and capital throughout the Community. There were chapters on agricultural, transport, and competition policy. Social policy was included, in the sense of policy relating to employment. A Social Fund and an Investment Bank were established. 'Overseas countries' (then colonies) and territories were to be associated. The policies were to be financed by a Community budget, whose income would eventually come from its 'own resources'—a euphemism for its own taxation which has persisted until now.

Euratom was given similar institutions to govern, like the ECSC, a particular sector of the economy: the 'nuclear industries' in their application to peaceful purposes. It was to promote research, investment, and infrastructure; create a common market for the sector; and ensure safety and the use of nuclear materials only for the intended purposes.

Euratom came too close to the heart of de Gaulle's concept of national sovereignty: his nuclear *force de frappe*. He marginalized it into an agency whose main function was to encourage research. Nor is it a coincidence that one economic power essential to a federal system with which the Economic Community was poorly endowed was the control of monetary policy, in particular the issuing of money by a federal bank, for this was seen as the citadel of economic sovereignty. The Treaties of Rome preceded de Gaulle's return to power as French President and champion of the cause of national sovereignty. But the forces defending the retention of this basic economic prerogative in the institutions of the member states were nevertheless too strong for the federalist-minded designers of the EEC Treaty to challenge.

Despite the eclipse of Euratom and the EEC's lack of monetary powers, the Community, as the three Communities collectively soon came to be called, forged ahead with the establishment of the customs union. With a booming economy and strong support from industry, the programme for tariff cuts was accelerated. At least part of the good performance of the Community economy in the EEC's early years was attributed to this wholesale removal of protection. The Community's external tariff, far from provoking protectionism in the international economy, was moreover the catalyst for multilateral tariff cuts on an unprecedented scale, particularly the Kennedy round of Gatt negotiations in the mid-1960s which led to cuts averaging one-third across the board by the industrialized countries. At the same time the common agricultural policy was put in place: a major political achievement even if it was later to become a sorcerer's apprentice, flooding the Community with wasteful expenditure and the world market with surpluses.

The successes of the ECSC and of the EEC in its early

period were reflected in the theory which the American political scientists who developed it called neofunctionalism.[8] Their idea was that, once the political decision had been taken to establish supranational institutions in one sector, a new constellation of political forces would extend the area of integration to other sectors until it covered the main fields of political activity. Political parties and interest groups would focus on the new institutions in the sectors of their initial competence. But the realization of their objectives would be frustrated by those institutions' lack of powers in related sectors, not yet integrated, where the effect of the supranational decisions could be negated. The new supranational political forces would help to resolve the contradiction by promoting the transfer of the related sectors to supranational competence.

The merit of this theory was to consider the novel circumstances of the Community, which has more federal elements than other international organizations but falls short of being a federation, whereas many federalists had concentrated on the idea of a federal constitution without giving much thought to the confederal system that was likely to precede it. The neofunctionalists also had the merit of going beyond a snapshot of the Community to treat it as a process of development over time. In the first period of euphoria about the Community, up to the early 1960s, their ideas had much influence in Europe. But their fascination with the new institutions, and their addiction to the 'welfarist' tendency then prevalent to underrate the strength of other values and of existing institutions, led them to ignore the power of national sovereignty and the nation-state. They even went so far at times as to suppose that the process of transferring powers from member states to supranational institutions, or 'spillover' as they called it, would be automatic. This notion was rudely rebutted by de Gaulle, the leading contemporary embodiment of national sovereignty.

Stagnation

General de Gaulle made his concept of the Community quite explicit: '. . . there is and can be no Europe other than a

Europe of the States—except, of course, for myths, fictions and pageants'.[9] Until 1962, de Gaulle was preoccupied with domestic French problems and with bringing the Algerian war to an end. This he succeeded in doing in that year, thus freeing himself to give his attention to his quarrels with the federalists in the Community and the 'anglo-saxons' outside it. His initial offensive was his veto, in January 1963, on Britain's first attempt to join the Community, negotiations about which were by then far advanced. This was a blow not only to the British, but also to the Community practice of taking decisions on EC matters collectively after thorough discussion, whereas de Gaulle's veto was announced at a press conference without discussion with his partners.

This episode was followed by a conflict over the financing of the Community budget, which was seen as a major French interest, since France had a strong agricultural production that the common agricultural policy was designed to help finance. But this interest would be secure only if other member states lost the power to cut off the funds for the agricultural budget: that is, if the Community was to have its own budgetary resources, instead of depending on contributions from the governments. The Commission and the Dutch, with support from other member states, insisted that if tax money was to go direct to the Community without the need for approval each year by member states' parliaments, its expenditure must be subject to the approval of the relevant elected representatives, that is of the European Parliament. This federalist logic convinced most of those who wanted further development of the Community. But it was anathema to de Gaulle. The Commission hoped that the French interest in securing the finance for agriculture would outweigh de Gaulle's concern for national sovereignty. But de Gaulle was not amenable to neofunctionalist spillover. He withdrew his ministers from the EC Council from 1 July 1965—the policy of the empty chair—and expressed his doubts about the future of the Community. Boycotted by its leading member government, the Community was in evident crisis. But in the first round of the French presidential elections in December, de Gaulle failed to get a majority. The French public was apparently not best pleased with what seemed like threats to withdraw from the Community. The second round was won by a de Gaulle who had started to speak less caustically about the Community; and in January 1966 he sent his ministers to Luxembourg to patch it up with his partners. The result was known as the Luxembourg compromise: a statement in which the French delegation asserted a right of veto in the Council 'when very important interests are at stake', while the other five maintained their stand in defence of the majority vote where the Treaties stipulated it. The issue of parliamentary control of the budget, which had ignited the quarrel, was shelved.

Some useful lessons can be drawn from this trial of strength between national sovereignty and federal reform. The first is that, even if some politicians may have grand notions of abandoning the Community for the principle of national sovereignty, the public is not keen to follow. This has been demonstrated in elections and referendums not only in France, but also in Britain. A second is that, with France's participation essential to the Community, neither spillover nor federal reform stood a chance when faced with de Gaulle's stand on national sovereignty. A third, first shown by the grant of budgetary powers to the European Parliament after de Gaulle's departure in 1969, is that the logic of reform can outlast the nationalist leaders. Yet ministers and civil servants of member states continued to show themselves more than comfortable with the practice of continuing discussion in the Council until unanimity was reached even if that should take a decade or more, which was one of the results of the Luxembourg 'compromise'. It was not until the Single European Act was signed in 1986 that the principle of majority voting began to become generally accepted in the Council.

The unanimity procedure, or, more crudely put, the veto, was a major reason why even after de Gaulle's demise the Community faced a lengthy period of only slow development, apart from its enlargement from six member states to twelve. The enlargement was certainly a very substantial achievement. The accession of Denmark, the Irish Republic, and the United

Kingdom in 1973, of Greece in 1981, and of Portugal and Spain in 1986 was a tribute both to the success of the Community, which made them want to join, and to its adaptability, which enabled them to do so. But the use of the Community's powers was dilatory and weak; and the development of its powers and institutions was limited, even though a number of steps were taken to strengthen them.

When Britain joined, with a grievance about the unfavourable bias of the Community's agricultural and budgetary system, the Regional Development Fund was set up, intended as a counterweight; and the Social Fund was expanded in the following years. The European Monetary System, which began to operate in 1979, was an important step towards monetary union. Institutional steps in a federal direction included powers of co-legislation for the European Parliament with the Council over part of the budget and the creation of the Court of Auditors to help budgetary control (1970 and 1975); direct elections to the Parliament (first held in 1979); and a steady growth in the role of the Court of Justice. The European Council of heads of state and government (from 1974) was a parallel innovation of an intergovernmental character, as was the 'European Political Co-operation' (from 1970) aiming to co-ordinate member states' foreign policies. With these and a number of other successes, some quite small but cumulatively significant, the Community arrived at the mid-1980s not only enlarged to include nine-tenths of the population of Western Europe, but also with its powers and institutions somewhat enhanced.

Apart from the Community's enlargement, however, the two decades from the mid-1960s to the mid-1980s can be seen as a long period of stagnation. Even if some steps were taken that strengthened the Community, its capacity to solve its principal problems was demonstrated to be dangerously weak. The agricultural budget in particular continued to consume between two-thirds and three-quarters of the Community's budgetary resources, aggravating the quarrel with Britain and the dissatisfaction of Germany, the other net contributor; provoking tension with the United States and others through the excessive subsidization of EC exports; pre-empting money that might have been used to finance new policies for the Community; and giving the impression of a Community that was incapable of action where it was really needed.

Enlargement brings with it objective problems: greater diversity and new interests to be accommodated. It also brought the British, less unyielding than de Gaulle but with a rooted objection to relinquishment of national sovereignty. The French, for their part, were only gradually to relax their attachment to de Gaulle's brand of nationalism; and as they did so, the Germans grew to feel more strongly that they were entitled to their share of autonomy too. Danes and Greeks proved awkward in various ways. Few were inclined to be amenable in a time of oil shocks and stagflation. All these things aggravated the fundamental problem of a polity confronted by growing pressures to take action on a wide front but depending heavily on securing agreement among a number of governments in order to do so.

It is not surprising that many observers concluded that the Community, after its initial flying start, had become stuck as a complicated intergovernmental organization, more powerful perhaps than most others but not essentially different. There was, according to this 'realist' school of thought, little prospect that it would become stronger in the future, let alone that there would be further steps in a federal direction. From the mid-1980s, however, this reductionist view, which had seemed to many plausible during the Community's years of stagnation, began to appear less realistic.

Regeneration

During the first half of 1984, when France occupied the Presidency of the Council, two long-standing problems were resolved: the terms of accession for Portugal and Spain, and the compensation for Britain to set against its net contribution to the Community budget. President Mitterrand also lent support to the European Parliament's federalist-oriented Draft Treaty to establish a European Union, which the Parliament, inspired by Spinelli, had approved by a large majority in

February of that year. A year later, the European Council approved the Commission's ambitious programme, strongly supported by leading industrialists, to complete the single market by the end of 1992; and under the impulse of this and of the European Parliament's Draft Treaty, the member states negotiated the first major revision of the Community Treaties, embodied in the Single European Act, which came into force in July 1987.

The Single Act extended the scope of majority voting in the Council to include most of the decisions required for completing the internal market, and gave the European Parliament the right, under a new 'co-operation procedure', to a role in relation to those decisions that went some way beyond consultation, though still well short of co-legislation with the Council requiring laws to be approved by both. The Parliament also secured the power to grant or withhold its 'assent' to association agreements and to the accession of new member states. The Single Act defined a Community competence in the fields of environment, technology, and conditions at work; set monetary union as a Community objective and gave the European Monetary System a basis in the treaties; formalized the system of foreign policy co-operation, and extended it to the 'political and economic aspects of security'. Importantly for the new members from the Community's South, the Single Act recognized the need for 'cohesion', or financial support for the weaker economies in the Community, lest they should lose out in the freer trade resulting from the single market.

Agreement on the Single Act and progress with the decisions required to complete the single market gave the Community the momentum it needed to bind up the running sore of its agri-budgetary crisis. The Commission's President, Jacques Delors, put forward a comprehensive proposal to deal with it. This included 'stabilizers' to keep agricultural expenditure under control; a new tax resource to provide additional revenue, more fairly distributed among the member countries than hitherto; continued compensation to reduce Britain's net payment to the EC budget; and a doubling of the 'structural funds', as instruments of the cohesion policy. The European

Council agreed a settlement along these lines in February 1988, resolving at least for a time a problem that had dogged the Community for a decade. Building on this success, the European Council in June 1988 charged a committee, chaired by Delors, to draw up proposals for an economic and monetary union (Emu). The project gathered support from businesspeople who saw it as a completion of the single market project; from public authorities that wished to reassert, collectively, the control over monetary policy that was being eroded by the opening of the economies and financial markets; and from those who saw it as a major element in political integration. So the Delors report led to an Intergovernmental Conference (IGC) to consider the treaty amendments needed to establish economic and monetary union.

While the IGC on economic and monetary union was being prepared, the countries of Central Europe began in 1989 to emerge from under the Soviet hegemony, to be followed by East Europeans and, in 1991, by the dissolution of the Soviet Union itself. One of the early consequences was the unification of Germany in October 1990. This led both France and Germany to seek closer political integration of the Community: France, in order once again to anchor Germany more firmly in the Community system; Germany, to balance this eastwards extension by consolidating the western relationship that had provided a framework for four decades of prosperity and peace. The proposal of Chancellor Kohl and President Mitterrand that an IGC on political union be held in parallel with that on economic and monetary union was adopted by the European Council in June 1990; and the two IGCs resulted in agreement on the Treaty on European Union (TEU), at the European Council meeting in Maastricht in December 1991.[10]

Maastricht and after

The IGC on economic and monetary union produced a highly structured design based on a single currency and a European Central Bank, together with a phased programme for establishing them by 1999, even if not all member states would then participate. The IGC on political union was less coherent. The main elements of political union were to be a common foreign and security policy (CFSP) together with a strengthening of the Community and its institutions, to which was added 'cooperation in the fields of justice and home affairs' to deal with the implications of open frontiers within the Union for matters such as asylum, immigration, and crime.

The Union was 'founded on the European Communities, supplemented by' the other 'forms of cooperation': the CFSP and the co-operation in justice and home affairs (Article A/1 TEU).* The institutional arrangements for the latter were to be more intergovernmental than those of the Community. The EEC, renamed the European Community, remained the centrepiece of the Union, with its institutions somewhat strengthened and competences enhanced. The European Parliament in particular gained some powers: the right to approve—or not—the appointment of the Commission; co-decision with the Council in a dozen fields of legislation; extension of the power of assent, to include some international agreements. The consultative Committee of the Regions was established. A form of Union citizenship was defined. In addition to the major new power over currency, the Community's competences were extended in more than a dozen fields, including education, vocational training, youth, social policy, culture, public health, consumer protection, trans-European infrastructure networks, industry, research and technological development, cohesion, environment, and development co-operation. At the same time the principle of subsidiarity was affirmed, restricting the actions of the Community to those where the objectives 'cannot be sufficiently achieved by the Member States and can therefore, by reason of the scale or effects of the proposed action, be better achieved by the Community' (Article 3b ECT).[11] Protocols to the Treaty provided that Britain and Denmark could opt out of the single currency project and Britain out of the 'social chapter' too.

The structure of the Treaty reflected the complexity of these arrangements. The bulk of it consisted of amendments to the EEC Treaty, including the change of name from European

* For explanation of the numbering of articles, see Note on p. ix.

Economic Community to European Community—though the term 'Community' is still normally used to denote the three Communities: ECSC, EEC, and Euratom. Thus the Treaty on European Union, in its Title II, amended but did not replace the European Community Treaty (ECT), which remains central to the whole construction. The Treaties establishing the European Coal and Steel Community and the European Atomic Energy Community were likewise amended in Titles III and IV. Title V then provided for the CFSP and Title VI for the co-operation in justice and home affairs. The aim of Titles I and VII/VIII was to link the whole together. The European Union encompassed all these elements; and the term 'Union' is now generally used to refer to any or all of them, including the Community. This practice is followed in this book, save where the term Union is inappropriate: for example, where the text refers to the time before Maastricht, when the Union did not exist; or where it relates to matters such as the Community's legal system, which has not applied to the CFSP or the co-operation in justice and home affairs. The Treaty on European Union is likewise called the Maastricht Treaty unless there is particular reason why the formal title should be used.

The Maastricht Treaty was signed in March 1992 but the process of ratification proved laborious. The Danes, whose government wanted to be the first to ratify, rejected the Treaty in a referendum in June 1992 by 50.7 to 49.3 per cent. This encouraged the Treaty's opponents not only in Britain, but also in France whose referendum in September approved it only by the 'petit oui' of 51.05 to 48.95 per cent. The debate in the House of Commons was lengthy and fraught, with the Conservative government's small majority countered by the substantial number of its backbenchers who opposed the treaty; it was not until August 1992 that the UK was able to ratify. The Treaty was challenged in an appeal to Germany's Constitutional Court, which took until October 1992 to deliver the judgment that it did not conflict with the German constitution. The other member states had ratified meanwhile, including Denmark, whose voters reversed their decision in a second referendum after their government had obtained a further opt-out with respect to defence and a reassertion of its opt-out from the single currency. The Treaty came into force in November 1993, nearly a year later than had been intended.

The strength of opposition to the Treaty, not only in Britain and Denmark, but also in France, which had from the outset been a prime mover in the Community's progress, undermined confidence in the Union's future development. The money markets, which had counted on the success of the single currency project, were shaken by the results of first the Danish, then the French referendum; and speculation disrupted the stability of the European Monetary System, first in September 1992 when Britain and Italy had to leave its exchange rate mechanism and then again in August 1993 when the mechanism had to be loosened to accommodate the fluctuation of the French franc. The currency instability was exacerbated by the transmission to other member states of the high interest rates that had resulted in Germany from the economic strains of unification, with a consequent depressing effect on the recession that the member states were already undergoing. The rise in the Union's rate of unemployment to over 10 per cent further soured the political atmosphere. Nor was the atmosphere improved by the Union's failure to work effectively for peace in Bosnia.

Disturbed by these things and finding the Maastricht Treaty hard to understand, citizens' support for the Union tended to weaken. Yet the Union remained attractive enough to encourage other Europeans to want to join. Four of the Efta states, Austria, Finland, Norway, and Sweden, concluded treaties of accession. Norwegian voters rejected theirs in a referendum, as they had previously done when their government sought to join at the same time as Britain, Denmark, and Ireland. But the other three joined in 1995.

The Hungarian and Polish applications for membership came early in 1994 and those of eight other Central and East European states followed. Starting in 1989, the Community had responded to their emergence from the Soviet system through trade liberalization and aid. It went on to associate them closely through 'Europe Agreements'. The next step was to make clear that they could join the Union once they had satisfied the economic and political conditions; and accession negotiations with a first wave, the Czech Republic, Hungary, Poland, Estonia, and Slovenia, together with Cyprus, were opened in March 1998. The number of member states will almost certainly reach a score or more in the early years of the twenty-first century; another five of the present applicants are likely to join a few years after that; and the membership may eventually exceed thirty.

Such a numerous and diverse membership will change the Union in many ways. Concern that it could make the institutions unworkable was one reason why the majority of member states wanted the Maastricht Treaty to provide that a further Intergovernmental Conference be held in 1996, 'with a view to strengthening the federal character of the Union.'[12] Owing to British and Danish opposition the word federal was deleted. But the IGC was held and resulted in the Treaty of Amsterdam, signed in October 1997.[13]

The prospect of enlargement was not the only motive for the Amsterdam Treaty. Many of the governments that had been ready to accept the word federal were frustrated by the British and Danish refusal to accept what they regarded as a sufficient strengthening of the institutions. The adoption of a powerful new federal instrument, the single currency, and the political impact of German unification lent urgency to this view. Thus the IGC was to consider reform of the institutions as well as, among other things, the arrangements for security and defence.

In the 'Reflection Group' of government representatives set up to pave the way for the IGC, the British representative was pitted against most of the rest on proposals for more majority voting in the Council and co-decision for the Parliament, which would move the institutions further in a federal direction. It looked as if the IGC would end in deadlock on such fundamental questions. The French and Germans began to envisage establishing a core group to press on with further integration, leaving the rest to catch up later should they so wish.

Amsterdam and after

Six weeks before the European Council met in Amsterdam in June 1997 to conclude the IGC, John Major's Conservative government, which had been blocking reform of the Union's institutions, was replaced by Tony Blair's Labour government, with a different approach to some of the main points at issue. A substantial extension of co-decision was agreed. The protection of fundamental rights was consolidated. Blair was also ready to accept a significant extension of majority voting, but this was prevented because of conflict between German Länder and the federal government. Some improvements were made to the arrangements for the common foreign and security policy. Disagreement remained, however, between Britain and those who wanted to incorporate Western European Union within the EU as its defence arm. An important part of the 'co-operation in justice and home affairs' concerning policies related to the free movement of people across the Union's internal frontiers was transferred into a new chapter of the EC Treaty (Title IIIa/IV); and the Labour government, while withdrawing the opt-out from the social chapter, opted out from this new one. But despite these continuing differences, the change of government in Britain had removed the heat from the conflict over the institutions, and it proved quite easy to agree a provision for 'enhanced cooperation' whereby those member states wishing to go farther than others in a particular field could, subject to unanimous agreement, use the Union's institutions to do so (new Title VI EUT).

Taken as a whole the Treaty, which includes many minor improvements introduced over a broad front, makes the Union's institutions more efficient and democratic. It has, however, been severely criticized, in particular because majority voting was only narrowly extended and because changes relating to the number of Commissioners and the weighting of votes in the Council, seen at least by the larger member states as essential before the influx of mostly small Central and East European countries, were not agreed. Agreement turned on a delicate compromise between the larger and smaller among the existing member states, and this was unravelled by the failure to extend majority voting. The outcome was a Protocol to the Amsterdam Treaty requiring that a further IGC be convened to carry out a 'comprehensive review' of the institutional provisions, 'at least one year before the membership of the European Union exceeds twenty', that is, before the next wave of enlargement is completed.

Meanwhile the Union is changing dramatically as the euro is being introduced in most of the member states in accordance with the timetable for economic and monetary union (Emu) laid down in the Maastricht Treaty. Scepticism had been widespread in Britain and the United States. Unemployment was stubbornly high in France, Germany, and other countries likely to participate, aggravated by the stringent policies required to meet the criteria for inflation, budget deficits, and public debt. Political pressures would, it was believed, throw the Emu programme off course. But the British once again underestimated the political will of France and Germany to hold to the project that they and their partners had set in train in 1950 in order to change the nature of their relationship for good. Their leaders were determined to fulfil the commitments under the Treaty, including the irrevocable locking of the participating countries' exchange rates to the euro together with a single monetary policy run by the European Central Bank from 1 January 1999, leading finally to the replacement of their currencies by euro notes and coins from 1 January 2002. The Labour government indicated its intention to hold a referendum on the question of participation after the next general election, expected in 2001 or 2002. If Labour wins that election, it is likely that Britain too will adopt the single currency, in which case all member states will probably participate.

With the single currency as well as the single market and associated policies such as the common agricultural, transport, competition, and external economic policies, together with its budget, the Union will have a range of economic powers and instruments not far short of what a federation would require to deal with the economic interdependence among its states. While the institutions too have progressively acquired federal elements, they have not come as close to those of a completed federal system as the economic powers have done. Nor will the Union become a federal state unless the member states give it the principal responsibility for armed forces and its institutions are made fully federal. The question whether the Union can over the long run sustain the combination of a fully integrated economy with separate defence and security policies is beyond the scope of this book, though if it is decided to integrate in those fields too, the story the book tells of the development by stages towards a federal system for the economy may well be found relevant. But the question whether the federal powers and institutions in the economic field can be sustained without more federal institutions to control them may arise in the nearer future. The next chapter shows how far the institutions have already been endowed with federal elements and what further reforms have been proposed.

2 Institutions or Constitution

The specific character of the Community institutions derives mainly from the conviction that, in order to achieve more than conventional international organizations, they need to have more independence from the governments of member states.

This is most clearly demonstrated by the Court of Justice. It is the Court's duty to ensure that Community law is observed. In doing so, it affirms the primacy of Community law if there is a conflict with the law of a member state. The Court must judge whether member states, which like the Community institutions are bound by Community law, do in fact comply with it; and in order to ensure that member states' citizens benefit from their rights and discharge their obligations under Community law, the Court ensures that it applies directly to them, without the member states standing in the way.

Part of Community law is embodied in the treaties. But a large part is enacted by the Community institutions, and here, too, there is a substantial element of independence, though less clear-cut than in the case of the Court. The Council, comprising representatives of the member states, still has the most powerful role in the legislative process. But the hold of a given government is weakened by the procedure of majority voting on most measures. The Commission has the sole right to table most legislative proposals. The European Parliament has the power of co-decision in fields that may, following the Amsterdam Treaty, amount to about a half of the legislation, and a significant influence on most of the rest. Once enacted, the Commission has major responsibilities for the implementation of Community law.

The member states, represented in the Council, are still the predominant force in the Community institutions. But their behaviour is conditioned by the other institutions; and the question whether the powers of the latter are to be further enhanced remains one of the most crucial facing the Union.

The Commission: a European executive

An independent executive was, for Jean Monnet, the keystone of the Community that he wanted to establish. The High Authority was the only institution about which the Schuman declaration was explicit. Monnet, in chairing the conference on the ECSC Treaty and then as the High Authority's first President, insisted on its multinational and independent character, which has been preserved in the Commission to this day.

The members of the Commission, although usually former ministers or high officials of member states, are bound by oath not to take instructions from governments or from any other outside body (Article 157/213 ECT). To ensure that it is multinational, the Commission contains one member from each of the smaller member states, two from the larger ones. Following the accession of Austria, Finland, and Sweden, the number of Commissioners rose to twenty; and the impending enlargement to the East would take it well beyond the number of significant portfolios available. So there was pressure for treaty amendment to keep the number within bounds. Each of the larger member states was ready, in negotiating the Amsterdam Treaty, to forgo one of its Commissioners provided the smaller accepted that Commissions would not in future include a national from each member state. But agreement on this was linked with a deal on the voting system in the Council; and because of the dissent about the extension of majority voting, the reform was postponed until the IGC to be held before the next enlargement.

The Commissioners are appointed by 'common accord' among the governments, subject, however, since the Maastricht Treaty, to the approval of the European Parliament (Article 158/214 ECT). However dissatisfied a government may subsequently be, it has no power to withdraw one of them during the term of office. This the Maastricht Treaty fixed at a period of five years, to start in the January six months after the elections to the Parliament so that the new Parliament can approve—or not—the appointment of the new Commission. The Amsterdam Treaty gave the Parliament the power to approve the nomination of the Commission's President too, who is to have the right to give—or withhold—his or her accord to the governments' nominations for the other Commissioners (Article 158.2/214.2). Taken together, these can be seen as significant steps towards an effective parliamentary executive.

The Commissioners have recruited an equally multinational body of officials to carry out their tasks; and the name Commission is in practice given to the Commissioners and officials collectively.

In line with its designation as the Community's executive, one of the Commission's main functions is to execute the policies decided under Community law. For a policy such as that relating to agriculture, this is a big and complex task. Another is to represent the Community in international trade negotiations (Article 113/133 ECT). Some of the Commission's tasks of implementation are given it directly by the treaties, rather than by decisions of the Council. An example is the competition policy (Article 89/85 ECT); and the larger scope given to the ECSC's High Authority than to the EEC's Commission stemmed mainly from the policies enshrined in the ECSC treaty in this way. Despite the extent of its executive job, the Commission has remained a small body, with fewer officials than have many local authorities in the member states. This it has done through delegation of much of the administration to the civil services of the member states, following an example that has worked well in the relations between the German federal government and the Länder.

The Commission's responsibilities go beyond plain implementation, in the duty that the treaties lay on it to ensure that their provisions and 'the measures taken by the institutions pursuant thereto' are applied (Article 155/211 ECT). In this capacity the Commission is sometimes called the guardian, or 'watch-dog', of the treaties. It brings infringements to the attention of those responsible, including member states, and if necessary takes them to the Court.

The most innovative among the functions given to the Commission is its role in legislation. Most governments, although called 'executives', in fact play a vital part in the legislative process, proposing draft laws that they expect the legislature to approve, in more or less amended form. The Commission is weaker in relation to the Council than most governments are in relation to their legislatures. But on most subjects the Council cannot act without a proposal from the Commission; and the Commission has the right to make legislative proposals on its own initiative (Article 155/211 ECT). These may take the form either of a Regulation, which is 'binding in its entirety and directly applicable in all member states'; or of a Directive, which is 'binding, as to the result to be achieved', but leaves it to the member states to choose 'the form and methods'; or of a Decision, which is 'binding in its entirety upon those to whom it is addressed' (Article 189/249 ECT). Since there must be unanimous agreement in the Council in order to amend the Commission's proposal, governments that want it changed may well have to persuade the Commission to withdraw and amend the draft itself. The Commission might stand a good chance of securing its passage instead, if this could be done by a simple majority. But where majority voting in the Council is stipulated, it is almost always by qualified majority, with over 71 per cent of the weighted votes; and for the most important matters the treaties specify unanimity, which the governments in any case usually prefer to seek. Thus the Commission, if it wants a decision, is often obliged to withdraw and amend, even if it judges that this will unduly weaken or delay the measure.

The Commission does not fill the shoes of a European government in the process of Community legislation. But it does play an essential part; and in the period of early EEC success, it was often called the motor of the Community, pulling the Council along behind it. Among the actions that evoked this metaphor were the acceleration of the customs union programme, the realization of the common agricultural policy, and the conclusion of the Kennedy round of trade negotiations.

Impressed by such achievements, neofunctionalists used the term engrenage (enmeshing) to express what they saw as the Commission's co-optation of member states' officials to help realize its European objectives.

The Commission was not as strong as the neofunctionalists had thought, when faced by a government that refused to be co-opted. The attack that de Gaulle launched in 1965 was against not only the European Parliament but also the Commission: 'this embryonic technocracy for the most part foreign'.[1] He did what he could to weaken it; and the practice of seeking unanimity in the Council, which lived on for nearly two decades after him, did more. There was less talk of motors and engrenage.

The Commission never ceased to be indispensable. However much nationalists might resent it, the laws and policies required for an integrating economy and the European co-operation that was generally desired would not be feasible without an institution designed to articulate the common interest. The Commission has been the architect, and often the initiator, of many of the Community's achievements: less impressive, certainly, during the more stagnant period from the mid-1960s to the mid-1980s, but then gathering strong momentum again. There were significant successes, even before the regeneration of the Community following the Single European Act: already in the late 1970s the initiative by Roy Jenkins, as Commission President, to relaunch monetary integration, resulting in the European Monetary System; the adoption of Lord Cockfield's single market programme; the influence of the Delors Commission on the Intergovernmental Conference that drew up the Single European Act.

The Single Act demonstrated the limits to the Commission's independence in relation to the Council. The Council had over the years encroached on the Commission's executive competence, in particular by setting up committees of member governments' officials to supervise its work. Seized of the consequent threat to the Community's efficiency, the Act required the Council to 'confer on the Commission . . . powers for the implementation of the rules which the Council lays down', but added the weasel words that the Council 'may impose certain requirements' (Article 10 SEA). The Council had to act in this on a proposal from the Commission, which proposed committees in a form that would not be obstructive. The Council could amend this text only by unanimity, and included representatives of governments that had supported a more federalist version of the Single Act. Faced with the prospect of fuller executive competence for the Commission, however, they unanimously agreed on a restrictive system of committees that the Commission and the Parliament found excessively restrictive.

Despite this setback, the Commission continued to expand its influence. It designed the crucial agri-budgetary reform of 1988. With the agreement of the USA and other OECD countries, it was given the responsibility for co-ordinating the assistance of the advanced industrial countries to the emergent democracies of Central and Eastern Europe. President Delors was central to the project for economic and monetary union and played a big part in the design of the Maastricht Treaty. With the enhancement of the Community's competences, the Treaty enlarged the scope of the responsibilities of the European Commission (as the Commission was formally renamed following Maastricht). The Treaty also gave the Commission the right of initiative with respect to the common foreign and security policy, though this is a right of co-initiative, shared with the Council, rather than the exclusive right of initiative that gives the Commission its strong position in the Community's legislative process; and the Commission was to be 'fully associated' with the work in this field. Maastricht gave the Commission a similar role with respect to the co-operation in justice and home affairs, but Amsterdam converted this into an exclusive right of initiative for legislation as regards the free movement of people across the Union's internal frontiers, together with related policies.

With the part he played in promoting the Single Act and the Maastricht Treaty as well as a number of other achievements, Delors has been the most influential federalist since Monnet in the development of the Community. The standing he gave to the office of President was reflected in the competition among present and former prime ministers to succeed him. But the difficulties that followed the success of agreement on the Treaty took their toll, and notwithstanding its creditable performance, the federalists' vision of the Commission as an incipient government for the Community has been frustrated. For all its significant federal features, the governments of member states still dominate the Community. To judge the strength, durability, and consequences of the intergovernmental structures, we must examine the Council of ministers and the European Council of heads of state and government.

The intergovernmental bodies: Council, Coreper, European Council

The membership of the Council is that of a conventional international organization: a representative at ministerial level from each member state (Article 146/203 ECT). Each minister is responsible to the government and parliament of his or her state. Most ministers also realize that they have a responsibility to try to reach an agreement that will be of some benefit to the Union as a whole. Otherwise, nothing would get done. But the structure of the Council makes such agreements difficult.

Each minister is backed by a government department that will usually have a point of view on the matter at issue, sometimes deeply rooted and often lent a certain self-righteousness by being termed the national interest. Where unanimity is required or sought, which was generally the case following the Luxembourg 'compromise' of 1966 until the Single Act of 1987, at least some are likely to resist the necessary compromises. Even a qualified majority may be hard to secure. Following the enlargement to fifteen member states, it requires 62 of the votes out of a total of 87, weighted so as to give more voting power to the representatives of larger member states: ten each for France, Germany, Italy, and the UK; eight for Spain; five each for Belgium, Greece, the Netherlands, and Portugal; four each for Austria and Sweden; three each for Denmark, Finland, and Ireland; two for Luxembourg (Article 148/205 ECT). A decision could be blocked by 26 of these weighted votes. Examples of such blocking minorities could be Italy, Spain, Portugal, and Greece, on matters of concern to the southern tier; Britain, Germany, the Netherlands, and one of the Scandinavians, on matters of northern or of liberal trading concern.

To secure agreement that is more than an empty compromise is a thorny political problem. In organizations dominated by a hegemonial leader, the others can often be led. But it is a rewarding feature of the Union, and a basis for a democratic system, that there is no hegemony: the larger states have been of similar size; and even the united Germany falls far short of being a hegemon. The government whose turn it is to be President of the Council can exert influence, particularly if it represents a major member state and is working well with the Commission. But the procedure of rotation allows each government only six months in the presidency; and this is too short for a full development of the leading role, even in the common foreign and security policy where the troika system provides for consultation with the preceding and succeeding presidencies.

Coherence is further undermined by the fragmentation of the Council on functional lines. So far from being a single group of ministers, the Council is a hydra-headed conglomerate of more than twenty functional Councils, each comprising the ministers with a given responsibility such as agriculture, finance, industry, trade, or transport. The foreign ministers sit as a General Affairs Council with the aim of co-ordinating the work of the other Councils. But ministers of agriculture, finance, etc. are not easily co-ordinated; and each Council when it meets has the equal right to act as the legislature for the Community. When the agriculture ministers have decided on a measure, the finance or foreign ministers have no power to rescind it; and it was not until 1988 that the agricultural budget began to be brought under control.

This unwieldy Council has enormous responsibilities. It has to enact the large volume of Community legislation. It has taken on itself the burden, much of which could be left with the Commission, of taking a multitude of executive decisions. It has to try to co-ordinate member states' policies in a wide area, such as foreign policy, where the Union's method is still co-operation rather than integration. So it combines legislative, executive, and diplomatic roles. An array of ministers, each flying into Brussels at intervals for a day or so, could not possibly come to grips with all this. In order to do so, and to reduce their dependence on the Commission, they have permanent delegations of their own government's officials stationed in Brussels, each one headed by a Permanent Representative, responsible for preparing the meetings for the whole set of that country's ministers. The Committee of Permanent Representatives, known by the French acronym as Coreper, meets weekly and goes as far as it can to reach agreement before the ministers come to meet in the Council. This it does to such effect that many measures are agreed without discussion in the Council.

Much of the work of day-to-day decisions which results from the Council's determination to keep the Commission on a tight rein is also delegated to member states' officials, sitting in the several hundred committees that the Council has set up for the purpose. Some of the committees are merely advisory, helping the Commission to take account of member states' views and circumstances. Others, such as many concerned with managing the common agricultural policy, can either persuade or force the Commission to think again if they can muster a qualified majority against the Commission's decision. Yet others can stop the Commission from acting unless it gets a qualified majority on its side, so that the Commission's implementation can be prevented by a blocking minority; and in the field of trade policy, some decisions can be referred to the Council by a single member state. All this adds to the responsibilities and influence of the permanent delegations.

Already in the 1960s the neofunctionalists' idea of engrenage, or the co-optation of member states' officials to the Commission's sphere of influence, was challenged on the grounds that the member states were the stronger, so the co-opting would be the other way about.[2] Although the Commission has maintained a creditable degree of independence, committees of the latter sort bear witness to the strength of the member states' official machines. The Commission, appointed by the governments, has lacked a political base that would enable it to be a match for them in any serious attempt to change the balance of political power. The European Parliament, with which the Commission has increasingly become allied, does not have the strength to offer such a base, at least as yet, although the powers given to the Parliament by the Maastricht and Amsterdam Treaties may point towards a change in the balance. Coreper ranks high in the federalist demonology. But if the system is unsatisfactory, the overburdened and dedicated Permanent Representatives are not to blame. It is they who have enabled it nevertheless to produce so many useful results.

With the intergovernmental method riding high, there were important developments in its institutions. One was the system of committees, with Coreper at the peak. Others were the European Council and the foreign policy co-operation initiated in the 1970s, then the Maastricht Treaty's 'pillars' for common foreign and security policy and for co-operation in justice and home affairs.

Co-operation among member states in their foreign policies should come readily in a Community with political aspirations and instruments of external economic policy. But it did not come in the 1960s, thanks to the quarrels between de Gaulle and his partners. It was in 1970 that the member states' foreign ministers and the political directors of their ministries began to have regular meetings for the purpose; and the European Political Co-operation (EPC), as it was called following the division of labour between political and economic departments within the ministries of foreign affairs, evolved to the point where the Single European Act brought it formally within the Community treaties.

The aim of the EPC was defined in the Single Act as 'to formulate and implement a European foreign policy', no less. But the means scarcely measured up to it: regular meetings of ministers and officials, and after the Single Act a small secretariat in Brussels. There were some useful results, such as many votes in common in the United Nations and joint declarations on a variety of topics. But they were modest compared with achievements of the EEC such as the Gatt rounds of trade negotiations, the Lome Convention, and the new relationship with Central and Eastern Europe. Although the Maastricht Treaty designed a more elaborate system for the common foreign and security policy, and gave a role to the Commission and the Parliament, the system remained predominantly intergovernmental, and ill-adapted to producing a really effective common policy. The same may be said of the Treaty's provisions for co-operation in justice and home affairs. But the Amsterdam Treaty's provisions within this field, for free movement of people and related policies, which give a bigger role to the Commission and the Court, are likely to be more effective.

The other intergovernmental innovation that was initiated after de Gaulle and later incorporated in the treaties by the Single Act (Article 2) is the European Council, in which the heads of state or government and the President of the Commission meet at least twice a year, assisted by the foreign ministers and a Commissioner. When President Giscard d'Estaing launched the series of regular meetings during the French presidency in 1974, he seemed to have in mind intimate chats among the political heads of the member states (the President in France, Prime Ministers in the other countries). But the European Council was quickly sucked into the political vacuum at the centre of the Community, to take decisions that the Council of ministers was unable to take. These ranged from small details, through the resolution of acute crises such as the British net contribution and the agri-budgetary imbroglio, to agreement on the Maastricht and Amsterdam Treaties. The European Council has approved package deals that carried the Community into a new stage of development, such as that under French presidency in 1984 which combined the mechanism for Britain's budget rebate with the green light for Spanish and Portuguese accessions; under German presidency in 1988 which decided on the expansion of funds to assist the EC's weaker economies together with reform of the budget and of the agricultural policy; and under Dutch Presidency which completed the negotiations for the Maastricht and Amsterdam Treaties in 1991 and 1997. Initiatives are also taken that lead to important steps in developing the Community: to prepare direct elections to the European Parliament (French presidency, 1974); to launch the European Monetary System (Germany, 1978); to convene the IGC that drew up the Single European Act (Italy, 1985) and to agree on the Act (Luxembourg 1985); to respond vigorously to the reforms in Central and Eastern Europe (France, 1989); to prepare for the incorporation of East Germany into the Community on its accession to the Federal Republic (Ireland, 1990); to convene the IGCs on Emu (Spain, 1989), and on political union (Ireland, 1990), which led to the Maastricht Treaty. The Maastricht Treaty states that the European Council is to give the Union 'the necessary impetus for its development' and is to 'define the general political guidelines' (Article D/4 EUT); and the record shows that it has indeed come to play a central part in taking many of the principal decisions. So the quality of its performance can best be judged in the context of the performance of the institutions as a whole.

Results of the intergovernmental system

The Community has notable achievements to its credit, such as the customs union and trade policy, the successive enlargements, the survival through difficult times, the resurgence that accompanied the launching of the single market programme; and the Union has continued with the launching of the single currency. The common agricultural policy must also be counted among the early successes, easing the reduction of agricultural employment by one-half in the original member countries and providing a cement that helped to keep France attached to its partners through the 1960s. So the existing institutions, with their intergovernmental predominance, have shown their ability to secure agreement on important matters, to continue working through the lean years, and to recover momentum when times are better.

This is incomparably superior to Europe's performance in the decades before the Community was established. But the question remains: is it good enough? Can the Community in its present form work well enough in bad times as well as good? Can it handle the political and economic consequences of the single currency or of enlargement to the East? Can it deal with current business in ways that satisfy the economic and political aspirations of its citizens?

The story of agriculture invites scepticism. Already in 1968 Sicco Mansholt, the Commissioner for agriculture who had been the architect of the common agricultural policy, produced a memorandum for the Council stressing the need for a major programme of structural measures to avert the looming crisis of high cost and over-production.[3] It was over four years before the Council approved some Directives, responding modestly to what Mansholt had proposed. Since Directives specify the result to be achieved but leave the member states to draft and enact their own legislation, another five years passed before they were actually applied in France; and in Italy there was still no action on some aspects of the Directives by 1980. Thus over ten years after Mansholt's warning shot, virtually no effective action had been taken to check the crisis, which as a consequence in the 1980s almost wrecked the Community. It was not until February 1988 that the European Council pulled back from disaster, with decisions that contained the problem for a time; and it was only in March 1991 that the Council decided on a reform which stabilized the situation for the time being, but remains inadequate to meet the challenges of the eastern enlargement or the rules of the World Trade Organization. The responsibility for the prolonged agony has been that of the Council and the European Council, and theirs alone. The European Parliament had little power in the field of agriculture; and the Commission's proposals, had the Council accepted them, would have stopped the haemorrhage long before.

In agriculture, the Council's delays had spectacular effects. But a period of gestation of ten to fifteen years is by no means abnormal for a Council decision on a tricky question in other fields. The decision on the structure of the value-added tax took that long even before enlargement had augmented the number of member states' positions that had to be reconciled.[4]

More recently, the programme of legislation to complete the single market acquired a remarkable momentum, thanks to the Council's use of the provision in the Single Act for majority voting on these matters (Article 18 SEA). But overload in the Council, together with the search for unanimity on many important matters, continued to cause delay. Nor, with the consequences of the single currency, is the pressure likely to abate. This can be seen as a result of the secular trend to economic interdependence; and when the interdependence links countries as diverse as the members of the Union already are, and with further enlargement increasingly will be, there cannot fail to be political consequences, which lend conviction to the argument that there will be a weaker Union, with loose co-operation and irregular application of its laws, unless there are stronger institutions.

Effectiveness is one arm of this argument. Democracy is the other. It is contended that laws made by ministers and not approved by an elected parliament transgress the norms of representative government. If such laws were not very important, they could be seen as examples of regulation delegated to the executive, which is widely practised in democracies. But with the volume and significance that the Community's legislative programme has attained, this justification wears thin. The criticism that laws are negotiated by interlocking technocracies, insufficiently accessible to the people's representatives, becomes more telling. The fact that the Council, as a legislature, conducts its proceedings behind closed doors has added to the unease. Thus there are grounds of both effectiveness and democracy that have led to demands for more federal elements in the institutions.

Against the pull towards intergovernmental methods, there has been a current flowing towards stronger federal elements in each of the institutions. The Single Act extended the scope for majority votes in the Council, stipulating qualified majority voting for most of the legislative harmonization required to complete the internal market, and for the decisions on the regional fund, on health and safety at work, and on specific research programmes; and the Maastricht Treaty provided for majority voting on most of the new Community competences. Majority voting is, indeed, now the normal rule for Community legislation, with some vital exceptions such as tax. This has not only made the Council more federal, but also strengthened the legislative role of the Commission, whose indispensability in resolving Community problems and crises has continued to be evident. The powers of the directly elected European Parliament were enhanced by the Single Act and the Maastricht and Amsterdam Treaties as well as in other ways. The influence of the Court of Justice has been rising steadily. All this has reflected awareness of a need for political integration, to set against the centrifugal tendencies of the intergovernmental method, which remains a powerful influence in Community business and predominant in the common foreign and security policy.

The Court of Justice and the rule of law

'The Court of Justice shall ensure that in the interpretation and application of this Treaty the law is observed.' Thus straightforwardly the EC Treaty (Article 164/220) sets down what the Court is for. Its full import can be grasped only if we remember that the member states had previously accepted no binding authority outside themselves. It was of course World War Two, seen as the ultimate consequence of allowing relations among nation-states to be determined by power rather than law, that had induced the member states to take this unprecedented step.

To provide a sound juridical basis for the Community and to gain the confidence of all the member states and their citizens, it was essential that the Court be incontrovertibly impartial. It comprises one judge from each member state. The judges have to be chosen 'from persons whose independence is beyond doubt' (Article 167/223 ECT) and the Statutes of the Court require them, before taking up their office, to take an oath to perform their duties 'impartially and conscientiously'. The Court is assisted by six Advocates-General, appointed in a similar way and likewise for six-year terms, to make 'reasoned submissions on cases brought before the Court' (Article 166/222 ECT). Thus composed, the Court of Justice has been remarkably successful in securing respect for Community law.

It was in order to 'ensure . . . that the law is observed' that the Court established the principles of the primacy and direct effect of Community law. For if member states' law could override Community law, and if governments could stand between the law and the citizens, the law would soon be applied divergently in different countries and it would no longer be possible to say that the member states and their citizens were bound by it. They would be sliding back to reliance on power relationships instead of law to settle their differences.

Having established the principles of primacy and direct effect for Community law, the Court applied them with as little European centralization as possible. The Court itself tries cases involving member states and Community institutions. But cases between individuals and between individuals and national authorities are tried in the courts of member states, with the Court of Justice intervening only to give a 'preliminary ruling' when asked to do so on a point regarding the interpretation of the treaties or the validity or interpretation of the acts of Community institutions (i.e. Community law). There have been few complaints that national courts are not impartial in applying Community law; and the member states have almost always complied with judgments of the Court which went against them, even if they have sometimes taken their time to do so.

Among the many hundred judgments made by the Court, some stand out as landmarks in the Community's development. In 1979, the judgment on Cassis de Dijon (case 120/78) initiated a new phase in the removal of barriers that fragment the EC market. The German authorities had forbidden imports of that French drink on the grounds that its contents did not comply with German regulations; but the Court found that the French regulations, which had been respected, were an adequate safeguard for health and must be recognized as such in other member states. This judgment rested on Article 30 EEC

(Article 30/28 ECT), which prohibited 'all measures having equivalent effect' to quantitative restrictions on intra-Community trade, and which the Court ruled should apply directly in member states in the absence of more specific legislation enacted by the Council. The sale of Cassis de Dijon on the German market went ahead, and set a precedent for the mutual recognition of member states' regulations, which became a major new strategy for completing the single market. A year later, in the isoglucose cases (138/79 and 139/79), the Court took a significant step towards establishing the European Parliament's legislative power. The Council had enacted a regulation for that substance without waiting for the Parliament's opinion; and the Court found the regulation invalid because the EEC Treaty required the Council to consult the Parliament. The Parliament could, thereafter, exert more influence on legislation, because it could delay the process until it was confident that its proposed amendments would be taken into account. In 1985, in a case (13/83) brought by the Parliament, the Court found that the Council was acting illegally in failing to decide on a common transport policy despite the duty clearly imposed on it by the EEC Treaty, over a quarter of a century before. This was the first sanction against the Council's habit of stunting Community development by indefinite delay.

Thus the Court has established itself as a significant actor in ensuring the development of the EC institutions as indicated by the treaties, as well as in promoting free movement within the Community and ensuring that Community law is applied in other ways. It has, like the Council, suffered from overload due to the expansion of Community activities; so the Single Act (Article 11) provided for a second Court, called a Court of First Instance because all its cases are brought directly to it rather than going first to the courts of member states, to deal with a limited range of cases. The Maastricht Treaty broke new ground by giving the Court of Justice the power to fine member states that fail to comply with its judgments. The Treaty excluded the new fields of common foreign and security policy and of co-operation in justice and home affairs from the Court's jurisdiction, but the Amsterdam Treaty did give it jurisdiction over much of the latter field. Thus the Court and the legislation it applies are proper to the Community rather than the Union as a whole. Given this limitation, the Court continues to win growing respect and an expanding role, helping to ensure that 'as far as its legal system is concerned, the Community now possesses most of the characteristics of a federation'.[5]

European Parliament and European democracy

The Schuman declaration contained no hint of a parliamentary assembly for the Coal and Steel Community. But on the suggestion of a French federalist member of parliament, the idea was introduced into the negotiations to establish the ECSC; and Monnet, in his inaugural speech for the High Authority, was able to say that 'the High Authority is responsible, not to the states, but to the European Assembly . . . the first European Assembly endowed with sovereign powers'.[6] Such a parliament was hardly necessary for the ECSC itself, but rather because it was seen as the first step towards a European federation; and in the same spirit the treaty provided that its members, initially designated by the member states' parliaments, would be directly elected by universal suffrage when the Council had decided how this was to be done.

The Council was to decide this by unanimous vote (Article 21 ECSC, followed by Article 138 EEC); and it was over a quarter of a century before the first direct elections were held. On becoming French President in 1974, Valéry Giscard d'Estaing consulted Jean Monnet on the steps he should take to put some new life into the Community, and decided to take the initiative on this, as well as on the creation of the European Council;[7] and the elections were duly held in June 1979. The authority of the European Parliament, as it was to be formally designated in the Single Act, was greatly enhanced. It 'increased its influence dramatically', according to Britain's Permanent Representative during the period following the elections.[8]

One argument that had helped to strengthen the case for direct elections was the Parliament's acquisition of budgetary powers through the amending treaties of 1970 and 1975; and it had been given these powers because of the need perceived for democratic control of Community expenditure. It was the Dutch second chamber that had bound its government to insist on control by the European Parliament if the Community was to be allocated its own tax resources. Although this federalist logic was rejected by de Gaulle, the Dutch Parliament and the federalist logic outlived him. The French government that followed his resignation in 1969 retained some of his attitudes, and managed to confine the Parliament to a mainly consultative role with respect to the agricultural budget and some other items of expenditure; but for the rest, the amending treaties made the Parliament and the Council a genuine two-chamber legislature, with the Parliament having the final say and hence the stronger power over that part of the budget (Article 203/272 ECT). Because the Council eschewed the unanimity procedure in voting on the budget, and because the EEC Treaty stipulated that the Commission 'shall implement the budget . . . on its own responsibility' (Article 205/274 ECT), thus giving it full executive power, this 'non-compulsory expenditure', as it is quaintly called, is subject to a fully federal relationship between the EC's legislature, executive, and judiciary: a bridgehead for federal institutions in a confederal or hybrid Community.

With agricultural expenditure predominant, the non-compulsory expenditure started small. But it grew steadily; and the expansion of structural funds agreed, to meet the needs of the weaker economies in the single market and the economic and monetary union, has brought it to about half the total budget. For this part of the budget, the Parliament has the right to add expenditure within limits prescribed by the treaties, which has enabled it to introduce new policies in matters such as research, education, and youth exchanges; give priority to food aid for the Third World; and increase the allocations for aid to Central Europe. The Parliament also has powers over the allocation of expenditure within the budget, which it has used, for example, to freeze aid to Turkey in reaction to violations of human rights.

The Parliament's powers over the budget as a whole are less impressive. It does have the right to adopt or reject the budget as a whole. But if it rejects the budget, the Community can continue to spend at the same monthly rate as in the previous year (Article 204/273 ECT). Given inflation, this means a cut in real expenditure, which is not usually in line with the Parliament's wishes. The Parliament has not, indeed, been able to secure effective power over the agricultural expenditure, although it has obtained the right, starting in 1988, to ensure that the Council keeps that spending within agreed limits during the periods of successive 'financial perspectives'.[9] The Parliament is also responsible for granting Discharge for the whole budget (Article 206/276 ECT), i.e. for affirming that a preceding year's expenditure has been properly implemented. Its capacity to scrutinize expenditure is strengthened by the Court of Auditors, which was created by the amending treaty of 1975, following cases of fraud and other improprieties that the Parliament had unearthed in the early 1970s. A Commissioner for the budget went so far as to say he thought the Commission would have to resign if Discharge was refused.[10] The Maastricht Treaty further strengthened the Parliament's budgetary control by giving it powers to demand information from the Commission about its execution of expenditure and systems of financial control, and by requiring the Commission to act on the Parliament's observations (Article 206/276 ECT).

The Parliament's budgetary powers give it significant influence over the Commission. The treaties have also given it other forms of control. Thus the Parliament has the right to dismiss the Commission by a two-thirds majority (Article 144/201 ECT). It was such a power, already incorporated in the ECSC Treaty (Article 24), that led Monnet to say that the High Authority was responsible to the Parliament rather than to the member states. But the Parliament has never used this power. It has usually regarded the Commission as its ally in developing the Community. If, moreover, the Parliament were to have dismissed the Commission, the Commissioners would nevertheless have stayed in place until the governments appointed a new one; and the Parliament would have had no influence over this process. The British Permanent Representative, cited earlier, nevertheless observed already in the 1980s that, as a result of fear of dismissal, 'the Commission pays a great deal of attention to the views of the Parliament, in its preparation of draft legislation, in the line it takes in Council ... and in budgetary matters'.[11] The Maastricht Treaty has, moreover, strengthened the Parliament's position in giving it the power of approval over each new Commission, and the Amsterdam Treaty consolidated this by requiring the Parliament's prior approval of the nomination for the Commission's President. The Maastricht Treaty also gave the Parliament the right to set up Committees of Enquiry to investigate cases of alleged maladministration (Article 138c/193 ECT). Thus the Commission's accountability to the Parliament has been considerably reinforced. The Commission has other reasons, too, to cooperate with the Parliament: it needs political allies to strengthen it in its relations with the Council; it needs, as we have seen, to secure the Parliament's approval with respect to the budget; and it needs the Parliament's support for its legislative programme.

The Parliament's legislative role has come a long way since the founding treaties gave it the right to be consulted about Community legislation. Until 1979 this consultation on non-budgetary legislation brought little influence.The Commission was polite. The Council was cavalier. With the direct elections following on the grant of budgetary powers, the Parliament's legislative role became more important. The Court's ruling in the isoglucose case secured for the Parliament the right at least to delay; and some types of legislation could be influenced by its budgetary powers. But it was the Single Act that brought the Parliament closer to the centre of the legislative process.

One of the impulses that gave rise to the Single Act was the European Parliament's Draft Treaty for European Union (1984), which proposed a federal reform of the Community institutions, making the Parliament a co-legislator with the Council. The Draft Treaty and the Parliament's role were strongly backed by the Italian parliament and government; and most of the other governments were open to the idea that the European Parliament's powers should grow as the scope of Community legislation was increased. So the Single Act did something to strengthen the Parliament's powers. Under what is called the assent procedure, the Council cannot act on an application for membership of the Community without the assent of the Parliament, nor can association agreements with third countries be concluded without the Parliament's assent (Articles 8, 9 SEA). Although this procedure does not give the Parliament the right of amendment, but only of acceptance or rejection, it did extend the Parliament's power to these two crucial elements in the Community's external relations. The Parliament has used this power to secure, for example, trade benefits for the Palestinians as a condition for accepting an extension of the association agreement with Israel; and, on giving its assent to the treaties of accession for Austria, Finland, and Sweden, it was able to secure in return a significant role with respect to the Intergovernmental Conference that led to the Amsterdam Treaty.

For most of the legislation to complete the single market and for some other matters, the Single Act laid down a 'co-operation procedure' whereby the Council, voting by qualified majority, had to co-operate with the Parliament without giving it the full power of co-legislation (Articles 6, 7 SEA). Under this procedure, if the Parliament rejected a measure that had been accepted by the Council, the Council could then enact it only by unanimous agreement. Thus if one government agreed with the Parliament, the law could not be enacted. A case in point was the measure to restrict exhaust emissions from small cars. Not only the Parliament but also the environmentally conscious Dutch government wanted a stricter limit than the majority of the Council had accepted. The combination of Parliament and Dutch would have been enough to bring the measure down. In fact the Parliament secured the enactment of a stricter limit by using its rights of amendment under the co-operation procedure. If the Commission accepted the Parliament's amendments, the Council could then change the revised text only by unanimous agreement, which was not likely to be forthcoming if, as in the case of the small car exhausts, there was a government that strongly agreed with the Parliament. So in such cases, the Parliament was well placed to persuade the

Commission to support its amendments, as the alternative to rejection of the measure as a whole. Thus the Commission did support the Parliament's amendments and the Council enacted the stricter limit for exhausts. With the Commission's general desire to avoid conflict with the Parliament, combined with the sanction of rejection in the background, the Parliament was able under this procedure to secure the passage of over half its amendments into Community law.

In order to deal with these complexities of the Single Act, the Parliament adopted new rules of procedure. Its performance rapidly won it respect in Brussels and made a considerable impact on the vast programme of legislation required to complete the single market by the end of 1992; and this paved the way to the substantial enhancement of the Parliament's legislative powers by the Maastricht and Amsterdam Treaties. The assent procedure was extended to apply to all international agreements with an institutional framework or budgetary implications and to those involving subjects where the Parliament has a power of co-decision with the Council. The Parliament's assent is also required to the procedure for European elections, sanctions should a member state seriously and persistently breach human rights, amendment of the statutes of the European System of Central Banks (ESCB) and of the supervisory tasks of the European Central Bank (ECB), and major decisions regarding the structural and cohesion funds.

The Maastricht Treaty also introduced the procedure of co-decision, which gives the Parliament the power to reject, by an absolute majority, a measure approved by the Council (Article 189b/251 ECT). But unlike the assent procedure, this gives the Parliament the right to propose amendments which, if not initially accepted by the Council, are considered in a conciliation committee, comprising the members of the Council or their representatives, and an equal number of members of the Parliament; and the Council cannot ignore the MEPs because, if agreement is not reached, the Parliament can reject the measure as a whole. Maastricht stipulated co-decision for fifteen provisions of the Treaty, including most of the single market legislation; and this was extended at Amsterdam to apply to over fifty provisions. In addition to the single market these cover, in full or in part, a wide range of policies: on employment, self-employment, right of establishment, free movement of workers, mutual recognition of diplomas, vocational training, the Social Fund; transport, environment, Trans-European Networks, the European Regional Development Fund, development co-operation; education, culture, public health, consumer protection; fraud; the treatment of foreign nationals; citizens' rights to move freely within all member states. Following Amsterdam, co-decision has replaced the co-operation procedure for all legislation save a few aspects of Emu; and the Amsterdam Treaty also improved the co-decision procedure by simplifying it.

The Parliament has by now acquired a very substantial legislative role. After the Maastricht Treaty came into force, co-decision applied to about a quarter of the number of laws enacted; and its extension following Amsterdam may bring the proportion to half.[12] This, combined with its power of assent and its powers over the budget and the Commission, carries the Parliament a good part of the way towards achieving equality with the Council as far as legislation and accountability of the Commission are concerned. It has also become quite effective as a forum, articulating European concerns, being addressed by such luminaries as Nelson Mandela, Mikhail Gorbachev and Ronald Reagan, and airing citizens' problems, with the latter function reinforced by the parliamentary Ombudsman introduced by the Maastricht Treaty (Article 138e/195 ECT). But the Parliament still falls short of being an equal partner of the Council in a two-chamber legislature. It was the subordination of the people's representatives to those of the governments that was a major motive behind Altiero Spinelli's resolve to persuade the Parliament to design and approve its Draft Treaty for European Union, following the first direct elections in 1979.

Intergovernmental institutions or constitutional government

Spinelli set out his critique of the Community's institutions in his Jean Monnet Lecture in 1983.[15] This focused on the dominance of the intergovernmental Council, which he attacked as both inefficient and undemocratic, ignoring the European Parliament wherever possible and resisting institutional reform. Moreover, the Council enacts Community laws without granting access to members of the public and without even a proper published record of its proceedings; the representatives of member states who do this have often been not ministers but their substitutes; and much of the legislation is passed on the nod, having been already agreed by the Permanent Representatives. Ministers could in theory be controlled by the member states' parliaments. But if such control were to be really effective, the *de facto* legislature would be the several parliaments of all the member states, and the legislative process would be impossibly cumbersome. As it was, Spinelli found the Council unacceptably inefficient. With the rotation of its presidency every six months, it could not effect a continuous development of policy, nor could a given member state achieve enough during its half-year in office; and the Council compounded its own defects by subjecting the Commission to detailed control by Coreper's web of committees. Yet the Council, Spinelli complained, insisted on arrogating to itself a load of political and executive responsibility which it was unable to carry. Spinelli's solution was the Draft Treaty for European Union, approved by the Parliament in 1984 for submission to member states, with its proposal for federal reform of the Community's institutions.

Spinelli made his critique at a low point in the Community's fortunes. The European Council has since made important decisions; and the performance of the Council improved along with acceptance of the principle of majority voting for much of the legislation, following the Single Act. But the Parliament continued to regard much of Spinelli's critique as valid. It reiterated in 1990 the principles on which the Draft Treaty of 1984 was based; and in 1994 it considered a similar Draft Constitution of the European Union.[14]

The Draft Treaty provided for a general system of co-decision between the Parliament and the Council voting by qualified majority, with respect to legislation, the budget, and the appointment of the Commission. The Commission would have full executive competences which, together with its right of legislative initiative, would enable it to fulfil the function of a government for the Community. The jurisdiction of the Court of Justice would be filled out in certain respects, including its role in the guarantee of fundamental rights and freedoms established in the Union's constitution. Thus the Community's institutions would be brought into a federal relationship with each other.

The basic principle of a federal system, that it is a union not only of states but also of citizens, was recognized in the provision that all citizens of the member states should also be citizens of the Union. The Draft Treaty proposed to give the reformed institutions competence not only to perform the Community's existing functions, but also to establish an economic and monetary union, to have power over Community tax as well as expenditure, and to conduct environmental and social policies. External policy and security were also to come within the scope of the Union, but were to be dealt with by the method of intergovernmental co-operation until a further decision should be taken to integrate them under the responsibility of the Union institutions. In order to prevent the creation of this federal Union from being blocked by one or two member states, the Draft Treaty provided that it should come into force when ratified by a majority of the member states containing two-thirds of the Community's population.

The member states did not accept the Draft Treaty, substituting for it the less ambitious Single European Act; and it is often argued, particularly in Britain, that the member states will never agree to federal reform of the institutions. But they have, in the Maastricht and Amsterdam Treaties as well as the Single Act, taken many of the steps that the Parliament proposed, in addition to adopting the name European Union. The Court has been given jurisdiction to guarantee respect for human rights by the Community institutions. The citizens of the member states are now also citizens of the Union, 'with the rights and duties imposed by the Treaty'. (Article 8/17 ECT) The Council enacts most of the laws under the procedure of qualified majority and the Parliament has the right of co-decision over some half of them. In addition to these and its budgetary powers, the Parliament has also acquired the assent procedure and the right to approve the appointment of the Commission. Emu is being established, though not for all the member states if Britain and Denmark continue to opt out; and there is competence in the environmental and social fields.

These reforms have brought the Community quite far towards becoming the federal system envisaged in the Draft Treaty. The essential further steps that would make its institutions federal are few: the extension of qualified majority voting and co-decision to cover all legislation; clear executive competence for the Commission; and the ability to amend the treaty without unanimous agreement among the member states, which, as the number of members rises, will become more and more difficult to reach. The common foreign and security policy remains intergovernmental, but that, for an indefinite transitional period, was also the proposal of the Parliament's Draft Treaty.

The Draft Treaty was an attempt to replace the predominantly intergovernmental relations in the Community institutions by a system of constitutional government based on the rule of law and representative government.[15] The rule of law is well developed within the sphere of Community competence. Law, including regular legal restraints on government, predominates over arbitrary power; and there is equality before the law, with access to impartial justice, for both citizens and public authorities. But the Community is not so near to applying the principles of representative government, which require that laws must be enacted by the citizens' elected representatives and the executive be clearly accountable to the legislature. In seeking the completion of such a constitutional government, the Parliament adopted a 'dual strategy', working for further steps towards federal institutions as well as promoting the project of a federal Community as a whole. The Parliament's Draft Treaty had substantial parliamentary support in a number of member states, including Belgium, Germany, Italy, and Spain, and was widely endorsed by Christian Democrat,

Liberal, and Socialist parties in the Community, as well as by interest groups and substantial sectors of public opinion.[16] The approach of the single currency and eastern enlargement has added urgency to the case for a federal constitution for the Union, or at least for its central, Community pillar. But the other track of the dual strategy, that of proceeding by steps, has already carried the Union a long way in the federal direction.

3 From Six to Fifteen and More

Britain, Denmark, and the Irish Republic joined the Community on 1 January 1973, fifteen years after the EEC was established and over two decades after the ECSC. Why the delay? Was it just that the British, whose lead the other two followed, needed time to adjust their relationship with the Continent after their very different wartime experience? Or had 'a thousand years of history', as the Labour Party's leader Hugh Gaitskell put it in 1962 when he came out in opposition to the Conservative government's first application to join, built differences into the British economy and polity that would make it hard for the British to co-operate with the Continentals in the Community institutions? The question is still relevant. Britain has often been seen as an obstructive partner in the Community and now the Union; and this gave rise to the idea that a core group of member states might have to move ahead on their own, leaving the British to catch up later if they wish. What does the story of the Community's enlargement tell us that can help to explain the effect of Britain, and of the other late arrivals, on the working of the institutions and on the prospects for development?

In June 1940, ten years before the Community was launched by the Schuman declaration, it was the British government that had offered union to France; and this was the crest of a wave of British public support for the federal idea that had swept the country in 1939 and the first half of 1940, to the extent that an Archbishop said it had made a 'staggeringly effective appeal to the British mind', and Churchill was astonished by the enthusiasm with which the Cabinet approved the offer.[1] Even if the circumstances were exceptional, the British did show that they were capable of embracing the idea of federation. Then the fall of France turned Britain towards America. The British became disillusioned about the Continent, reliant on the United States and, after the war was won, confident in the capacity of the British nation-state to do what was necessary for the British people.

The 1950s: Britain exclusive

After the war Jean Monnet, who was head of the French planning commission, began to seek an opportunity to create new institutions for European co-operation. He looked first to Britain, exploring the scope for economic integration between the two countries. But the British were not receptive. So Monnet turned to the Germans, who were ready to accept the sort of integration that he had in mind. Having experienced, as its Deputy Secretary-General, the weakness of the pre-war League of Nations, he was determined that post-war Europe should have institutions that would not be emasculated by subordination to the governments of the member states. When Schuman on 9 May 1950 announced the proposal for a High Authority to control coal and steel production, the participants were to be France, Germany, and such other European countries as were prepared to be bound by the High Authority's decisions. Italy and the Benelux countries accepted. Britain did not.

The post-war Labour government's reaction was uncompromisingly negative. The project was seen, not as an opportunity to plan the coal and steel industries in common, but as a threat to give foreigners the right to shut down British mines and steelworks. Britain was perceived as a world power, a cut above its Continental neighbours, regarded as unreliable countries with which one would not care to have a particularly close association. So there was no serious interest in exploring exactly what the project might involve. It was seen as a 'rather fancy arrangement that the European constitutional theorists were indulging in', or as a 'federal Europe' in which British participation was out of the question.[2]

In 1950 France and Germany were bold to act without British participation or even approval, so soon after the war which had left Britain as the strongest West European power. But the success of the Coal and Steel Community demonstrated that the Continentals could go ahead without the British. The next Community venture showed that this ability still had its limits. In France, opposition to the Treaty for a European Defence Community (EDC) extended beyond the Gaullists and Communists to many politicians of the centre parties who were reluctant to accept such complete integration with Germany in the absence of any form of British association. But although the Conservatives had criticized the Labour government for their negative reaction to Schuman's proposal, they maintained, once in office after the election of 1951, a similar aloofness towards the nascent Community. Not only did the Conservative government regard membership of the EDC as out of the question, but no association or support was offered, such as might have encouraged the French National Assembly to ratify the Treaty; and in August 1954 the Assembly voted to let it drop.

This encouraged the British government to relapse into the comfortable assumption that the Continentals could not accomplish an important project without British help. The negotiations to establish the EEC and Euratom were, therefore, almost complete before the British government realized that it should act to protect British interests in relation to this new and potentially powerful entity. Membership was still regarded as out of the question, with the Community institutions similar to those that had been too strong medicine for the British when the Coal and Steel Community was created; and some of the economic provisions of the new treaties were inconvenient. The government therefore devised an ingenious scheme, known as the Free Trade Area, which would give British industry free access to the Community market without submitting to the Community's institutions or to the awkward economic stipulations.

The Free Trade Area, to which almost all of Western Europe, including the Community, would have belonged, would have been an intergovernmental organization without the federal elements of the Community's institutions. It would also have excluded some of the Community's functions, in particular the common external tariff and agricultural policy, which would cut across British trade with the Commonwealth, and the provision for 'social harmonization', i.e. harmonization of some elements of labour legislation. Compared to the Community, the idea was minimalist: free trade in industrial goods, with no alteration to tariffs on imports from outside the area.

France's five partners were, for the most part, eager for British involvement. But the more federalist among the Community's protagonists feared that the Free Trade Area might dissolve the Community 'like a lump of sugar in a British cup of tea'. France, which by the time the Free Trade Area negotiations came to a head in 1958 was led by General de Gaulle, had more traditional motives for opposing an arrangement that might give the British a leading role in Western Europe at the expense of the French. The British were exposed because their proposal was widely seen as solipsistic: tailored to British interests without regard to those of others, and in particular of France. The negotiations dragged on until they were broken off by de Gaulle in November 1958.[3]

The 1960s: Britain excluded

After their original Free Trade Area proposal had failed, the British went on to initiate the setting up of the European Free Trade Association (Efta), which applied the same minimalist free trade principles to Denmark, Norway, Sweden, Austria, Switzerland, Portugal, and the United Kingdom. But at the same time the British were rethinking their relationship with the Community. Much had changed since the initial rejection of Schuman's proposal. The British economy was becoming weaker than those of the neighbours on the Continent. The British Commonwealth was in the process of transformation into a loose association that might give Britain some influence, but not the sort of power that had set it apart from its neighbours in the past. The Continent, on the other hand, was no longer weak and unreliable, but had made impressive economic and political progress, and was evidently capable of realizing such an important project as the Community had become. British industry wanted full access to this rich market nearby; and people in government did not want to see Britain 'relegated', internationally, 'to the second division'.[4] Prime Minister Macmillan decided to turn British policy around and seek membership of the Community.

Negotiations began in 1961 between the Community and Britain, together with two other Efta members, Denmark and Norway, and the Irish Republic. This time Britain accepted the Community's institutions and negotiated only to change some of its economic arrangements. Agriculture and Commonwealth trade were, as in the design of the Free Trade Area proposal, two of the main concerns, to which were added Britain's obligations to the other Efta members, which would be met by free trade with the Community for them as well. Macmillan justified the change of front regarding the institutions by aligning himself with de Gaulle's 'confederal' concept against those who were working for a federal system. Macmillan avoided any clear definition of these concepts, however, and the Permanent Under-Secretary of the Treasury was at the same time indicating that the idea of moving towards 'some kind of a federation' was acceptable.[5]

Most of the leaders in British government, business, and media soon swung round to support the idea of Community membership. But the public remained divided, and Macmillan had difficulty with the farmers' and Commonwealth lobbies, both influential with Conservative Members of Parliament. This made the British negotiators in Brussels cautious, looking over their shoulders towards London: from the point of view of the chief British official there, 'a sort of Whitehall exercise'.[6] The negotiations dragged; and, with Labour Party supporters increasingly doubtful, Gaitskell led Labour into opposing membership in October 1962. This did not pass unnoticed by de Gaulle, who could argue that the Party which was likely before long to form the next British government was against

British accession. His relationship with Adenauer and his political position in France were at the same time strengthened, so that he was well placed to veto the continuation of the negotiations in January 1963.

Britain had moved far from its earlier post-war stance of aloofness from Europe; and the government had accepted the Community institutions, even if with the proviso that de Gaulle was a guarantee against their becoming more federal, at least for some years ahead. But there was still much opposition, both to the European entanglement and to the federal elements in the Community. It appeared, for a time, that the rebuff of de Gaulle's veto might turn the British away from Europe again. But the Labour government, which had replaced the Conservatives in 1964, again applied for membership in 1967, only to encounter another veto from de Gaulle. The government held to its new policy, however, and began to prepare a new application when de Gaulle resigned in 1969.

Georges Pompidou, who succeeded de Gaulle as President of France, did not share his rooted objection to British membership. German Ostpolitik was, moreover, raising French fears of a more independent and powerful Germany, to which Britain within the Community could act as a counterweight. At the same time the French seized the opportunity to get the other Community member governments, which had been keen supporters of British entry, to accept conditions that were of interest to France. Above all, this meant agreement on securing the Community's 'own resources', i.e. its own tax revenue, with which to finance the common agricultural policy that France saw as a principal French interest in the Community. This was elegantly called 'completion', since it would complete outstanding Community business. At the same time, it was agreed that British entry would be accompanied by 'deepening' of the Community through the extension of its competences in monetary integration. Willy Brandt, by then Chancellor of the German Federal Republic, was a keen promoter of the project of monetary union; and European monetary integration to countervail the dollar and underpin the agricultural policy had for some time been a French concern.

The French now had another motive. They had, from the beginning, feared that British participation would make the Community a looser and weaker organization. So the idea of deepening the Community at the same time as widening it seemed a suitable antidote—which would moreover lock Germany more securely into it. But the French government could not, so soon after de Gaulle, accept stronger Community institutions: functional integration, in the monetary field, appeared to be the perfect answer. The story of the ensuing attempt at monetary union is told in Chapter 7. Ironically, it failed in large part because France was not then ready to accept that monetary integration should have institutional consequences, on which Germany insisted. Equally ironically, the condition of 'completion', which was seen as a French interest in a more traditional sense, did lead to a strengthening of the Community institutions, because the payment of tax revenue direct to the Community, escaping the control of member states' parliaments, was accompanied by significant new budgetary powers for the European Parliament. Here, however, we need only note that enlargement of the Community does not have to result in its dilution through the greater diversity among the member states: it can be accompanied by the strengthening of the policies, powers, or institutions.

First enlargement: Britain, Denmark, Ireland

Although the Labour government had prepared Britain's ultimate, and successful, application to join, it was Edward Heath who carried it through after he became Prime Minister with the Conservative election victory in June 1970. He had long been convinced of the case for membership on both political and economic grounds. Politically, it was not just a matter of avoiding 'relegation to the second division', but of the positive merits that he saw in European unity. Economically, the argument was difficult. Since the common agricultural policy had been designed for the six founding members, it was ill adapted to the needs of Britain, with its small agricultural sector and large imports of foodstuffs. It would impose high prices on the British consumer and, with the financial regulation that France was so eager to see completed, a heavy burden for the British taxpayer. A number of economic studies foresaw a direct, 'static' loss to Britain of 0.75–2 per cent of gross domestic product, with a central estimate of 1.25 per cent.[7] There were some predictions of much heavier cost, in the belief that deflation would be required to stem losses to the balance of payments. But other studies suggested that the 'dynamic' effects of competition, innovation, and investment would, over the medium term, outweigh the static loss—which should build up gradually over a transitional period. Industrial leaders held fast to this view and continued to support entry. The White Paper with which Heath presented the case for membership to Parliament after the substance of the negotiations had been completed in July 1971 likewise emphasized 'improvements in efficiency and competitive power'.[8]

Heath had no doubts about the case and drove the negotiations forward as fast as possible. Solutions to many of the difficult problems relating to agriculture, the Commonwealth, and Efta had already been found during the first negotiations in 1961–3. Heath took care to establish a good relationship with Pompidou, insuring against a repetition of the veto of 1963. The European Movement ran a massive campaign to turn the public round from its initially hostile stance. Yet the negotiation was by no means plain sailing.

The main issue for the British economy was the cost of the agricultural policy. A transition period of seven years was agreed, during which Britain would be eased incrementally into full participation in the Community budget. By then, it was argued from the Community's side, there would be new policies that would benefit Britain, offsetting the British loss on the hitherto predominant agricultural expenditure. But what if the burden on the British should still be excessive? Britain's negotiators did not succeed in getting any commitment to remedial action written into the Treaty of Accession. But the Community side assured the British, in the course of the negotiations, that if 'unacceptable' situations should arise 'the very survival of the Community would demand that the institutions find equitable solutions'; and this assurance was duly recorded in the White Paper.[9] The 'British budget question', though thus circumvented in the negotiations, was to remain an incubus for the Community until the mid-1980s.

The House of Commons remained sensitive about sovereignty, and the White Paper asserted that there was 'no question of any erosion of essential national sovereignty', adding however that there was to be 'a sharing and an enlargement of individual national sovereignties in the general interest'.[10] This, like so many of the formulations about sovereignty, glossed over the hard questions. What national sovereignty was regarded as 'essential'? How much sovereignty was to be 'shared and enlarged' and how? The answers would depend on the future development of the Community and behaviour of the member states; and this would depend on the attitudes of their governments. Heath's attitude was favourable to integration; that of the British governments which succeeded his from 1974 onwards, less so.

The decade that followed the first enlargement lent support to those who had predicted that widening would be the enemy of deepening. Some significant steps were taken, such as the first direct elections to the European Parliament and the creation of the European Monetary System (EMS). But such steps were relatively few. The Community experienced a period of stagnation rather than development; and some aspects of the behaviour of new members were blamed for this.

Britain and Denmark, together, through much of the 1980s, with Greece, resisted proposals that they felt would erode national sovereignty; and the attitude of the British Labour government which replaced Heath's administration in 1974 was soured by the growing opposition in the Labour Party to the principle of membership itself. The government first tried to renegotiate the terms of membership, obtaining however only cosmetic adjustments. British membership of the Community was placed in question by a referendum on the issue in 1975. The electorate voted two-to-one for staying in. But ministers who had campaigned against remained in the government, continuing to represent Britain in the Community's Council. It is not surprising that they were often seen as obstructive, nor that Britain chose, when the EMS was created in 1979, to stay out of its central element, the Exchange Rate Mechanism. In 1980, the year after the Conservatives replaced Labour in government, the Labour Party Conference voted for unconditional withdrawal; and the Party campaigned for it in the 1983 election, which was, however, again won by the Conservatives. It was not until towards the end of the decade that Labour under Neil Kinnock's leadership returned to a more positive policy.

Although Britain, as a new member, did little to help cure the Community of its malaise in the 1970s, it was by no means the sole cause of the stagnation. French governments during that period were still in a post-Gaullist phase of vigilance against any federalist encroachment by Community institutions. Underlying many of the Community's difficulties, moreover, was the stagflation that pervaded the world economy, which had been initiated by the quadrupling of oil prices at the end of the year of the first enlargement. With rapidly rising inflation and unemployment, the mood of member states was protectionist rather than integrationist. Hopes of monetary integration were also set back by the divergence of economic performance among the member states. Britain and Italy, in particular, proved much more prone to inflation following the oil shock than most of the other member states, while Germany became the model of stability. The idea of closer integration threatened inflation for the Germans, deflation and more unemployment for the Italians and the British. Divergence among the member states' economies became a key concept in the 1970s, causing concern about the future of the Community.[11]

When Mrs Thatcher won the 1979 election for the Conservatives, who had claimed to be 'the party of Europe', a more positive British attitude to the development of the Community was widely expected. After a further lapse of five years, this proved justified in one important respect: British support for the single market programme. But negotiation of the Single European Act in 1985 was hampered in many ways by British reluctance, and the Community's development had, for five years, been blocked by the conflict over Britain's net contribution to the budget. There were good grounds to argue that, since new policies had not gone far to rectify the imbalance, the agricultural budget was causing an 'unacceptable situation' such as had been discussed during the entry negotiations; and Britain's partners were not quick to agree to a reduction in the net contribution that a British government could accept. But however the blame may be apportioned, the widening of the Community had hampered its deepening for a further five years. Apart from the commitment to the freeing of trade through the single market programme, moreover, Mrs Thatcher's pronouncements as well as some of her actions in the later 1980s confirmed, for many among Britain's partner countries, the impression they had gained during the budget negotiations, that her view of the Community was reductionist, confined mainly to deregulation and freer trade; and though the style of her successor, John Major, was different, they were to find that less had changed in the substance.

It was President Mitterrand who, at the meeting of the European Council at Fontainebleau in June 1984, presided over the taking of decisions that led to the resolution of the British budget problem. At the same meeting he secured the breakthrough that brought Portugal and Spain into membership in 1986. This time, it was to be shown that enlargement need not impede the Community's development.

Southern enlargement: Greece, Portugal, Spain

Whereas the British had, initially, doubted the political stability of the Community countries, the southern members which brought its number from nine to twelve in the 1980s started from a diametrically opposite perspective. Greece, Portugal, and Spain had all become free of dictators in the 1970s. To them, the Community was a stronghold of democracy that could help to consolidate their own recently established democratic systems. Whereas Britain had, moreover, been richer than the member states when the Community was founded, for the new southern members it represented the prosperous, modern economy to which they aspired. Their perception of the Community was thus more favourable than that of the British had been.

There were problems, of course. The southern enlargement brought with it a new kind of economic divergence, after the economies of the existing member states, recovering from the shocks of the 1970s, had themselves begun to converge. The Greek, Portuguese, and Spanish economies were at a lower stage of development than that of the Community's mainstream. Among the existing members, only the Irish Republic was comparable. Average incomes were lower; a higher proportion of people worked in agriculture; industry was technologically less advanced. The integration of such economies with those of the existing members raised fears on both sides. The higher-paid existing members feared competition based on cheap labour—not only in manufacturing but also, for France and Italy, in Mediterranean agricultural products. The new member states feared they would be unable to compete with the stronger industries of the North. Greece and Portugal had, admittedly, already been open to the competition of Community industries, in the Greek case under an association agreement and, for Portugal, through the free trade relationship that the Community had negotiated with each member of Efta. But membership of the Community would make this free trade more complete and rigorous, and less reversible. For Spain, which, because of the Community's objection to the Franco regime, had not qualified for a free trade arrangement, a wide range of industries that had been developing fast would have to face a new, chill north wind of competition.

For the existing members the southern enlargement presented no profound economic challenge. The acute fears were confined to a limited sector of agriculture in France and Italy. The worry was, rather, political. Would the Community, with this new diversity of interests and divergence of economic performance, be able to take the decisions necessary for the future? Or would its institutional machinery, at least partly unblocked by the resolution of the British budget problem, again become too difficult to operate? Solutions were sought in two directions. Federalists called for the institutions to be strengthened, so that there would be less chance for a small minority of governments to block decisions in the Council. Pragmatists considered various techniques, under names such as two speeds, two tiers, variable geometry, and Europe à la carte, to enable some member states to act while others opted out.[12] The new members from the south, with their weaker economies, were faced with more formidable economic problems, to which they reacted in different ways.

The Greek reaction was coloured by a political event, similar to that which the British had experienced after their accession. Entry had been negotiated by a Conservative government, which was soon after replaced by the Socialist opposition. As in Britain, the new Greek government was not enthusiastic about the Community. It gained the reputation of tending to obstruct Community business whenever a problem arose for it. It made the negotiations for the accession of Portugal and Spain more difficult—and more difficult, it was contended, than the real problems of Iberian competition with Greece could justify. Greek demands did have a concrete result for the development of the Community, however. Its policy for the promotion of economic growth in the weaker regions was strengthened through what were called Integrated Mediterranean Programmes because they provided funds for regional development in a more co-ordinated way. With this and other experiences of working in the Community, the Greek government's attitude towards it evolved; and subsequent governments were yet more favourable.

Neither Spain nor Portugal suffered any such political inhibition after their accession in 1986. Their entry coincided with the regeneration of the Community following the solving of the British budget problem and the launching of the single market programme; and they provoked no accusations that they were obstructing the Community's development. The solution that they secured for their problem of divergence was similar in principle to the Integrated Mediterranean Programmes that had been devised for the Greeks, but on a grander scale. The first step was taken before they had actually joined. The juridical basis for the single market programme was formulated in the negotiations for the Single Act, in the last few months of 1985. But working closely with the Commission, they managed to secure provision in the Single Act for a policy of 'cohesion', that is for 'reducing disparities between the various regions and the backwardness of the least-favoured regions' (Article 23 SEA). Their argument was that, since the single market would expose them to more rigorous competition from stronger economies, they should be compensated with measures that would assist their economic development. The argument was accepted in principle by most of the governments; and it was recognized that discontented members could make it hard to enact the complex legislation that the single market programme required. But it is one thing to secure agreement on a principle, quite another to ensure that the Community applies it adequately in practice. In this, too, the southern members and the Irish, who have a similar interest, succeeded, again with the Commission playing an essential part. By the first half of 1988, the Community could no longer delay a general reform of its budget. The chronic deficit caused by its agricultural spending had to be tackled and the arrangement to compensate Britain for its excessive contribution renewed. The opportunity was seized to turn the principle of cohesion into a major financial commitment, with the doubling of the Community's 'structural funds' (regional development fund, social fund, and fund for 'agricultural guidance') by 1993. Along with agreement on economic and monetary union in the Maastricht Treaty, the Cohesion Fund was added and the allocation for structural actions was then increased again, rising to over ecu 30 billion by 1997.

Thus the southern enlargement was accompanied by a significant enhancement of the Community's policy instruments.

Austria, Finland, Norway, Sweden, Switzerland

Austria's application for membership, presented in 1989, and those of Finland, Norway, Sweden, and Switzerland, which followed it, raised quite different questions. There were no doubts about the solidity of their democracies or the contribution that their economies could make to the Union and its budget. The main concern was, rather, whether they were ready to accept some political implications of membership: whether the neutral status of all save Norway would inhibit their participation in the common foreign and security policy and, in particular, in 'the eventual framing of a common defence policy, which might in time lead to a common defence'; and whether they would resist the further sharing of sovereignty implied in the federal goal which the majority of member states had wished to affirm in the Maastricht Treaty. Switzerland, indeed, shelved its application following the referendum in 1992 when its citizens rejected the milder medicine of the European Economic Area. But the governments of the other four accepted participation in the CFSP without reserve, as well as all other elements of the Maastricht Treaty and of Community law, given some transitional arrangements and provision for special aid for less-favoured agricultural areas. Despite fears in the European Parliament and elsewhere that the Union's institutions or the CFSP would be weakened by divergent attitudes in the new member states, the Parliament gave its assent and the treaties of accession with the four applicants were signed by June 1994. In each of them ratification depended on a referendum. While the result in Norway was negative, the other three acceded in January 1995.

Mediterranean applicants

Turkey lodged its application in 1987. Part of Turkey is geographically in Europe and the country is a member of the Council of Europe, although its membership has been troubled by failures to maintain the standards of fundamental rights, rule of law, and representative government to which its political élites generally aspire. Such principles of constitutional government are an essential condition for membership of the Community, in which the rule of law based on fundamental rights has to apply evenly throughout, elections to the European Parliament have to be freely and democratically conducted, and the ministers who enact laws and take other decisions in the Council must all come from properly representative governments. Doubts whether these principles are solidly based in the Turkish political system have clouded reactions to Turkey's application, and compounded worries about the Turkish economy which, though growing fast, is still at a lower level of development than that in the Community and prone to growing pains such as treble-digit inflation. While the Portuguese and Greek economies are also much less developed than that of the Community in general, these are smaller countries; Turkey's population is as big as those of the Community's larger members and still growing fast. The strain caused by economic divergence would be correspondingly greater.

Against doubts such as these, there are strong strategic arguments for consolidating Turkey's relationship with Western Europe which, even if the end of the Cold War may have weakened them, can be reinforced by instability in the Middle East or Central Asia; and there are political grounds for giving what encouragement outsiders can to Turkey's still fragile democracy. These will certainly weigh with existing member states; and some will not mind if further enlargement should place new obstacles in the path that would lead to a federal Europe. Other governments and parliaments would, on the contrary, object to this; and since treaties of accession must be ratified by all member states, their objections could prove decisive. Likewise the European Parliament, which can be expected to be punctilious about the principles of fundamental rights, rule of law, and representative government, could well withhold its assent.

The first step in the Community's procedure after receiving an application is for the Council to request an Opinion from the Commission. In 1990, three years after Turkey applied, the Commission produced its Opinion to the effect that despite significant progress, Turkey's economy and polity had some way to go before the Turks could meet the conditions for membership. The Council had no difficulty in accepting the Commission's view. In December 1997, when the European Council decided to open accession negotiations with five Central and East European states as well as Cyprus, it also indicated that Turkey, while eligible for accession, was not yet ready for it.

Two other Mediterranean countries, Cyprus and Malta, presented their applications for membership in 1990. Both already had association agreements with the Community and neither presented any serious economic difficulty. Following a change of government, the Maltese application was withdrawn. But although the Turkish occupation of part of Cyprus remains, a major political problem, accession negotiations with Cyprus began, like those with five Central and East European states, in March 1998.

Central and Eastern Europe

After they emerged from under Soviet hegemony in 1989–90, Central and East European countries too became potential members. East Germany chose a fast track into the Community by uniting with the Federal Republic in 1990. In the following years the Community concluded Europe Agreements with the Czech Republic, Hungary, Poland, Slovakia, Bulgaria, Romania, Estonia, Latvia, Lithuania, and Slovenia. The phased movement to industrial free trade and the close economic and political co-operation for which these association agreements provide could be seen as a form of preparation for membership: the preambles to the first agreements already recognized 'the fact that' the ultimate objective of the associates was 'to accede to the Community, and that this aim, in the view of the parties, will help [them] to achieve this objective'.[13] This convoluted wording was the result of disagreement within the Community because some member states, echoing French reservations when the British applied to join in the early 1970s, feared that enlargement would weaken the institutions and undermine policies such as those concerning agriculture and the structural funds. These fears were reflected in a report of the Commission which emphasized that 'widening must not be at the expense of deepening.'[14] Nevertheless, the European Council at Copenhagen in June 1993 affirmed that 'the Associated countries in Central and Eastern Europe that so desire shall become members of the European Union', and went on to list the conditions: the candidates must satisfy the political and economic conditions of democracy and market economy; they must demonstrate 'adherence to the aims of political, economic and monetary union'; and enlargement would also depend on 'the Union's capacity to absorb new members while maintaining the momentum of European integration'.[15]

While the candidates faced an enormous task in transforming their polities and economies from the Soviet to the democratic and market model, that condition was at least reasonably clear. But the words 'political . . . union' and 'maintaining the momentum of European integration' meant very different things to the nationalist British government and the more federalist among its partners. These differences about deepening became explicit after the European Council in June 1994 decided that the IGC which was to lead to the Amsterdam Treaty should create 'the institutional conditions for ensuring the proper functioning of the Union' after its enlargement.[16] As we saw in Chapter 1, the British government was stubbornly opposed to many of the aspects of deepening that most of the others regarded as essential. They feared that a need for unanimity would lead to deadlock in the Council as the number and diversity of member states increased, and that the movement from intergovernmentalism towards a parliamentary democratic system would be reversed unless co-decision becomes the general rule. To the contrary, Britain's Conservative government looked to enlargement to create a less constraining Union by leading back towards intergovernmentalism.

Despite this divergence between the British and most of the rest, progress continued on other aspects of the enlargement process. The European Council at Essen in December 1994 agreed on a 'route plan for the associated countries as they prepare for accession.'[17] The ten candidate countries had to fill in a vast questionnaire about all aspects of their progress towards meeting the conditions of membership. Following the Commission's analysis of this, the European Council decided in December 1997 that negotiations should be started early in 1998 with the Czech Republic, Estonia, Hungary, Poland, and Slovenia, which were seen to have progressed far enough with their economic and political transformation to be ready to play their part in the single market and the Union's institutions. Negotiations with the other five would come later; and meanwhile a European Conference, meeting for the first time in March 1998, would bring together annually for political discussions the heads of state or government of each of the applicants for membership, including Cyprus, which joined the five Central and East Europeans in the first wave of negotiations, and Turkey, should it wish to participate.

Meanwhile the Union itself was making less progress in adapting its own policies and institutions to the needs of enlargement. The impact of the candidate countries on the common agricultural policy and the structural funds will be very costly unless these policies are radically reformed. The Commission has estimated the cost for agriculture alone at ecu 9–12 billion;[18] and there have been higher estimates. Britain and Germany have been leading the member states that resist easing the path to enlargement through an increase in the Union's budget. The Commission set out its proposals for reforming the agricultural and structural policies in its 'Agenda 2000' report.[19] The agricultural reform, based on a transfer of budget expenditure from price support to income support, will encounter stiff resistance in France and Germany as well as other member states; and any reduction of the structural fund spending in Greece, Portugal, and Spain will be stoutly resisted. There will be protectionist pressures, not only from farmers but also from manufacturers of products such as textiles; and free movement of labour from countries such as Poland will be hard for Germany to accept.

Such resistance to change in existing arrangements is nothing new. It was encountered in negotiating previous enlargements and has been overcome, with the help of transition periods of up to seven years to make the necessary adjustments, when there was enough political will to bring in the new member states. For Germany, the contribution of enlargement to stability among its eastern neighbours is a vital political interest, bolstered by the expected economic advantages. So Germany will almost certainly accept uncomfortable but necessary changes in Union policies. Britain strongly favours enlargement on more general political grounds. France has feared that the Union would be weakened by the enlargement and that its centre of gravity would shift towards Germany. The need to maintain its partnership with Germany, together with more general political considerations, overrode these fears, but France may be less inclined than Germany to make concessions in order to conclude the negotiations. The same applies to Spain, determined to maintain its receipts from the structural funds and conscious that its own accession negotiations lasted seven years, partly because of the French government's determination to protect French farmers. But such reservations notwithstanding, there is a consensus among the member states that enlargement is a necessary condition of Europe's stability and security. The specific problems are therefore likely to be overcome, eased by the device of lengthy transition periods, provided the consensus is not disrupted by divergences about the political structure and future of the Union.

Negotiations in the 1996 IGC about 'the institutional conditions' for enlargement focused on the balance between larger and smaller member states as regards their representation in the Council and their nationals among the Commissioners. The larger states wanted heavier weighting for their votes in the Council to offset the growing number of small states due to join the Union. There was also pressure to reduce the number of Commissioners to correspond with the number of significant tasks to be performed, implying that the Commission would not, after enlargement, be able to include a national of each member state; and naturally the smaller states feared that they rather than the larger ones would face the prospect of a Commission without one of their nationals in it—not that the Commissioners are supposed to act as representatives of their state, but they do bring to the Commission knowledge of their country's circumstances and political culture.

When the European Council met in Amsterdam, a compromise seemed to be in sight. The five larger member states would each forgo one of the two places traditionally reserved in the Commission for their nationals, thus leaving room for Commissioners from five more of the smaller states than would otherwise have places; and the smaller states would accept a re-weighting of the votes in the Council in favour of the larger. For the Belgian Prime Minister, Jean-Luc Dehaene, however, these arrangements were linked with an extension of the procedure of qualified majority voting, seen as necessary if enlargement is not to lead to gridlock in the Council. But Chancellor Kohl, concentrating on the domestic German politics of maintaining adequate support for the replacement of the mark by the euro, failed to resolve a dispute between the federal government and the Länder about voting arrangements for the Union's environmental and immigration policies, with respect to which both federal government and Länder can claim some competence under Germany's Basic Law. So Kohl did not accept the expected extension of qualified majority voting; Dehaene withdrew his support fot the re-weighting of votes in the Council; and the compromise fell apart.

This contretemps illustrates the negative interaction between domestic politics and the Union's decision-taking when the latter is as heavily intergovernmental as it is for treaty amendments, which have to be ratified by all the member states. But it will probably also come to illustrate the Union's capacity for recovery from such setbacks, through taking the necessary decisions when they can be delayed no longer. In order to facilitate this, a protocol was added to the Amsterdam Treaty stipulating that a further IGC be convened in time to be completed before the next wave of enlargement.

The Amsterdam Treaty was severely criticised for failing to resolve this issue. But there were more fundamental questions about the Union's institutions. The substantial extension of the European Parliament's power of co-decision and its right of approval over the appointment of the Commission's President were important steps in the direction of parliamentary democracy. The Treaty, with its provision for sanctions against a member state perpetrating 'a serious and persistent breach' of human rights, provided reassurance that the Union would not be undermined by any member states that should fall short of the necessary standards of democracy and the rule of law. But the limited extension of qualified majority voting was a setback for hopes of enhancing the Union's effectiveness. Proposals to deepen the Union by making qualified majority voting and co-decision the general rules for enacting Union legislation and by strengthening the arrangements for foreign and security policy will doubtless be made during the 'comprehensive review' of the Union's institutions to be undertaken at the next IGC; and the drafting of a constitution that would make the Union not only more effective and democratic but also more comprehensible to the citizens is also likely to be proposed. The prospects for the Union after enlargement will depend on the extent to which it is strengthened in such ways. A Union which, after the eastern enlargement has been completed, will have half a billion citizens could, if its institutions are indeed adequately reformed, be an enormous force for prosperity and stability, not only within Europe but also in the wider world.

4 From Customs Union to Single Market and Open Frontiers

Free trade versus protection is the classic issue of international economic policy. Britain's industrial supremacy in the nineteenth century was based on free trade. Germany and the United States sought to promote their industries by protecting them against British industrial power. Until the 1930s, both policies could show evidence of success. But in the 1930s, the rise of protectionism and autarky was associated with the world economic depression and the approach of war. When the war was over, there was a widespread determination not to let such things happen again.

The Americans led in establishing the liberal international economic order, in which the General Agreement on Tariffs and Trade (Gatt) was to ensure non-discriminatory tariffs and freer trade. But the founder members of the European Community wanted to go farther. Having suffered grievously during the war, they were ready to go to greater lengths to ensure that protectionism did not become a cause of future conflicts among them. Looking across the Atlantic at the wealth and power of the United States, they reasoned that Europe's divisions were a cause of their relative backwardness. In order to produce cars or planes as efficiently as the Americans, they wanted to have a unified continental market too.

The success of the customs union

Such were the motives that underlay the support for the idea of the customs union, which was the central economic feature of the EEC Treaty. The economic arguments went beyond the classical free trade case for cutting out production that was high-cost and concentrating it where there was a comparative advantage. Attention was drawn to the dynamic effects: the scope in the larger market for scale, specialization, and stronger competition; and the consequent opportunities for higher investment, more innovation, and faster economic growth.[1] The political arguments went beyond the reduction of friction between states. Merit was seen in a new relationship between the citizens of the states, in which for certain purposes they would all be equal before the law, without discrimination on grounds of nationality, thus planting deeper roots for the growth of peaceful relations among them. So the project itself went beyond a bare customs union, with tariff-free trade inside the union and a common tariff on imports from outside, to an area in which the 'four freedoms' prevail, that is free movement not only for goods but also for services, capital, and people going about their business; and the whole was to be the responsibility of institutions that could ensure the enactment of laws required for these purposes, together with the rule of law through the Community's judicial system, and any necessary executive action.

Despite the reaction against the autarky of the 1930s, there were still fears about the impact of free trade. The Germans and the Dutch were the most liberal among the six founders, the French and Italians the most protectionist. When the common market project was first mooted, it seemed far from certain that the French would be ready to accept the removal of protection for their industry against German competition. So the designers of the EEC Treaty devised an ingenious method of allaying such fears while at the same time ensuring that the customs union would at the end of the day be completed. The removal of tariffs and quotas, or quantitative restrictions, from trade among member states would not be imposed at one swoop, but would be phased in incrementally over a transitional period of 12–15 years. Each member state would be able to adjust the rate of tariff reduction on individual products, freeing the imports of sensitive sectors more slowly, provided that the state's tariffs as a whole were reduced on average at the agreed rate. Similarly member states were to align on to the common external tariff by a series of three steps during the transitional period. In these ways protectionist pressures that could have impeded acceptance of the EEC Treaty were deflected; and France like the other five members entered a new phase in the development of a more open economy, with the first tariff cuts of 10 per cent at the end of 1958.

Had the expected economic gains not materialized, Monnet's idea of uniting Europe step by step might have progressed no farther. But evidence of economic success came surprisingly quickly. In the first couple of years after the EEC was established, the Patronat, which represented French industry, swung round from its earlier suspicion of the idea of opening the French market to support for accelerating the timetable of liberalization. The proposal for acceleration had political motives. The Commission wanted to maintain the momentum generated by its early success in sorting out the initial problems of launching the customs union. The Germans and the Dutch, together with the Commission, wanted the Community to start playing its part in a wider process of international liberalization; and they also wanted to make concessions to ease the impact on the British and other Efta countries of the Community's moves towards its common external tariff, which required them to raise their own relatively low tariffs on imports from those countries. The French, on the contrary, wished to ensure that the common external tariff remained intact, and to remove from the Dutch and the Germans any temptation to avoid imposing it on the trade partners in Efta. The resolution of this conflict of interests lay in acceleration of both the Community's internal tariff reductions and the first move towards the common external tariff, whose level was at the same time cut provisionally by one-fifth. This gave the Dutch and Germans faster progress towards internal free trade and towards international negotiations with a liberal orientation, while the French secured the commitment they sought to the external tariff's implementation. The acceleration was strongly promoted by the Commission and the federalists. But the support of industry, including French industry, was also decisive.

Once they had been convinced that the customs union was going to be established, industrialists had begun to make their plans for doing business in the larger market. Having started to invest to produce for it, the delay that had been designed to meet protectionist fears became an irritant, standing in the way of early success for the new investments. Their support for acceleration indicated that the dynamic effects were materializing, and helped to give the customs union a clear run in the 1960s. Instead of a reduction of 30 per cent of the internal tariffs by 1962 or one of the two following years, as provided in the Treaty, the tariffs were in fact cut by half by the middle of 1962.[2]

The customs union continued to fulfil high expectations through the 1960s. Trade among the member states grew twice as fast as trade in the wider international economy, quadrupling in the first decade after the Community was established in 1958. Gross domestic product expanded in the Community at 5 per cent a year, twice as fast as in Britain or the United States. Economists did not know how much of this growth had been due to the creation of the customs union, which was completed well ahead of time in mid-1968. The general expansion of international trade certainly helped. But the Community had evidently provided a framework in which the growth had been possible. Although the economists were unable to estimate dynamic effects, industrialists had been acting on the assumption that these existed. Their support for acceleration had soon been followed by the backing of British industry for the attempt to join the Community in 1961–3. The nature of the growth of trade within the Community in the 1960s consolidated industrial support. Protectionists had feared that whole sectors of industry would be competed out of existence in their own country. But trade expanded on different lines. It was predominantly intra-sectoral trade, with each member state's exports and imports both growing in each sector. This was the consequence of greater specialization within each sector, and of larger scale in the production of these specialized products than would have been possible in the protected national markets. It was easier to adjust to this kind of change, because most people could continue to work in the same sector and place as before.

Politically, the Community suffered in the 1960s from de Gaulle's attack on its institutions. Expectations of steady progress towards political union on federal lines were dissipated. But the success of the customs union ensured that the Community would be valued for its existing achievements, not only for its potential as a step towards a federal union. This enabled the Community to weather the difficult period of stagnation in the 1970s and early 1980s, to double its membership, and to be ready to react to the problems of the 1980s with a further stage in the creation of a single market; and this in turn made further big strides towards union appear politically feasible.

The need to complete the internal market

The dynamic phase of the late 1980s, with the single market programme as its focus, was the Community's response to the difficulties that had arisen in the 1970s. At the beginning of that decade, the hopes for Community development in the post-de Gaulle period had been placed on the combination of the first enlargement and the project of monetary union. But while the enlargement was realized, the attempts to promote monetary integration, already weakened by disagreement between French and Germans over the relationship between monetary union and other elements of political and economic union, were blown off course by instability in the currency markets, which was an early warning of rough seas ahead.

After the exceptionally long boom of the 1950s and 1960s, inflation was starting to take hold of the international economy; and it hit very hard at the end of 1973, with the quadrupling of the price of oil. This injected a strong inflationary impulse into the European economies, and imposed heavy deficits in their external balances as they paid the new prices for their oil imports. Their main weapon to stem the inflation and correct the deficits was deflation, causing large-scale unemployment. For some time they suffered both inflation and unemployment; and by the time inflation was generally under control, there was a second oil shock, when prices were doubled in 1979.

Quite apart from the political problems of accommodating the new entrants, and in particular the British, the Community was not well placed to promote further integration while its members were struggling against inflation and unemployment. On the contrary, they were tempted to lapse into measures of disintegration, as governments sought to protect their hard-pressed industrial sectors: not with tariffs or quotas, to be sure, as these were not allowed by Community law which the member states did not wish to defy, but by subsidies to firms in trouble and, sometimes, by regulations which were overtly for purposes such as safety or consumer protection but which were in fact protectionist devices. Thus the fragmentation of the Community's tariff-free internal market by non-tariff barriers was intensified. Wherever they stood in the way, whether in the form of subsidies maintaining high-cost production or other government interventions, the more efficient firms were inhibited from producing for the wide Community market.

The pressure of unemployment which pushed the Community into this dangerous phase was intensified by new competitors from outside Europe. Japan, during the 1960s, had been establishing itself as an exporter far beyond its earlier image as a producer of cheap textiles with cheap labour. The Japanese had mastered the techniques required for the second industrial revolution, which had been pioneered by the Americans and applied in particular to the production of cars, consumer durables, and standard machinery. Their exports of such products began to make inroads into the European market. Hard on their heels came other, newly industrializing countries such as South Korea, Taiwan, Hong Kong, Singapore, Brazil, Mexico, China, and India. While these still had cheap labour, they were climbing behind Japan up the ladder of technology, moving from textiles and shoes through consumer electronics to steel, shipbuilding, cars, and a range of capital goods. Protectionist pressures in Europe grew as Europeans began to doubt their ability to compete with these 'new Japans' in the products of the second industrial revolution.

Europeans sought a way out through more advanced technological development. But here they came up against the superiority of the Americans and Japanese in the new technologies, based on microelectronics and with information technology at the epicentre. By the early 1980s fears were widespread that Europe might become an industrial museum, the term Eurosclerosis was current coinage, and Europe's ability to compete in the world economy replaced unemployment as the focus of economic concern in the Community.

Various reports were produced on the declining competitiveness of the European economy.[3] They demonstrated how Europeans were losing ground to Americans and Japanese, both in the Community market and outside it, in many sectors where the newer or higher technologies were the key to success. They also drew attention to the fragmentation of the Community market caused by the non-tariff barriers and suggested that the Europeans, if they were to compete with the Americans and Japanese in the industries of the future, would have to follow the example of these most formidable competitors in establishing a single, barrier-free internal market.

This diagnosis and prescription were not just the brainchild of economists and officials. They were shared by leading industrialists in the most relevant sectors. Wisse Dekker, the head of Philips, one of Europe's foremost electronics manufacturers, went so far as to publish a report that recommended a programme for the Community to sweep away the non-tariff barriers by 1990. Not long after, in June 1985, the Commission published its White Paper, *Completing the Internal Market,* which set out a detailed timetable for enacting nearly three hundred measures to remove the barriers by the end of 1992.[4]

Like the idea of the customs union that was embodied in the EEC Treaty, the 1992 programme to complete the single market was supported by both economic liberals and federalists. But whereas in the 1950s the liberals had been concentrated mainly among the Germans and the Dutch, with French industry and government on the protectionist side, by the 1980s a liberal attitude towards trade, at least within Europe, was widespread throughout the Community. The leading industrialists, in France as elsewhere, strongly supported the 1992 programme; and a liberal view of economic policy was spreading among the governments. Nowhere had it taken a stronger hold than in Britain, where Mrs Thatcher was distinctly unenthusiastic about most proposals for further development of the Community. However, she came to see the 1992 programme as a vast exercise in deregulation, led in the Commission by a former member of her government, Lord Cockfield, so she too championed the project. Thus it was supported by most member states as well as by Europe's leading industrialists.

Federalists in the European Parliament had meanwhile taken an initiative that was to lead to the Single European Act, which gave the 1992 programme its juridical form. This was the European Union Draft Treaty, which was the product of Spinelli's more general analysis of the Community's malaise, attributing it to the intergovernmental dominance in the institutions. The Draft Treaty proposed a thoroughgoing reform of the institutions to make them efficient and democratic, and thus capable of launching new projects such as monetary union as well as completing unfinished business such as the removal of the non-tariff barriers within the internal market. The European Parliament approved the Draft Treaty in the first half of 1984, when France held the presidency of the Council. President Mitterrand went out of his way to emphasize his sympathy with the Parliament's aims; and he persuaded the European Council to set up an *ad hoc* committee to recommend what should be done about it. The committee's report commended many of the elements in the Draft Treaty, though with key reservations from the representatives of Britain, Denmark, and Greece in particular. But by the time the report came to be considered by the European Council, under Italian presidency in June 1985, Mitterrand was preoccupied by the political situation in France among other things, and failed to maintain his earlier support for the Parliament's project. The political momentum was however sufficient for the Italian presidency, itself then the Parliament's strongest advocate among the governments, to push through the decision to hold an Intergovernmental Conference to consider amendments to the Community treaties. At the same meeting the European Council approved the Commission's White Paper on the completion of the internal market. Since this was agreed by all of the governments, whereas other aspects of the Parliament's Draft Treaty were not, the 1992 programme became the central element in the Single European Act that emerged from the Intergovernmental Conference. Spinelli and many other federalists saw this as a grossly inadequate outcome, or even an undesirable distraction from the main task of creating the European Union. Yet it was the Single Act and the 1992 programme that lifted the Community from its stagnant to its dynamic phase in the late 1980s, opening out new opportunities for the proponents of Union; and it was the confluence of the political momentum generated by the Draft Treaty and the economic pressures for the 1992 programme that brought the Community to the point where the necessary decisions were taken.

The single market programme

The Commission's White Paper, with its nearly three hundred measures for completing the single market, proposed a vast programme of Community legislation. The Commission divided the barriers into three categories: physical, fiscal, and technical.[5]

The physical barriers were those that confronted people or goods as they cross the frontiers, that is, customs and immigration controls. The Commission argued that these were, for the citizen, a manifestation of division within the Community, and that they imposed heavy costs on business. One of these costs was the time that lorries had to await clearance at the Community's internal frontiers, often for hours and sometimes for days. The lorry drivers were aggravated to the point of bringing such trade to a halt by a strike in the winter of 1983–4. The clerical work on providing documents for customs might be less uncomfortable, but was likewise costly. A study for the Commission on the costs of fragmentation of the market calculated that the cost of frontier checks on a consignment exported from Britain to France was ecu 131, while on one imported into Britain from Italy it was as much as ecu 280; and the total cost to the economy, including the public cost of the frontier controls, was estimated at ecu 8–9 billion.[6] The Commission proposed that these controls be abolished within the Community.

The fiscal barriers that the Commission proposed to tackle were the indirect taxes: value-added tax, levied on most sales of goods and services; and excise duties, on alcoholic drinks, tobacco, and petrol. The Commission argued that wide differences in these taxes from one member state to another were a cause of frontier controls to prevent tax evasion through importing goods from a state with a lower tax rate to a state with a higher one, and that they also distorted trade in other ways. The Commission was to propose that member states harmonize their rates of value-added tax within two bands, one of 14–20 per cent for the normal rate and one of 4–9 per cent for lower-taxed goods such as food, while excise duties would be aligned on the average of the member states' existing rates. These proposals were controversial. It was argued that indirect taxes have both revenue-raising and social functions that are better left to the member states and that the problem of tax evasion can be approached in other ways, while the British government insisted on fiscal sovereignty. The Commission subsequently accepted many of the criticisms; and the Council agreed in June 1991 on a minimum general VAT rate of 15 per cent, with lower rates for some special items, but without an upper limit. In 1993, minimum rates were also agreed for excise duties on alcohol, petrol, and tobacco.

The third category, which the Commission called technical, was wide-ranging and by far the most important. The barriers that can more correctly be so called are the technical regulations and standards: these regulations (not to be confused with the term Regulation used for a general form of EC legislation) are statutory instruments that define the specifications of a product to assure the consumer of its quality and safety, while standards are defined by private standards institutes to similar ends. Where products have to fit each other in order to be usable, as a plug has to fit its socket, the specifications may also ensure what is called 'plug compatibility', which is also most important in the field of information technology. Guarantees of safety are wanted not only for products such as toys, electrical appliances, cars, and many articles of capital equipment, but also for services such as banking or life insurance, where the customer may be unable to judge whether savings or premiums are at risk because the financial institution is not maintaining proper standards of honesty or prudence.

Member states had developed their own standards and regulations for a vast range of goods and services. As these differed from country to country, and it was often not possible for a product that met the specifications of one country to meet those of another without substantial adaptation, they constituted barriers that could be more costly than a tariff to overcome. Products could be adapted to meet the other country's specification, but that cost money and lost time while the product was tested and certified in the other country; and the need to spend this money and time made the producer less competitive than an American or a Japanese firm that could establish its product rapidly and economically in a less fragmented home market. An estimate for the Commission put the cost of adapting a volume car to all the EC markets at ecu 286 million on top of the cost of development for a single market.[7] Such a sum took more than the edge off a European manufacturer's competitiveness. The time and cost required to meet differing specifications bore most heavily on new technologies, where the development of new products can rapidly make the existing ones obsolescent. Getting such products on to the market without delay and selling enough to pay for the costs of development before the next generation of products renders them unsaleable is a condition of survival.

New technologies have also been, and remain, hard hit in Europe by the other types of barrier that the Commission called technical, but which could more appropriately be called political. These result from the nationalistic bias imparted by public purchasing, state enterprises, and government subsidies to industry. It was estimated for the Commission that public purchases from other member states were less than 2 per cent of the size of the market that should be open to them if there were no discrimination; and 'state aids' (or subsidies and other government assistance having equivalent effect) to industry had amounted to between 5 per cent and 10 per cent of total industrial costs in France, Italy, and Britain, with 2–5 per cent in Germany and over 15 per cent in Belgium.[8] The problem was not just a deficiency in Community legislation, but also the difficulty of ensuring that the laws are enforced. Discrimination in public purchasing can be quite hard to prove. As for the state aids, the Commission is given powers by the EC Treaty to find out whether they are being used as a form of protection against imports from other member states and, if they are, to prevent their use in this way. But the Commission needs, in much of its work, the co-operation of the governments, so it has often been reluctant to antagonize them by demanding cuts in state aids that would cause them serious political problems. Thus state aids were allowed to grow, during the difficult 1970s, to levels that substantially fragmented the Community market. But since the 1980s, with governments themselves seeking to cut public expenditure, the Commission has felt able to pursue a more rigorous policy in this field.

With the regulations and standards, it was not so much the difficulty of enforcing the law as the difficulty of enacting it that had been the cause of fragmentation in the Community market. The Commission initiated a systematic effort to remove these obstacles in 1969; but by 1984, when preparations for the White Paper were being made, it had been able to secure measures of harmonization at a rate of only about ten per annum.[9] Not only was this too slow to tackle the whole problem by the end of the century. In some sectors, where technological progress was fast, new regulations were being generated by member states faster than the Community was harmonizing the old ones, so that the market was becoming increasingly fragmented precisely in those sectors where the Europeans had most need to develop their industry as fast as the Americans and the Japanese.

The Commission's White Paper put forward two methods for breaking this legislative bottleneck. The first was a new approach to the harmonizing of member states' regulations. The Community's harmonized regulations had hitherto usually been bulky documents, defining every detail of the specifications required, which had been the subject of interminable negotiation among member states' officials and were then enacted by the Council, where the ministers doubtless had only a remote idea of the significance of these lengthy texts. On one occasion, however, a Directive had been agreed which employed the much simpler method of 'general reference to standards'. This was the 'Low Voltage Directive' of 1973 and it laid down the general objective of safety, leaving it to the European Committee for Standardization, bringing together the authorized standards institutes of member states, to draw up the detailed harmonized specifications.[10] The Commission proposed that this method be generally used where harmonization was required.

The Commission also asked, however, whether harmonization was indeed generally required. This question had been stimulated by the Court of Justice, which had been frustrated by the Community's inability to give effect to Article 30 EEC, prohibiting 'all measures having equivalent effect' to quantitative restrictions. Many of the technical regulations and standards clearly had an equivalent effect, reducing imports or preventing them altogether. But in the absence of harmonized regulations, the Community had for over two decades found no way to make this prohibition effective. In 1979, however, the Court set a precedent when it ruled that the German regulation which prevented the import of Cassis de Dijon into the Federal Republic was illegal, on the grounds that the French regulations provided adequate assurance that it was safe for the consumer to imbibe. Such 'mutual recognition of other member states' regulations' could, the Commission suggested, be much more widely applied, thus circumventing the laborious process of harmonization. With this 'new strategy', putting the emphasis on deregulation rather than re-regulation, the Commission hoped to ease the burden of legislating for the 1992 programme.

Most of the measures proposed in the White Paper did, nevertheless, involve the re-regulating process of harmonization, even if with the simplification of the new approach. Whatever the attractions of the ideology of deregulation, the member states with stronger protection for health and safety have not been willing to rely on the regulations of those where protection is weaker. Thus the legislative programme envisaged by the White Paper remained formidable; and it was far from certain that the Commission's new approach and strategy would suffice to ensure its success. A new political impulse and more efficient procedures for enacting Community laws were also needed. It was a principal aim of the Single Act to provide them.

The Single European Act and open frontiers: 1992 and beyond

Although the EEC Treaty established the principle that measures such as technical regulations or standards should not be allowed to restrict trade among the member states, the Treaty lacked two elements that would have helped to put the principle into practice. It contained no timetable for this, such as it had for the removal of tariffs and quotas; and there was no provision for majority votes to harmonize such measures as laws, regulations or administrative action in member states that 'directly affect the establishment or functioning of the common market' (Article 100/94 ECT). Failing these two elements, the search for unanimous agreement could be prolonged indefinitely.

The Single Act committed the member states to complete the internal market by the end of 1992, as 'an area without internal frontiers in which the free movement of goods, persons, services and capital is ensured in accordance with the provisions of this Treaty' (Article 13 SEA). This, together with the Commission's White Paper, provided the timetable. The Single Act went on to introduce majority voting in the Council for a number of cases that the EEC Treaty had left with the unanimity procedure, including Article 100 on harmonization, which was central to the single market programme, though fiscal harmonization (Article 99 EEC) still depends on unanimous agreement among the governments. Those states with high standards in matters such as health, safety, or the environment are moreover protected against having their standards harmonized downwards because they can opt out of Community laws that would have such an effect, provided that the Court of Justice did not find that they were making 'improper use' of this right, i.e. using it for the purpose of trade protection (Article 18 SEA); and the Amsterdam Treaty passes this responsibility to the Commission (Article 100a/95 ECT). While this does not give the states with high standards a veto over Community legislation, it does warn the partner governments not to override such a state when it has a convincing case. Nevertheless, the agreement to extend the scope of majority voting was followed by a sharp increase in its use and in the rate at which Community legislation was enacted.

A major political impulse was needed to launch the single market programme successfully; and the new provision for majority voting contributed significantly to it. The Single Act as a whole also helped by embodying agreement on a range of treaty amendments to develop the Community's powers in the economic and social fields and to formalize the co-operation in foreign policy as a Community activity; and the enhanced role for the European Parliament in internal market legislation gave it a higher political profile. All these things added to the sense of political momentum. But the Commission still feared that, after political agreement on the grand principle, protectionist interests and bureaucratic inertia might impede the programme in practice. So they decided to demonstrate the general economic benefits that could be set against the particular interests and resistances.

The result was known as the Cecchini report, after the name of the former Commission official who directed it.[11] It was a massive study, based on research undertaken by over a score of institutes and consultancy firms throughout the Community, including surveys of particular sectors and problems as well as macroeconomic surveying and modelling. In these ways it was possible to estimate some of the dynamic effects of creating the single market, which economists working on the basis of customs union theory had previously not been able to do. The result boiled down to an estimated addition of around 1 per cent a year to the rate of growth of the Community's gross domestic product for a period of five years or more, if the single market programme should be fully realized. This estimate was well publicized and helped to engender confidence in the programme.

The political and business support for the programme was enough to move it forward at least as fast as could be expected. By the end of 1992, over nine-tenths of the measures had been adopted. Once enacted, the Directives have to be passed into the legislation of member states, some of which have been dilatory about it; and the European Committee for Standardization has found the translation of Community laws into detailed standards burdensome and time-consuming. Five years later, moreover, some important measures had still not been adopted in fields such as energy, transport, and financial services, where the problems were complex and protectionist pressures strong. But despite such obstacles, the single market legislative programme has been a clear success; and its momentum generated an investment boom in the late 1980s. This was followed by a recession which evoked complaints that the forecast dynamic impulse had not materialized, to which the Commission responded with a further study providing evidence that growth was nevertheless higher than it would otherwise have been in time of recession. Business interests confirmed the positive assessment by maintaining their strong support for the single market.

The successful launching of the single market programme had a snowball effect on other policies for developing the Community. The doubling of structural funds was a first example. The member states with weaker economies, led by Spain, insisted on getting such assistance towards their development to meet the challenge of the single market, securing first acceptance of the principle in the section on 'economic and social cohesion' in the Single Act, then agreement on the budgetary allocations. The idea of a Social Charter was promoted by labour interests in the richer member states, where there was fear that the single market could bring with it 'social dumping', i.e. cheap competition from member states where labour legislation is less developed. It was also argued that the integrated capital market would have to be accompanied by an integrated monetary policy. The Single Act introduced the objective of economic and monetary union into the treaties; and the freeing of capital movements through the single market programme strengthened the case for the single currency. Chapter 7 shows how this led to the Maastricht Treaty and the programme to establish the euro by 1999.

Free movement of people

The Single Act also went beyond the EEC Treaty, which had provided for free movement across the Community's internal frontiers for economic purposes, by stating that the internal market 'shall comprise an area without internal frontiers' (Article 13 SEA). This was generally interpreted as requiring the removal of all internal frontier controls and hence the free movement of people for any purpose. The British government resisted this idea and a core group of France, Germany, and Benelux bound themselves in the Schengen Agreements of 1985 and 1990 to remove their mutual frontier controls and take accompanying measures relating to visas, asylum, and police co-operation against drug traffic and other crime. All the other member states save the United Kingdom and Ireland, which is closely linked with the United Kingdom by far-reaching bilateral arrangements for free movement, subsequently signed the Agreements. The Maastricht Treaty also included such matters within the area of its 'third pillar', on co-operation in justice and home affairs, which provided for judicial, customs, and police collaboration to combat international crime such as terrorism, drug-trafficking and addiction, fraud, and co-operation on asylum, immigration, and treatment of nationals of third countries. But it was a weak structure with intergovernmental institutional arrangements and dependent on the unanimous ratification of conventions. By 1997 none had been ratified and the 'pillar' had scant achievement to its credit.

This was not acceptable to the states that were committed through Schengen to abolish their frontier controls. They insisted on stronger arrangements in the Amsterdam Treaty, which brings policy on visas, asylum, immigration, and some other matters relating to the free movement of people into the European Community over a five-year transitional period after the Treaty enters into force. The Commission is to have the exclusive right of initiative for legislation in that field, though sharing it with the member states during the transitional period; the Court of Justice is to have jurisdiction, except for matters relating to law and order and security within the member states; and after the end of the transitional period, the Council 'shall take a decision' to introduce co-decision for part or all of this field, though this has to be done by unanimity. The Amsterdam Treaty states rather grandly that the aim of this new Title IIIa/IV of the EC Treaty is 'to establish progressively an area of freedom, security and justice'. The arrangements for this were accepted by all the signatories to the Treaty save the Danish, Irish, and British, who obtained protocols allowing them to opt out while providing that they could opt in for specific measures, subject to the unanimous agreement of the other member states.

The signatories to the Schengen Agreements, which had already generated some three thousand pages of rules on free movement and related policies, found it highly inconvenient that these should remain separate from the arrangements within the Union, so a protocol to the Amsterdam Treaty gave responsibility to the Council, excluding the representatives of Ireland and the United Kingdom which were not signatories, to place the Agreements and rules 'within the institutional and legal framework of the European Union'. The Council is to decide, by unanimous agreement, the 'legal basis' of each of the rules, thus determining which of them should come under Title IIIa and which under the third pillar's intergovernmental arrangements; but until these decisions have been made, which the track record of the unanimity procedure indicates may take a long time, the rules are to remain subject to the third pillar. Denmark, anxious to avoid the more federal commitments, opted out from participation in any of the arrangements within the Community.

Title IIIa/IV of the ECT and the Schengen Protocol have dealt with much of the field covered by the Maastricht Treaty's third pillar. So the Amsterdam Treaty reduced the latter to the subjects of police, customs, and judicial co-operation together with 'approximation of rules' to prevent and counter crime, although the Schengen rules will, when the Amsterdam Treaty comes into force, remain with that pillar unless and until they are transferred to the Community.

Negative integration and positive integration

The ECSC Treaty already contained provisions to ease the adjustments forced on firms and workers by the freeing of trade in coal and steel. Jan Tinbergen coined the term 'positive integration' for this, in contrast with the removal of trade barriers which he called 'negative integration'.[12] Towards the end of the 1960s, following completion of the customs union, it was suggested that there was a more general case for complementing the negative integration through policies with aims that go beyond the removal of barriers.[13] Examples of such positive integration in the EEC Treaty were the European Investment Bank and Social Fund for purposes of what has come to be called economic and social cohesion, and the common agricultural policy with its aim of a better life for farmers. The Single Act and the Maastricht and Amsterdam Treaties, in addition to decisive measures of negative integration in the form of the single market and the single currency, provided for many further examples of positive integration, including the cohesion, social, consumer protection, education and training policies; environmental, industrial, research and technological development policies; human rights and other policies relating to citizenship and the free movement of people.

Because positive integration implies value judgements, it is a very political activity, requiring democratic institutions. With the negative integration of single market, single currency, and free movement of people, the Union is not likely to rest in stable equilibrium. Either, if the needs for positive integration are not met, it will tend to become less integrated again, as the Community market did in the 1970s. Or, if the positive integration continues to develop, it is likely to require more effective and democratic institutions: a more federal structure. The Maastricht and Amsterdam Treaties included a number of steps in that direction. If the new technologies, and the specialization that goes with them, continue to press the European economies towards greater interdependence, the cost of resisting movement towards such a structure could be high.

5 Agricultural Policy: Formation, Crisis, Reform

It was harder to create a common market for agriculture than a customs union for industry. Simple tariffs were not deemed adequate by European states to protect their farmers against the sometimes violent fluctuations in world markets; and they had already devised a variety of complicated forms of price and income support instead. Member states were not ready to let their own supports be undermined by free imports from other member states with differing price systems. If agricultural trade within the Community was, like industrial trade, to be free of tariffs and quotas, the existing national systems would have to be replaced by a Community-wide system of support. Given the importance of the farm vote at the time when the Community was founded, this was a formidable political task.

The British proposal for a Free Trade Area sought in 1957 to evade this task simply by excluding agriculture; but the proposal failed because it was not acceptable to the French. Such a solution could not be contemplated for the Community, for which, in Britain's absence, France was essential as a counterweight to Germany. The French, fearing German industrial strength, were reluctant to open their own industry to German competition. But French agriculture was a strong competitor; and the French saw their potential gains in agricultural trade as an indispensable counterpart to the risks they would take in the industrial common market.

The Community's common agricultural policy can thus be seen as the product of national interest secured by the use of bargaining power. But any such diplomatic success would have been short-lived had it not been part of a general bargain that satisfied all the member states. For the benefits they all derive from the Community depend on the proper working of its institutions; and these do not work well if they contain representatives from member states that feel seriously aggrieved. It is a cardinal principle of Swiss federal practice that no part of the country should feel that its interests are neglected by the federal system. The Community itself has developed the technique of the package deal to ensure a balance of interests at any phase of its development, and the initial EEC bargain, satisfying French agricultural and German industrial interests, can be seen as the first major example. The bargain might not have endured had either French industry or German agriculture been seriously damaged; but French industrialists rose to the challenge of the common market and the common agricultural policy was arranged so as to satisfy German farmers too. Later on, the agricultural interest was to be pressed to the point where it endangered the Community's equilibrium. But at the outset it was an essential element in the balance. The question was not whether, but how to establish it.

Formation of the common policy

The form of the common agricultural policy was too complex and difficult a matter to be settled in the negotiations for the EEC Treaty. The Treaty provided, in essence, that there should be an agricultural common market without barriers to trade among the member states, that it should be established by the end of the transitional period of 12–N15 years from 1958, and that it should be determined by the Council, on a proposal from the Commission, acting by a unanimous vote among the member states' representatives during the first two stages of the transitional period but by a qualified majority vote thereafter. Thus there was an aim, a deadline, and a procedure, but the hard decisions remained to be taken.

The Germans wanted a policy which was market-orientated and which allowed them to continue importing from the low-cost world markets, with the somewhat contradictory proviso that there should not be too much sacrifice of the high, protected prices that German farmers enjoyed. The French wanted a Community market organization in a form that would enable them to sell a lot to the Germans. These wishes of the two most powerful member states appeared hard to reconcile. But the Community's first Commissioner for agriculture, Sicco Mansholt, identified a first key decision on which they could agree: to base the protection needed for the common price support on the instrument of the variable import levy.

The import levy was familiar to Mansholt, as it was the form of protection used by the Netherlands and he had been the Dutch Minister for agriculture. It secured a stable price for the farmer by making the importer of a competitive product pay a levy to meet the difference between the world market price and the domestic support price. So it would be the level of the Community's support price that would determine how much the high-cost German farmer would be protected, and hence how much he would produce and what share of the German market would be left for imports from France. But the conflict of interests could be resolved later, when the Community's common price level was fixed—as it would have to be when the barriers within the Community were removed and the common import levy was introduced. Meanwhile, Mansholt asked for agreement on the principle of the import levy.

The French and Dutch governments supported Mansholt in this, seeing it as the key to the decisions required to open the Community market to their farmers' exports. The Germans resisted. But the Dutch made agreement on the levy a condition of their acceptance of the Community's passage to the second stage of the transitional period. This could be delayed for up to three years by any member state which could claim that the objectives of the first stage had not been fulfilled; and the Dutch claimed that they would not be fulfilled unless agreement was reached on this step towards the common agricultural policy. The Germans were keenly interested in passage to the second stage, which would bring further liberalization of the Community's internal market; and they did not want the Community's political success to be jeopardized. So they finally accepted the levy—but not before the Council resorted to the device of 'stopping the clock' at midnight on 31 December

1961, until agreement was reached after a marathon session lasting until 14 January 1962.

Two more key decisions had to be taken before the common agricultural policy could be put in place: the level at which prices were to be supported and the source of the money to pay for the support.

The price level was another bone of contention between the Germans, who wanted higher prices, and the Commission, Dutch, and French, who wanted them lower. The price of wheat was the crux, determining the price of bread and, through its influence on grains for feeding animals, of meat and other livestock products. Two forms of pressure were brought to bear on the Germans. They were much concerned, both for industrial interests and for their good relations with the United States, to secure a successful outcome to the 'Kennedy round' of international trade negotiations, which were to initiate a new phase of liberal world trade. The French government was ready to accept this, but also prepared to make its acceptance conditional on German agreement to a Community price for wheat. This was another example of a major package deal—or rather a further instalment of the Franco-German deal that lay behind the success of the negotiations to establish the EEC. But de Gaulle was impatient to secure what he saw as France's prime interest in the Community, and disinclined to follow the Community way of doing things by seeking a consensus based on a balance of interests. He preferred the classical methods of power politics. He knew that the Germans set great store on the Community's institutions, which had helped to give them their respected place in the post-war Western system, whereas he felt that the destruction of those institutions would be no great loss, and was certainly in favour of weakening them. He therefore issued threats, in the second half of 1964, that without satisfaction on agriculture France might leave the Community; and he must have felt that this rough tactic succeeded, because agreement on the wheat price was reached before the end of the year.[1] With hindsight it may be doubted whether his tactics paid off. The EEC Treaty provided that until 1966, when the Community passed to the third stage of its transitional period, decisions on agricultural policy had to be taken by unanimous vote in the Council; and the German vote was obtained in 1964 only by conceding a wheat price that was considerably higher than the Commission or the French wanted. This, through its effect on the agricultural price level as a whole, not only helped to protect German farmers from French competition, but was also a cause of the general over-production that was eventually to impose such problems on the Community and its members, including France. Nor was the new price in fact to be introduced until mid-1967, by which time it could have been determined by a qualified majority vote, thus weakening the Germans' ability to exact such a high price—had de Gaulle not by then undermined the principle of majority voting. The high-handed methods preferred by de Gaulle also stiffened the Germans' resolve to resist his next offensive against the Community's institutions, when the third main element in the common agricultural policy, the way in which it was to be financed, came up for decision in 1965.

Money would be needed to support the prices fixed by the Community. Should the price of a product fall below the support level, it would have to be bought and stored. Storage would cost money, and, should it not be possible to sell the stocks later in the Community market for that product, they would have to be exported at subsidized prices or used for purposes that brought a lower return within the Community. The Commission estimated that the Community's customs duties and import levies should at first suffice, with additional contributions from the member states if required. The EEC Treaty provided that the Community should have its own 'resources', i.e. taxes, to finance its budget; and the French government saw this as an important national interest because it would ensure that the cost of the common agricultural policy was borne by the Community as a whole and not just by the member state that produced the surpluses. But the Commission espoused another principle with which the French government of the day did not agree: that since these taxes would pass to the Community without the resulting expenditure being scrutinized by the member states' parliaments, democratic accountability required that the Community budget should be approved not only by the Council, but also by the European Parliament acting jointly with it.[2]

This proposal provoked an epic conflict between the Community and de Gaulle. He was set on securing the common financing of agriculture. France's partners accepted that this was necessary for a Community agricultural policy, while agreeing with the Commission that it must be managed by Community institutions which transcended the intergovernmental. But de Gaulle saw this as a threat to French national sovereignty. When his partners failed to submit, he withdrew his ministers from policy-making in the Council, and held to this policy of the 'empty chair' throughout the second half of 1965. This time the Germans and the other four governments were resolute. They continued Community business; and the French electorate showed, in presidential elections towards the end of the year, that they did not like to see risks taken with the Community. In January 1966, de Gaulle decided to return to normal working in the Community, after sending his ministers to a meeting in Luxembourg to announce to their partners that he would not accept majority votes on 'very important interests': the so-called Luxembourg 'compromise'. While de Gaulle accepted that he could not get the others to agree to any formal weakening of the Community institutions, the Luxembourg 'compromise', which might more accurately have been called the Luxembourg veto, led to the general use of the unanimity procedure in the Council for about two decades, thus consolidating the dominance of the intergovernmental method of operating the Community and diminishing its capacity for action.

When the agricultural common market was introduced in mid-1967, it was at first financed with the help of member states' financial contributions. After de Gaulle resigned two years later, his successor secured the agreement on the Community's own resources as part of the package deal for the first enlargement, conceding in part the institutional conditions that had been anathema to de Gaulle. The customs duties and import levies were supplemented by a tax of up to 1 per cent of the value-added of taxable goods in the Community, which was enough to finance the excessive production through the 1970s, which led to the crisis that debilitated the Community until the mid-1980s.

Thus the common agricultural policy was created as required by the EEC Treaty. Unanimous agreement on the three main decisions, the levy, the price, and the financing, was extremely hard to achieve, each time harder than the last, culminating in the conflict over financing that was the occasion for de Gaulle's challenge to the Community in 1965. It was the French interest in the agricultural policy that enabled the Community to survive that challenge. But the settlement at Luxembourg weakened the institutions when it had already become clear that the search for intergovernmental unanimity was an unpromising basis for common action on the scale of the agricultural policy. By making them more intergovernmental, not less, de Gaulle's institutional legacy was a major reason why the policy was not to be reformed until nearly two decades after it had become evident that reform was required. Meanwhile the agri-budgetary crisis did untold damage to the Community.

The sorcerer's apprentice

The single market for other farm products followed soon after the achievement of the single market for cereals in July 1967. Mansholt and DG VI, the Commission's Directorate-General for agriculture, realized that the price levels which the Council had agreed would stimulate production. Yet the average holding, at some 13 hectares, was too small to enable most farmers, even with the higher prices, to avoid falling further behind the rising incomes in other sectors in the Community. So long as farms remained so small and so many people therefore continued to work on the land, Mansholt reasoned, they could survive only with prices that were increasingly out of line with world prices, stimulating surplus production that would burden the Community's budget. He concluded that the structure of Community agriculture would have to be rapidly developed, so that fewer people would work on larger, more modern farms, earning much higher incomes.

The Mansholt plan, as it came to be called, was presented to the Council in a Commission Memorandum in December 1968.[3] Its central aim was to reduce the number working in agriculture in the Community by about half in the 1970s, to 5 million by the end of the decade. The main method was to be the modernization of farms, encouraged by Community grants and loans for farm development. For this, the member states would have to accept a big increase in the Community's resources for its structural policy, or for 'guidance' as it is called in the title of the European Agricultural Guidance and Guarantee Fund.

Mansholt put his great energy and talent into a campaign to gain support for his proposals.[4] He hoped that his vision of a modern, prosperous agriculture would attract the more dynamic among the farming interests as well as consumers, taxpayers, and others who would benefit. But the farm lobbies were up in arms against the idea of cutting the number of their members in half. Mansholt could argue that more than 5 million had left the land in the preceding decade. But this was one in three of the number at the beginning of that decade, not one in two; it had not cut so close to the hard core of farm people who were most fiercely attached to the land; and it had occurred without being the aim of a specific Community policy that the lobbies could oppose.

The governments were also against him. All, and not least the Germans, were influenced by the lobbies; and the French government, still strongly Gaullist, was keenly opposed to the enhancement of the Commission's role that the proposed policy would imply. They had accepted that the Community should be responsible for a common agricultural market, because that had been agreed in the EEC Treaty and was the interest of the French government. But there was no enthusiasm among the governments for handing responsibility for a large slice of structural policy to the Community. They wanted to keep it for themselves. The result was the attrition of the Mansholt plan over more than three years of discussions, until the Council decided, in April 1972, to provide only some modest finance for development loans to farmers, incentives for early retirement, and assistance for information and training intended to raise efficiency. The budget for 'guarantee', i.e. for price support, was great and growing; that for 'guidance' remained small.

Not only were the Council's decisions long delayed and quite inadequate when they came. They were also applied unconscionably slowly by the member states. The decisions took the form of Directives, which leave it to the member states to make their own laws to achieve the agreed results; and this often takes a couple of years, with another year before their application begins to have an effect. In this case the decisions were not being applied in France until 1977, five years after they had been taken by the Council; and in Italy there were still no farm development plans at all at the end of 1978, ten years after Mansholt had presented his Memorandum to the Council and alerted the governments to the dangers ahead if action was not taken.

Not surprisingly, the size of farms changed little in the 1970s, rising by only one hectare to an average of 13.7 hectares. The number working in agriculture did fall by 2.6 million; but in the absence of an effective structural policy and with the cushion of high prices this spontaneous drift from the land was, at half the rate that Mansholt had deemed necessary, not fast enough to resolve the problem he had diagnosed. The poor farmers remained poor. The richer ones prospered, responding to high prices and incomes with a rapid growth of productivity based on technological advance. Production outran consumption. Community production of cereals as a percentage of consumption grew from 91 per cent in 1973/4 to 116 per cent in 1983/4, of meat from 96 per cent to 101 per cent, and of butter from 98 per cent to 134 per cent. Between 1975 and 1984, the Community's agricultural exports grew by 256 per cent, imports by only 14 per cent.[5] This caused disruption in world markets, hitting hard some Third World countries as well as trading partners such as Australia, Canada, New Zealand, and the United States. With Community prices around half as much again as world prices in the early 1980s, the exports were heavily subsidized; and the Community had to finance the growing stocks of products that could neither be exported nor consumed at home. Thus the common agricultural policy had become very costly; it disrupted international trade; and instead of assisting the poor it did more to help the rich. The poor farmers suffered while the rich flourished.

Had it not been for the entry of Britain in 1973, and the diversion of imports into its large market from its traditional overseas suppliers to the Community farmers, together with the large British contribution to the Community budget, the burden of surplus production would have become intolerable for the Community sooner; and the decision to allocate to the Community budget revenue of up to 1 per cent of value-added also prolonged the period in which the Community could spend instead of reform. The Council was therefore able, despite rising surpluses, especially of dairy products, to sidestep the Commission's exhortations during the later 1970s to pursue a more rigorous price policy. It was not until 1982 that the first serious measures to control expenditure were taken; it was only in 1988 that a more general improvement of agricultural and budgetary policy was introduced; and it was not until 1991 that a fairly adequate reform was accepted—over two decades after Mansholt had drawn the Council's attention to the necessity of reform. Meanwhile, the Community had been divided and enfeebled by quarrels over the budget and had fallen in public esteem. It is worthwhile to consider why, when the Commission had so clearly diagnosed the problem, the Community had been allowed to drift so dangerously and so long.

Institutional weaknesses

The Mansholt plan was the work of people who were concerned about the problems of the agricultural common market as a whole. They foresaw that, without structural reform, the common agricultural policy would become untenable. The remedy they proposed was to modernize farming so that rapidly growing productivity would bring farmers adequate incomes without high prices. It was a bold vision. Perhaps they should have put more emphasis on the control of the costs of price support. But this was not what the ministers in the Council, in mutilating the Mansholt plan, proposed. They decided to continue fixing common prices without either a common structural policy or a mechanism for controlling costs. How could ministers act so irresponsibly?

Each minister was responding to the pressures of the political situation in his own member state which were generated by the interests in that state. The ministers' prime concern was not the impending problems of the system as a whole. When, early in 1971, it was time to fix the prices for the coming farm year 1971/2, Mansholt tried to induce them to take his structural reform proposals seriously by linking these to his proposals for prices. But the ministers reacted by merely promising to take some measures the following year, which were in the event only a token of what Mansholt had originally proposed. They had the power of decision; and they were not going to give the Community's needs, important though they might be, priority over political convenience at home. The member states showed the same low regard for the needs of the Community as a whole with their long delays in implementing the Council's Directives.

This order of priorities and its consequences during the 1970s and 1980s demonstrated the contradiction between a common political objective on the scale of the agricultural common market and the intergovernmental method that dominated the taking of decisions to achieve and maintain it. This contradiction has been at its most obvious where unanimous voting has been required, as we saw with respect to the prices and the financing. With the practice of unanimous voting entrenched during the two decades after the Luxembourg 'compromise', prices continued to be fixed by the Council at levels higher than the Commission had proposed, inducing over-production and heavy support costs. Along with this voting procedure went a concern for the special interests of member states that overrode the general interest in the single market, a prime example being the monetary compensatory amounts (MCAs). This is the bureaucratic name for the mechanism whereby special exchange rates for agricultural trade in the Community—also known as 'green currencies'—have insulated farmers and consumers from the immediate effects of exchange rate changes. First introduced as a temporary measure in order to protect the German farmers from a cut in their prices that would otherwise have followed from a revaluation of the mark in 1969, MCAs eventually became a general system of border taxes and subsidies that could shield either farmers or consumers from the normal effects of parity changes. They have persisted for over a quarter of a century. The single market requires their elimination and decisions were taken to that effect. But it is economic and monetary union that will finally put paid to this abuse.

The Council's structure as well as its voting procedures has undermined its effectiveness as a legislature. In no case has the division of the Council into a number of functional Councils, each empowered to enact laws in its own fields, caused greater confusion than in agriculture. The Council of finance ministers is responsible for the Community budget. Yet the Council of agriculture ministers, when it fixed the prices, took the decision that determined the size of the predominant part of the budget. Since they had no responsibility for financial matters, it is not surprising that their price decisions were financially irresponsible. The agriculture ministers have been subject to pressures quite other than financial constraints. They are the prime targets for agricultural lobbies, whose influence is particularly strong in election years; and a year seldom passes in which at least one of the member states is not going to have an election. Even if the others did not sympathize with those about to enter an election campaign, with unanimous voting their special interests had to be respected—another cause of higher prices. The agricultural ministries in most member states are close to the farmers' organizations; and the Agriculture Council, as it is usually called, has been advised by a Special Committee on Agriculture, comprising officials from those ministries, which meets more frequently and takes many day-to-day decisions without reference to the Council. Thus farm lobbies, officials, and ministers formed a tight circle, fairly impervious to the influence of other interests such as consumers or taxpayers when decisions were to be taken by the Council. Agriculture ministers in a national context are, of course, subject to similar pressures in making policies; but they have to justify financial implications to the finance ministers in their governments. No such coherence was built into the Community's institutions. The structure of the intergovernmental Council did not encourage responsibility for the budgetary consequences of agricultural decisions, any more than for the problems of the Community as a whole.

Both the Commission and the European Parliament have been responsive to the agricultural lobbies. But the Commission has, since Mansholt presented his Memorandum on reform in 1969, produced more responsible policies than the Council and proposed more moderate price increases than the Council decided. Before the direct elections in 1979, the Parliament was highly susceptible to agricultural pressures. But since the mid-1980s, it has been more inclined to represent the nine-tenths of the population who are not in the farm sector and thus to check the excesses of the decisions that the Council continued to take until the agri-budgetary reform of 1991. But when the Parliament's budgetary powers were determined in the treaties that introduced the Community's own resources in 1970 and 1975, the French government, in a rearguard action of the then retreating Gaullism, insisted that the Parliament's power to enact the budget jointly with the Council should not extend to the agricultural expenditure. Responsibility for the agricultural budget was therefore that of the Council alone. The Parliament, which took a wider view of the Community's interest than the Agriculture Council, had little influence over the decisions.

Common sense indicates that people working in institutions whose responsibility is for the Community as a whole are likely to give a higher priority to its general interest than those whose main work is in the institutions of a member state, devoted to the interests of that state. The interests of the member state and of the Community will often coincide, at least in the longer term. But there will be crucial occasions on which the longer-term general interest and the shorter-term national interest diverge; and it is to be expected that those who work in national governments will often be guided by the shorter-term national interest, even if in the long term the national and the general interests would converge. This has been the case with the common agricultural policy. The annual decisions of the Council on price have responded to the shorter-term national interests while leaving the longer-term Community interest—which was also the longer-term interest of the member states—to look after itself. It is fully understandable that the ministers should be mainly influenced by the context in which they mainly live and work. The fault is not so much theirs as that of the Community's constitution which has given so much power to them and so little to the Commission and the European Parliament, where people's main work is in an institution whose function is to produce laws, policies, and decisions for the Community as a whole.

Reform

Despite the defects in its institutions, the Community can take decisions when it has to, even if the result is often too little and too late. The overspending on agriculture could continue so long as the money available to the Community held out. But when, after over a decade of swelling budgets, spending began to approach the limit of the 1 per cent value-added tax plus the customs duties and agricultural import levies, which together comprised the 'own resources', action clearly had to be taken. In 1982, 'price quotas' were introduced to stem the flow of funds into price support for sugar. The full support price became payable only for production required for the Community market; there was a lower price for 'normal exports', or rather for exports that had become normal during the time that they had been dumped on world markets with Community export subsidies; and beyond that, the going price on the world market would obtain. But bringing some discipline into the regime for only one product was not enough. By

1984, the limit of existing own resources was reached.

The first half of 1984 was the time of the French presidency when Mitterrand assembled a package that included agreement on the Iberian enlargement and on Britain's budgetary rebate. The rebate was the key to a bargain that included British acceptance of the increase in the value-added tax contribution which was necessary to finance the agricultural policy. Increases in own resources have to be approved by all member states (Article 201/269 ECT), and the British government wanted to be satisfied on two counts before conceding its approval: the rebate; and agreement to bring the agricultural expenditure, which was the main cause of Britain's high net contribution, under control. Unfortunately for the Community, the rebate was evidently the higher priority, as the British government, while ensuring that two-thirds of Britain's net contribution would be reimbursed, accepted decisions on agriculture which failed to ensure an adequate control. Following the price quotas for sugar, a quota regime was introduced for milk, which had until then taken a particularly large share of expenditure. From 1984, production of milk beyond quota was subject to a penal levy; and this caused the notorious 'butter mountain' in storage to melt away, at least for a time. It was also agreed that agricultural expenditure should rise no faster than gross domestic product; and this decision was respected in the price decisions for the next farm year. But by 1988, agricultural spending had increased by more than ecu 6 billion, or by 30 per cent since 1984. Once again, the money had run out—indeed, creative accounting was required to finance a good part of that increase. This time, British agreement to more own resources would not be forthcoming without a firmer system for the control of expenditure.

The Commission produced proposals for reform of the agricultural policy and the budget in two reports in 1987, known together as the Delors package;[6] and the European Council took decisions on this basis under German presidency in the first half of 1988. 'Stabilizers' were introduced for products accounting for a large part of the budget. After the examples of sugar and milk, these provided for price cuts when an agreed quota was reached, thus reducing the cost of price support and, it was hoped, discouraging farmers from over-production. Some structural measures were taken in addition to these central decisions on price discipline. Farmers were to be paid for leaving arable land to lie fallow, provided that they 'set aside' one-fifth or more of their arable land for five years or more. There was to be compensation for early retirement. A start was made in providing income support for poorer farmers, related to their need and not their production, in order to avoid stimulating them to produce more. The structural funds, which were to be doubled by 1993, were to include among their objectives the stimulation of new sources of rural employment. Community expenditure on agriculture as a whole was to grow less fast than gross product; its expansion was to be kept within 74 per cent of the rate of growth of GNP. Price decisions were to respect this limit; and if the limit should nevertheless be approached, special action was to be taken to prevent it from being breached.

These measures appeared better able to keep the agricultural expenditure under control. So the British government as well as its partners accepted a further increase of the Community's own resources, to 1.4 per cent of value-added together with a new resource related to gross national product, enough to finance the slower growth of agricultural expenditure up to 1992 and the doubling of the size of structural funds. It seemed at last that the Community could be released from the agricultural incubus that had weighed it down for so long.

This success brought with it some strengthening of the institutions. The prestige of the Commission was enhanced and its capacity was demonstrated to devise proposals that served the Community's general interest while at the same time taking account of the particular problems of member states. In order to protect their commitment to double the structural funds, moreover, the member states accepted an Inter-Institutional Agreement whereby the Parliament would gain influence over the size of the agricultural budget in return for accepting the proposed size of structural funds; and the Council resolved that none of its decisions could require expenditure that had not been authorized in budgetary appropriations, hence determining to bring the agriculture ministers at last under budgetary control.

With quarrels over agriculture and the budget behind it for the time being, and the prospect of the completed single market ahead, the Community was better placed than it had been for many years to consider further steps towards Union; and at the same time as the agri-budgetary reform was agreed, economic and monetary union was placed on the Community's agenda, through setting up the Delors committee to recommend the stages by which it could be achieved. But the reforms of 1988, too, were soon to prove inadequate. With world prices low and Community production high, surplus stocks and expenditure were again getting out of hand; and conflict over agricultural trade was undermining the Uruguay round of Gatt negotiations, which were designed to maintain a generally liberal system for world trade in the years ahead. In March 1991 Ray MacSharry, the Commissioner for agriculture, proposed to do what economists had long recommended: shift the focus of policy from price support towards income support. Although the Council took over a year more to reach a decision, it was eventually agreed, in May 1992, to cut the intervention price for cereals by nearly one-third and that for beef by 15 per cent. Farmers were to be recompensed for this, and for new limits set on the buying of some products into intervention, by 'compensation payments' unrelated to quantities produced, including fairly generous payments for set-aside of 15 per cent of arable land. There would also be further aids for early retirement, for environmentally friendly production techniques, and for afforestation of agricultural land. This was not expected to reduce agricultural expenditure in the short term. But the longer-term budgetary prospects would be eased; and although agriculture continued to be the principal cause of conflict in the Uruguay round for yet another year and a half, it was the MacSharry reform that made final agreement possible.

The Uruguay round concluded with agreement to limit export subsidies within the context of the new World Trade Organization (WTO); and fresh negotiations are due to begin in 1999. EU prices for many farm products remain well above world prices and without more reform the Union would be unable to meet its commitments. This is one source of pressure for a further instalment of reform. Another is the prospect of enlargement, estimated by the Commission to add at least ecu 6 billion to the cost of an unreformed common agricultural policy and, by raising prices in Central and Eastern Europe, to generate unmanageable surpluses and to hit the consumers hard. Yet another pressure is the cost to the taxpayer, which is still about half the Union's budgetary expenditure for the benefit of 5.5 per cent of its working population. The Commission accordingly launched its proposals for the next instalment of reform.[7]

The Commission has proposed a further shift from price support to direct payments to farmers, together with a stronger rural policy. In order to meet the commitment to limit export subsidies, the support prices of wheat would be cut by about one-fifth in the year 2000. The support prices for beef, with production expected to recover by then from the shock of BSE which hit the market in 1996, would be cut by nearly one-third between 2000 and 2002. For milk products, the proposal was a more modest reduction by 2006. Farmers would be compensated by more generous income support; and sustainable development in the countryside, where farming is no longer the main basis of the economy, would be promoted by a rural policy including support for afforestation, rural tourism, small and medium enterprises, and most particularly policies to improve the environment. As with the MacSharry reform, the Commission proposed a moderate increase, not a cut, in the agricultural budget. But it hoped to enable the Union to meet its commitments within the WTO, to pave the way for enlargement, eased by suitable transition periods, and to sustain a viable agricultural policy over the longer term.

The history of the common agricultural policy demonstrates that big decisions such as this reform do not come easily. The Community took almost a decade to establish the common agricultural policy—more, if the time required to secure its financing on a permanent basis is included; then it took up to two decades to launch a reform that Mansholt had foreseen would be necessary once the agricultural common market had been established; then, when this proved inadequate, the delay in deciding on a more adequate reform threatened the stability of the world trading system. These inordinate delays, the second of which endangered the future of the Community and the third, that of world trade, were caused by the weakness of the institutions, with the dominance of the member states through the Council, and the subordinate roles of the Commission and the Parliament. The necessary decisions for enlargement and the WTO negotiations will probably, as in the past, eventually be taken. But it is doubtful whether the Maastricht and Amsterdam Treaties have strengthened the institutions enough to ensure that the decisions are taken without yet another delay, which will be damaging for the process of enlargement and the world trade system, as well as for the internal politics of the European Union itself.

6 Industrial, Social and Environmental Policy

Free market competition is the principal means of promoting economic efficiency and development in the European Union. By opening up the member states' markets to each other, the scope for scale and specialization has been multiplied. Spurred by the competition, firms have reduced costs and invested in new technologies. The way in which the Community created first the customs union, then the programme for completing the single market in the increasingly complex modern economy, was outlined in Chapter 4.

Because of this complexity, the single market is a far cry from the nineteenth-century liberal ideal of laisser-faire. Numerous standards and regulations needed to be harmonized for the protection of health, safety, or the environment. But even this does not ensure a level playing field. Firms can agree to fix high prices or abuse a dominant position in other ways. Governments can give firms subsidies and hence unfair advantage over their competitors in other member states. If it is to have a properly functioning market, the Union must deal with distortions such as these; and this is the logic of the policies for competition and 'state aids'.

While opening the markets and ensuring that they function freely has been the main thrust of the common policies affecting industry, and until Maastricht the Treaty had no specific provision for 'industrial policy', there have also been policies to correct what are seen as inadequacies or undesirable effects of the markets. It is not that the Union is particularly interventionist. Member states are more so, as witness the efforts through the common policy on 'state aids' to reduce their industrial subsidies. Despite the return to more market-oriented liberal attitudes in the 1980s, all industrialized countries have continued to act in this way, and the choice for the Union is whether to let its market be fragmented by the different policies of member states or to devise a common policy to prevent this. It is reasonable to argue that imperfections in modern markets justify some actions of this sort, even if it must also be recognized that imperfections in governments may cause such actions to do more harm than good. But this is not the place to tread the well-worn path of that argument.[1] Here we need note only that if the Union did not act in some such cases, the member states would, thus fragmenting the single market.

The most prominent of such common policies have been directed at old industrial sectors in trouble, where employment has been falling fast. Here, as in steel, textiles, and shipbuilding, there have been policies to temper the pain for those working in the industry by combining protection against imports (see Chapter 9) with aid from member states and from the European budget, while at the same time encouraging adjustment towards competitive activity. The previous chapter, on agriculture, showed some of the difficulties that can arise if such a task on such a heroic scale is given to institutions as weak as they have been up to now. Fortunately, none of the other sectors has presented quite such daunting difficulties as that.

In some fields of technological research, the resources of single member states are not enough to compete with the efforts that can be mounted by countries such as the United States or Japan. Public authorities support such research because the resources of individual firms are likewise not enough, and also because the innovations which result can bring benefits that spread wider than the organization in which they are made. So the economies of scale may point towards a Union-wide effort to supplement those of the member states; and there have been some programmes of this kind.

The Union also has policies that aim to protect the environment or standards of health and safety at work. Pollution from one country can damage the environment of its neighbours; and the products of those who care less about health and safety may undercut the products of those who raise their costs by caring more. Such effects of free markets can be unacceptable to those who suffer them, so the Union tries to prevent them. More controversial have been the attempts to improve working conditions beyond the limited objectives of health and safety, with the British government in particular arguing that this makes Europeans uncompetitive and increases unemployment. In Union parlance the whole range of policies relating to the conditions of employees is known as social policy. How far such policy should go has been a source of sharp conflict, although some of the industrial policies have been less controversial.

Steel

France has a historic tradition of the use of public power in the economy. There was no question but that the state would have a strong role in rebuilding the French economy after World War Two. But at the same time the French wanted to break the vicious circle of low growth and low expectations that had left France less developed industrially before the war than neighbours such as Germany and Britain. This was the context in which Monnet, as head of the French planning commission, developed the system that became known as 'indicative planning'. The planners, working with industrialists, published the production targets that appeared achievable and industry was expected to invest to achieve them. There was no compulsion—no question of Soviet-style imperative planning—but the planners could offer incentives such as low-interest loans to firms that agreed to help fulfil the plan. When the European Coal and Steel Community was established it was natural that Monnet should envisage policies of this kind for it. Since France then had the leading role, the ECSC Treaty provided for instruments to enable the Community to do so.

The wording of the Treaty gives the flavour of the time. 'To provide guidelines . . . on the course of action to be followed by all concerned', the High Authority was to 'draw up programmes indicating foreseeable developments in production, consumption, exports and imports' and to lay down general objectives for modernization and expansion (Article 46 ECSC). But such indications and targets would have been whistling in the wind had the High Authority not disposed of instruments with which to influence the firms. It could impose a tax of up to 1 per cent of the value of production of coal and steel as well as raise money on the capital markets; and with these resources it could offer cheap loans to firms that were ready to invest in line with the objectives and programmes, and subsidies for technological research. Since the development of the industries would require workers to change their jobs, and since Monnet was concerned that the Community should have a social as well as an industrial policy, thus earning support among workers and the general public, the High Authority could also provide money for training those who needed new skills and for housing those who had to move.

The Treaty also provided for liberal policies to ensure the proper functioning of the market. The coal and steel industries had been famous for their cartels; and, following the example of American Anti-Trust, the ECSC gave the High Authority power, subject to the ultimate authority of the Court of Justice, to prevent abuses by cartels or monopolies, and mergers that would lead to excessive concentrations of power. Since many of the abuses had been reflected in prices, moreover, transactions could take place only in line with prices and conditions of sale that the firms had to publish.

The ECSC was founded at a time of post-war shortages, and when memories of pre-war depression and over-capacity were still much alive. So the Treaty provided for the allocation of supplies if there was a 'serious shortage', as well as regulation of the market in the event of a 'manifest crisis' due to a 'decline in demand' (Articles 58, 59 ECSC). The High Authority could not declare that there was a manifest crisis without the assent of the Council, voting by a majority that gave greater weight to the larger producers of coal and steel. But once it had been declared, the High Authority could stabilize the market by imposing maximum production quotas on firms and fixing minimum prices. Thus the Community could impose a fairly strong regulatory system should the market be seriously disturbed.

The removal of barriers to trade within the Community had a substantial effect on the efficiency of these heavy industries, which had been distorted by frontiers that had cut across the logic of production based on iron ore from the Lorraine, coke from the Ruhr, and steelworks that used them both.[2] The industrial policies provided under the Treaty also had significant influence at first. But by the 1960s they became less relevant, for two opposing reasons. The coal industry, declining under the impact of competition from oil, was in crisis by 1958. But the Council rejected in May 1959 a comprehensive plan which the High Authority had proposed to deal with it; and from then on coal was protected by individual member states with subsidies which fragmented the Community market again and outweighed the effect of Community policies. Steel, on the contrary, was prospering in a free market like other manufacturing industries, and had less need of the special industrial policies which the ECSC Treaty had provided for it, but which were not available, or provided to a lesser extent, under the EEC Treaty that applied to other industries. It was not until the 1970s, when steel was hit by a severe recession, that the ECSC Treaty again came to the fore. Then in May 1977, the Commission (as the High Authority had become, after the three Councils and executives of the three Communities were merged in 1965 into a single Council and a single Commission) initiated a major episode in the history of the Community's industrial policy when it began to enforce, with the agreement of the Council, a regime of minimum prices for reinforcing bars.

The steel industry had run into difficulty after the oil shock of 1973–4 had led to deflation and recession, at the same time as the Japanese and some newly industrializing countries that could make steel more cheaply were taking shares from the Europeans in world markets. With the high fixed costs of a capital-intensive industry, steel firms incurred heavy losses when production fell. But waiting for bankruptcies to solve the problem by reducing capacity to the level of demand would be a lengthy process. Much of the steel was produced by large firms with correspondingly big resources and borrowing power; and the jobs they provided gave them a political clout that caused governments to subsidize them rather than allow them to fail. That, if it continued unchecked, would have been dangerous for the Community, because the more efficient producers, damaged by subsidized competition from other member states, would have ceased to find the Community of benefit. The spread of subsidization threatened the Community's integration in a number of sectors, and notably in steel.

The minimum prices were extended to other products in 1978. But this was a fragile expedient in the absence of any control of production, because firms would produce in quantities that made the minimum prices hard to hold. When the second oil shock induced a new recession, the Council accepted, in October 1980, the Commission's proposal to declare a manifest crisis; and the Commission introduced a regime for steel that became known as the Davignon plan, after the name of the then Commissioner for industry. In addition to the minimum prices, the Commission imposed maximum production quotas on firms. But this arrangement too would have been insufficiently robust without control over the supply of imports from the saturated world market. Yet whereas the Council could assent to the manifest crisis by majority vote, unanimity was required to ensure the control of imports. The German steel industry had modernized itself ahead of the crisis and the Germans felt that the Davignon regime shielded the less efficient producers in other countries at their expense. They therefore accepted the restriction of imports only on condition that their partners accepted a programme for bringing their subsidies to an end; and the Council agreed, in June 1981, that firms should qualify for state aids only if they were implementing a restructuring programme that would lead to the reduction of high-cost capacity.

This incident exposed a weakness in the Community's crisis regime, compared with the system of recession cartels practised in Japan. There, when a sector suffered from the sort of difficulties encountered by Community steel, the Japanese organized, as the Community did, a regime of minimum prices and production quotas. But while such a regime may ease the pain for the sector, it does little to relieve society of the burden of the high cost of the supported production. The Japanese therefore added an essential element: the firms were allowed to operate the cartel only on condition that they reduced capacity and modernized or diversified production to the point where they were again competitive without special support.[3] Thanks to the Germans' use of their voting power with respect to the import restrictions, the Community from 1981 did require restructuring and capacity reduction as a condition of state aids. But because of the political weakness of the Commission in relation to the governments of the member states, the cuts in capacity were too little and too late to avoid the continuation of the crisis regime until 1988, not far short of a decade after it had been introduced.

With the recession of the early 1990s, it was not long before the steel industry was in trouble again; and the Commission sought a further reduction of capacity. But agreement was again hard to secure, with private steelmakers in Britain and Germany resentful about the government subsidies that the Italians and Spaniards demanded for their producers as a condition of the capacity cuts. The industry's difficulties had not been resolved, despite the qualified success of the crisis regime in keeping trade conflict between member states within bounds while securing major reductions in capacity. The Japanese would surely have carried through the adjustment to a leaner, more competitive industry more thoroughly and in half the time. Japanese firms are more amenable to such arrangements than the Europeans: less individualistic, not divided by national rivalries, more apt to co-operate with government. Equally important, they have a government with which to co-operate. The weakness of the European institutions, with the Council unable to act decisively as an executive and preventing the Commission from doing so, raised the question whether it would not be wiser to refrain from embarking on such ambitious policies, at least until the institutions should be strong enough to conduct them effectively.

The Treaties provide for such market regulation only for

steel, coal, and in a different way for agriculture. With the rise of free market philosophy through the 1990s, such policies anyway became less fashionable. But in practice the Union does continue to apply some of these principles to help the adjustment of sectors in difficulty, making use of the instruments of industrial policy that it has available, including financial incentives and competition policy.

Competition policy, state aids

The policies to ensure competition among firms and to control state aids had an important place in the EEC Treaty. By the time that it was negotiated, in 1956–7, Germany had gained economic and political strength and German views about economic policy carried more weight. The German government was committed to the liberal ideas of the social market economy and hostile to the French style of intervention that had influenced the ECSC. The prominence of competition and state aids policy in the EEC compared with other forms of industrial policy reflected this German preference, acknowledged in Article 3f EEC (Article 3g ECT), which affirmed the aim of undistorted competition.

The EEC Treaty gave the Commission a strong position in the competition policy. After the Council had adopted the regulations, on proposals from the Commission, to give effect to the prohibition of restrictive practices and abuses of dominant positions stipulated in Articles 85 and 86 EEC (81 and 82 ECT), it was up to the Commission to enforce them subject only to appeal to the Court of Justice. Since the Commission deals in this with firms, not governments, and since it can impose heavy fines on firms that break the rules, it is at least as well equipped to act as the cartel offices in member states. It can be argued that such powers would be better held by an independent body that did not also possess, as the Commission does, responsibilities in other fields such as regional, social, or other aspects of industrial policy. But the appeal to the Court is some safeguard; and the record indicates that, even if an independent body might be better placed to exercise such powers objectively, it is better that the Commission should have them than that nobody should have them at all. In the absence of any such body at the European level, firms perpetrating abuses such as price fixing, output restriction, and market sharing across frontiers within the single market could probably escape the control of member states' competition authorities—even where effective authorities exist, which is not the case in all member states. As it is, the Commission's record, even in the difficult 1970s and early 1980s, was described as 'extremely impressive';[4] and its strong performance has continued through to 1998, when it fined Volkswagen ecu 102 million for compelling its dealers in Italy to refuse to sell cars to foreign buyers, mainly from Germany and Austria where retail prices were higher. The main cause for complaint has been delay in reaching decisions: ten years to give British brewers preliminary clearance for their agreements with tied pubs; five years to decide that a cement cartel was illegal and the companies involved be fined; and over a thousand cases outstanding at the end of 1997. The Commission needs more staff, which the member states have been reluctant to allow it.

While the EEC Treaty gave the Community competence to deal with restrictive practices and abuses of dominant positions, it did not include mergers that would lead to excessive concentrations of industrial power, as the ECSC Treaty had done. Since concentrations in coal and steel had become acutely controversial in the inter-war period, some being accused of facilitating the arms race and the drift to war, it was natural that the ECSC Treaty should seek to prevent them. In other sectors, at the time when the EEC Treaty was negotiated, they seemed less of an issue. But firms grew in size between then and the 1980s; and the imminent completion of the single market led to a spate of cross-frontier mergers within the Community in the last years of the decade, which made it more evident that the Community should be able to control them in all sectors, not just in coal and steel. The Council had been sitting on a Commission proposal since the early 1970s. But the Court ruled in November 1987 that the prohibition of restrictive practices (Article 85/81 ECT) could apply where a firm acquires control over another with its agreement (cases 142/84 and 156/84), and could thus lead, by direct application of the treaty, to the Commission acquiring a substantial power of merger control without any framework of specific legislation agreed by the Council. Spurred by this, and with the momentum of the single market programme, the Council agreed in 1989, sixteen years after it had started to consider the matter, on a law giving the Commission power to approve or block mergers of firms with a combined worldwide turnover over ecu 5 billion and a turnover in the Community of over ecu 250 million each on the part of at least two of the merging firms.

Just as the impending single market brought a wave of mergers in the late 1980s, so the prospect of the single currency helped to stimulate a new wave of mergers in the mid-1990s. In 1997 some 150 cases of mergers came before the Commission, two-and-a-half times the number five years earlier. But this has not caused delays, because the merger regulation requires the Commission to complete a preliminary investigation within one month to determine whether there is any serious doubt that the merger is legitimate, and any further investigation that may be required within four more months before deciding whether to initiate proceedings. Business has welcomed the speed and clarity of the procedure, compared with the scope for confusion and delay if trans-border mergers are subject to the authorities of more than one state. The Commission has also earned credit for its vigorous conduct, for example in imposing conditions on the acquisition by Boeing of McDonnell Douglas Corporation. Although both were American companies, the Commission had jurisdiction because of the size of their business in the Union, where they together had a share of two-thirds of the market for commercial aircraft. The Commission required Boeing's commitment to cease its exclusive supply deals, to license patents to other producers of jet aircraft, not to abuse its relationships with customers and suppliers, and to report annually on its receipts of public funding for research and development.

The Commission often permits mergers subject to conditions,

as it did in the case of Boeing; and many others have, as did Boeing, accepted them rather than be subject to proceedings. The EC Treaty likewise authorizes the Commission to allow agreements among firms where they contribute 'to improving the production or distribution of goods or to promoting technical or economic progress, while allowing to consumers a fair share of the resulting benefit' (Article 85/81 ECT). Thus the Commission can set conditions that firms are to meet if their agreements are to be allowed; and when a number of sectors were hard hit by recession and over-capacity in the late 1970s, it occurred to Davignon and the then Commissioner for competition, Raymond Vouel, that crisis cartels could improve production, provided that the minimum prices and production quotas were accompanied by reduction of capacity and modernization. In 1978 the case for a crisis cartel in the man-made fibres sector was being considered by the Commission, and Davignon and Vouel proposed that a regulation to legitimize crisis cartels be presented to the Council for its approval. But the Commission as a whole discarded this idea as likely to lead to a proliferation of restrictions; and the man-made fibres agreement was not approved by the Commission on the grounds that minimum prices and production quotas would not benefit the consumer.[5] It is possible, however, for consumers to obtain 'a fair share of the benefit'; and the Commission was later to look more favourably on arrangements of this sort. Thus the existing powers offered the scope for a variety of forms of industrial policy, when the institutions wished to exercise them in such ways.

The Treaty accords the Commission a similar role in the control of state aids as it has in the competition policy. State aids, that is subsidies or any other form of aid given to firms by member states, are prohibited in principle by Article 92/87 ECT. Once the Council, on proposals from the Commission, has adopted regulations to give effect to this prohibition, the Commission has the power to prevent a member state from granting such aids in any given case, or to require the state to alter the terms of the aid. The Treaty allowed that aids were legitimate in regions with low living standards or high unemployment; and this has led to rules that limit the levels of aid for investments in the more prosperous regions. Casting the net wider, it went on to allow aids 'to facilitate the development of certain economic activities or of certain economic areas', where such aid does not distort trade 'to an extent contrary to the common interest'. This widens enormously the scope for interpretation in what then become political rather than judicial decisions. The interpretation which the Commission has often given, in line with its thinking about recession cartels, is that aids to troubled sectors can be allowed provided they reduce capacity and promote adjustment into competitive activities. This has been its policy with respect, for example, to textiles, shipbuilding, and man-made fibres.

The policy has been sensible and logical. The problem has been to enforce it. In the hard times of the 1970s, state aids grew enormously. If the Commission had prohibited them, it would have incurred the wrath of wide sections of the workforce and endangered the standing of the Community institutions among the public. Outright defiance of member states' policies would have been risky. Since the Commission needs the governments' co-operation in many matters, including the enactment of its legislative proposals, it was not inclined to provoke them. It may also have feared that, if pushed too far, a government could refuse to respect Community law, with unfortunate consequences for the future of the Community. Even if individual Commissioners were not concerned about their chances of nomination again when the Commission came up for renewal after its (then) four years, the Commission had enough reasons to moderate its rigour with respect to state aids in the 1970s. In other words, its control then was not very effective. The balance of power in relation to the governments is far less favourable to the Commission than in relation to the firms with which the competition policy is concerned. But from the mid-1980s, with the recovery in the Community's economy and in the Commission's standing, its approach became more robust and it has taken some tough decisions in sectors such as the motor industry, for example with respect to such major firms as Renault and Rover.

The control of state aids is a powerful policy instrument, if the Commission's position can be strong enough in relation to the governments. In the main, this is a political question as to how far the Commission gains the capacity to act as a government for the Community or to what extent governments of the member states succeed in preventing it. One way in which they have clipped its wings is by denying it room in the budget for more staff. Just as there was a backlog of over a thousand cases for the competition policy, so at the end of 1997 not far short of one thousand decisions were pending on state aids. Member states tend to be more generous with such aids when unemployment is high, but they are not correspondingly generous in allowing the Commission the staff to fulfil with reasonable dispatch the obligations they have placed on it. The effectiveness of the Commission in this field may, however, also depend in part on how far it is confined to the negative power to prohibit member states' aids or how far it can also offer Community aids for adjustment and development; and in the field of technological research, its ability to do this has been growing.

Research and development

Monnet was concerned that the Community should not just be able to deal with problems from the past, such as curbing the power of steel barons or weathering a deep recession, but should also help to create a modern industry. The ECSC High Authority had the power to promote research and development and to provide finance for it; and when the relaunching of the Community was being planned after the failure of the Defence Community project, he was more interested in the idea of the European Atomic Energy Community (Euratom) than in the common market. A main consideration was political: the Assemblée Nationale would more readily accept the former than the latter. But he also saw advantage in building Community structures in new fields where national vested interests were less deeply entrenched. While he was wrong both about the common market, which was a great success, and Euratom, which was a failure, the validity of his basic proposition has been learnt the hard way: if less resources had been put into the old agricultural sector and more into the development of new technologies, some of the subsequent stagnation and conflicts could have been avoided.

Monnet was wrong about Euratom because it encountered a formidable vested interest: de Gaulle's idea of French military power. The Fourth Republic still existed when the Treaties of Rome were signed in March 1957; and had it continued to exist, the fate of Euratom might have been quite different. But de Gaulle came to power, replaced it by his Fifth Republic, and was determined to cut Euratom down to a small size so that it would have no chance of encroaching on the field he wanted France to occupy: atomic research as the basis for his nuclear *force de frappe*. Euratom continued to run four research centres, with some useful results, but without political significance. In addition to de Gaulle's resistance, the nuclear power plant manufacturers presented national obstacles to collective Community developments. The project which no member state could pretend to finance on its own was however the effort to generate power from nuclear fusion, which the Community mounted at Culham, near Oxford. This brought European scientists much prestige and raised high hopes that it might help to solve the world's energy problem in the next century. But there was no chance of an early economic return from the project.

As in the nuclear power industry, 'national champion' firms in other sectors together with governments ensured that the Community's research policy remained on a small scale and with little effect through the 1970s. But the results of national policies in that decade were disappointing. In the crucial field of microelectronics all the European states were decisively outdistanced by Japan with its programme that resulted in the mass production of chips. With the approach of Japan's fifth-generation computer programme, to be launched in 1981, it was becoming clear that the EC member states, acting separately, would not provide the resources or the framework to enable their information technology (IT) sectors to compete; and this would presage a long period of European industrial weakness.

In 1979 Davignon, as Commissioner for industry, produced a document that analysed the situation of European IT industries and concluded that fragmentation into national markets was a fatal flaw which had to be overcome. He realized that the member states and their bureaucracies, enclosed in their national frameworks, would be hard to shift. So he started with the leading IT companies, where consciousness of the danger of their situation was acute and resistance to far-reaching cross-border collaboration less. He invited the heads of twelve IT companies, accounting for three-quarters of Community production, to lunch in Brussels, told them he had a modest budget to promote co-operation, and asked their advice about what should be done to deal with the situation outlined in his document.[6] They agreed that they would like their firms to co-operate in research, starting at the easy end known as pre-competitive because the results are not close enough to development to be regarded as commercial secrets. This was also easier for Davignon, because the Commission had granted a 'block exemption' for such research with respect to the competition policy, and it could not be impeded as was the case with his idea of crisis cartels.

Davignon's initiative, based on the idea of working as the Japanese Ministry of Trade and Industry was perceived to do, helping industrialists with projects that they found useful to undertake co-operatively rather than imposing government policies on industry in the European tradition, was off to a good start. The heads of companies continued to meet, and agreed that the division of responsibility for standards in their sector among some sixty standards institutes within the member states was an intolerable defect, fragmenting the market and taking five to ten years to produce a common standard for an industry where the products, and hence some key standards, could become obsolete within a year. They established, by 1983, a Standards Promotion and Application Group, which proposed standards that were accepted by the Commission and adopted by the Council. This was not only an essential element in the single market programme. It was also seen as the catalyst for a process of merging and co-operating that shifted

Europe's IT sector from its cul-de-sac of national champions to a multinational structure better placed to compete with the Americans and Japanese.[7] Esprit, as the Commission's programme was called (acronym for European Strategic Programme for Research in Information Technology), was moreover appreciated by industry to an extent that the governments could not ignore. They accordingly accepted that it be expanded and followed by other similar programmes.

The Commission's success provoked reactions from the more nationalistic government machines, in particular in Britain and France. They countered with the Eureka scheme, launched by Mitterrand in 1985, which relied on intergovernmental organization, outside the Community framework, of projects bringing together different countries with a capacity and an interest. This did not, however, prevent a build-up of the Community's collective effort, with half-a-dozen programmes similar to Esprit. After a confrontation between Presidents Delors and Mitterrand at the European Council meeting in Milan in June 1985, a *modus vivendi* for Eureka and the Community programmes was embodied in the Single European Act, which gave research and technological development a general base in the EC Treaties that it had lacked hitherto, and provided for a multiannual framework programme setting out all the Community's activities in this field. Specific Community actions within the framework programme were to be decided by the Council voting by qualified majority, although the programme as a whole required unanimity.

The importance of the programme depends in part on the size of the Community's budget for research; and this, for the period 1987–92, was reduced from the level of ecu 7.7 billion, which was acceptable to the other governments, first by resistance from Britain and Germany, then by Britain alone. The decision was further delayed for nine months until a British general election was out of the way. Then the British government finally accepted a budget of ecu 5.7 billion: an average of some ecu 1 billion a year. With growing concern about European competitiveness in the global economy, President Delors secured a near doubling of the annual allocations for the

1993–7 framework programme, with the focus on IT, energy, industrial technologies, and life sciences and technologies. The budget for 1997 was ecu 3.2 billion; and for the period 1998–2002, the Council favoured a budget of ecu 14 billion, implying a significant reduction in real terms, and the Commission intended to focus on subjects relevant to employment, competitiveness, and the quality of life.

The Maastricht Treaty strengthened the articles on research and technological development and Amsterdam introduced qualified majority voting for the framework programmes. Maastricht also introduced an article on 'industry', in response to those who wanted a more explicit industrial policy for the Union (Article 130/157 ECT). Those governments that were suspicious of the idea were vigilant enough to ensure that the concept of competition was mentioned no fewer than three times in the fairly short article and that voting here too would be by unanimity, so that they can keep control over what the Union may do.

More significant than this general concept of industrial policy are the specific provisions that affect industrial development. Building on actions already undertaken under Article 235/308 ECT, which allows the Council to decide by unanimous agreement on 'action . . . necessary to attain . . . one of the objectives of the Community' for which the Treaty has not provided the necessary powers, the Maastricht Treaty not only firmed up the legal basis for research and technological development but also provided for action in some other important fields: trans-European networks, comprising cross-border infrastructures in the fields of telecommunications, transport and energy, which are central to the needs of industry in the coming century; education and training to help people gain the skills increasingly required in the modern European economy; small and medium enterprises, which generate the most employment opportunities but also have the most difficulty in taking advantage of the cross-border opportunities in the single market. The Union has significant programmes in each of these fields. Industry is also affected by the social provisions introduced in the Maastricht Treaty and by the Amsterdam

Treaty's new chapter on employment (Title VIa/VIII), which are intended to protect citizens from some of the consequences of the single market and single currency.

Social and employment policies

Many fear they will be hurt by the freeing of trade. The exposure of high-cost production to competition is, of course, one of the principal purposes; but the pain can be mitigated and the process of adjustment speeded if those who work in the high-cost activities are helped to move into more competitive jobs. It was in view of this, and in order to secure the support of trade unionists for his project, that Jean Monnet ensured that the Coal and Steel Community would be able to help people undergoing redeployment with housing and training for new skills.

More generally, when a common market is established the weaker economies may fear they will be crushed within it by the competition from the stronger; and those with higher pay and social standards may fear undermining by those whose level is lower. Thus when the EEC was established, the French feared that their standards of social legislation could be at risk. They had, for example, a textile sector with many female employees who had gained a right to equal pay, which would have to compete in a free market with textiles from other member states where women were paid less than men. France therefore insisted that the EEC Treaty contain the right to equal pay. Italy, on the other hand, still industrially less developed than the other members, sought help for developing to meet their competition; and the Treaty provided for the Social Fund to facilitate the employment and mobility of workers by training and other means, and the Investment Bank to promote economic development. Later, when Britain joined the Community, it secured the creation of the Regional Development Fund for similar purposes. Spain in particular pressed hard for the policy of 'cohesion' to accompany the establishment of the single market, which was to double the structural funds between 1988 and

1993 for the benefit of the weaker economies of the Community; and a similar increase was secured for the period of 1994–9, in the run-up to the single currency.

People in the richer and stronger economies also have their worries about the single market. The Danes and Germans in particular wanted to protect their standards of legislation relating to working conditions and to the environment. They insisted that the Single Act stipulate that harmonization of member states' measures should 'take as a base' a high level relating to health and safety at work, and to environmental and consumer protection. The further provision which allows a member state to opt out of a measure that threatens a decline in its standards has not led to fragmentation of the market, because harmonization has set high enough standards to avoid it.

The Single Act also required the Commission to encourage a dialogue between management and labour at European level, reflecting a concept of co-operation between the social partners that prevails in a number of member states, and in Germany in particular. This has taken the form, in the Federal Republic, of the system of co-determination, the best-known aspect of which is the legal right of employees to be represented on the boards of companies. This gave rise to a conflict over the status of workers in the European company statute on which the Council has long been trying to reach agreement, in order to facilitate the development of genuinely European firms. The German unions argued that if employers could choose a European statute that did not provide for co-determination, they would tend to do so, abandoning the German form of company and the obligations towards workers that go with it. British employers were among the foremost who resisted the spreading of the co-determination idea. The result has been a lengthy stalemate.

A similar conflict arose over the Social Charter, introduced by the Commission in order to provide reassurance for labour that the single market would be accompanied by improvement in the standards of social legislation (in the sense of legislation concerning employment conditions). The Social Charter contained provisions with which all member governments agreed, such as freedom of movement for workers, health and safety protection, and the right to join—or not to join—a union. But it also set out aims such as maximum working hours, a 'decent wage', and a right for workers to participation, which the British government contested. The Social Charter was approved by the European Council in December 1989, with Mrs Thatcher dissenting. But it was a statement of intentions, not a draft law; and the Single Act, which had provided for the Council to vote by qualified majority on only those measures of social policy that concern the health and safety of workers, had left other measures subject to the unanimity procedure and hence to the veto of a dissenting government.

The eleven governments that had approved the Social Charter wanted at Maastricht to incorporate its principles as a 'social chapter' in the Treaty and to provide for qualified majority voting in the Council, together with the co-operation procedure for the European Parliament, for laws on a number of subjects: not only improvement of the working environment to protect workers' health and safety, but also 'working conditions' more generally, 'the information and consultation of workers', 'equality between men and women with regard to labour market opportunities and treatment at work', and 'the integration of persons excluded from the labour market'. The British government refused to go along with this; and the member states adopted the new device of agreeing, in a protocol to the Maastricht Treaty which excluded Britain from its effect, that the other eleven could use the Community institutions—but without the participation of the British government in the Council—to take their decisions in the field. This, together with the protocol allowing Britain and Denmark not to adopt the single currency, set a precedent for opting out that led to the Amsterdam Treaty's general provision for opting out under the new chapter on 'closer co-operation'.

The protocol on social policy did not give rise to much legislation: only the directive of 1994 requiring firms with over one thousand employees, with at least 150 in at least two member states, to set up works councils or procedures for informing and consulting employees, and the parental leave directive of

1996. While Britain was exempted from these, the working time directive of 1993, stipulating that employees could not be required to work for more than 48 hours a week on average, did apply to Britain because it was enacted, not under the protocol, but under the Single Act's article on health and safety at work, which the Thatcher government had accepted and which provided for voting by qualified majority. The Court of Justice turned down an appeal on the basis of evidence that longer hours could lead to illness or accidents, although the British pointed to the much longer hours worked by, among others, the people who prepared and enacted the legislation. The directive did, however, allow a member state a derogation for ten years, provided that the work is voluntary and there are safeguards to prevent abuse.

The Labour government which came to power in time to conclude the negotiations for the Amsterdam Treaty had a different policy from that of the preceding Conservative government and accepted the Maastricht social chapter, which was therefore promoted from the status of protocol to that of new Articles 117/136–119/140 ECT. The text remained largely the same, save that 'equal pay for male and female workers for work of equal value' was specified as an additional aspect of equality subject to qualified majority voting in the Council, and the European Parliament's power was upgraded to co-decision for this as well as for the items to which qualified majority already applied. The new Labour government insisted, however, that unanimity be retained for other areas listed in the chapter, such as social security, social protection, representation of workers including co-determination, and protection of redundant workers, indicating continued British resistance to increased regulation in this field.

Having experienced growing regulation up to the 1980s, and linking this with its poor economic performance, Britain had moved farther than its EU partners towards what has been called the anglo-saxon model of flexible labour markets, with less regulation than is normal on the Continent.[8] Through the mid-1990s the British could point to declining unemployment, shared by the Irish as well as by the Americans, whereas with the notable exception of the Dutch, unemployment in most of the Continental countries, with their varying combinations of state regulation and consensus between the social partners, continued to rise relentlessly. The British emphasis on deregulation and competitiveness and that of many Continentals on social protection and solidarity became a further source of tension in the relations between Britain and other member states.

Delors sought to synthesize measures of macroeconomic policy, industrial policy, and labour market policy, designed to enhance both competitiveness and solidarity, in the Commission's White Paper on *Growth, Competitiveness, Employment*.[9] But a combination of recession and the continued conflict between Britain and its partners soured the atmosphere, and the White Paper, though well received, had little impact on events. Unemployment bore heavily on the politics of most member states and began to threaten the single currency project, because the associated squeeze on budget deficits, necessary though it might be over the medium and longer term, was widely blamed as one of the causes. One of the first initiatives taken by Sweden, after its accession in January 1995, was to propose that the treaty to come out of the forthcoming IGC should contain an employment chapter and a commitment to full employment.

The Amsterdam Treaty did indeed include the employment chapter (new Title VIa/VIII ECT) and the aim of 'high', though not 'full', employment. The chapter provides for a 'coordinated strategy for employment' and for an Employment Committee to advise the Council. The Council, voting by qualified majority, is to issue annual guidelines which the member states are to take into account in their employment policies; and the states are to provide annual reports on what they have done about it, which are to be the basis for a consolidated report to the European Council and for any recommendations that the Council, voting again by qualified majority, may choose to make to a state. The Council and Parliament may, by co-decision, adopt 'incentive measures' to encourage co-operation between member states and promote 'innovative approaches'. 'Incentive' in this context is a codeword for budgetary expenditure; and the more sceptical governments, particularly the British, Dutch, and Germans, made sure that this provision was hedged around with indications that the expenditure would be modest. The chapter relies, therefore, on the new procedures to give a higher profile to employment policies in the Union, but throws little light on what those policies might be. When the European Council held a special meeting on the subject in Luxembourg in November 1997, it was clear that one priority on which all were agreed was education and training to prepare the Union's citizens for the economy of the twenty-first century.

Environmental policy

Environmental protection is also a field where the Single Act not only guarded against the undermining of standards as a result of the single market, but also gave the Community a wider competence to 'preserve, protect and improve the quality of the environment'. Pollution carried by air or water does not recognize frontiers, so member states have a common interest in its mutual control. As ecological deterioration has become aggravated and public concern correspondingly sharpened, this field of competence has become increasingly important. Over 200 Directives and Regulations have been adopted relating to most fields of environmental management, including air and water pollution, waste disposal, dangerous chemicals, noise, and wildlife. One of the most important was the acid rain Directive of 1988, which committed member states to cut their emissions of sulphur dioxide and nitrogen oxides by stages over fifteen years, amounting to a reduction of 58 per cent over the period. Another was the reduction of exhaust emissions from small cars. Quality standards for drinking and bathing water are having a major impact in member states, including particularly Britain. There are noise limits for products such as aircraft, motor vehicles, construction plants, and lawnmowers. In 1985 a Directive required impact assessments to be made of projects likely to affect the environment, before member states' authorities allow development to proceed. A European Environmental Agency was established in 1994 to collect data and monitor the state of the environment. Two Directives have encouraged environment-friendly behaviour by industry: one which sets targets for the amount of packaging going to waste (1994), and one to oblige firms to minimize damage caused by their processes to the environment as a whole (1996). The 1994 Directive on conservation of habitats and of wild flora and fauna has created a broad framework for the protection of nature and requires member states to identify special areas of conservation. The accession of Sweden in 1995 enhanced the growing green influence in the Council, among other things rapidly inducing the Community to raise its standards with respect to hazardous chemicals.

The Union is a party to many international environmental conventions. It negotiates on chlorofluorocarbons (CFCs) and other ozone-depleting substances on behalf of the member states, and it can reasonably be claimed that it was the EC's approach which, in 1986, broke the international negotiating deadlock on depletion of the ozone layer in the stratosphere, which would result in penetration by the sun's ultraviolet rays to a degree that could have catastrophic consequences for life on earth.[10] The Union has likewise played a leading part in the other major international negotiations concerning the environment: those on global warming, which likewise threatens disaster over the longer term if emissions of greenhouse gases such as carbon dioxide (CO_2) are not sharply reduced. In the negotiations in 1997 for the Kyoto Protocol to the Framework Convention on Climate Change, the Union sought a reduction of 15 per cent in emissions of CO_2 by 2010, while the USA proposed only a standstill for a wider range of gases. In the event the American Administration accepted a cut of 7 per cent for three greenhouse gases while the EU committed itself to 8 per cent. The EU's own efforts to ensure compliance with its targets for greenhouse gas emissions by the member states rely mainly on voluntary rather than legally binding procedures. The mandatory element is a requirement that each member state must 'devise, publish and implement national programmes for limiting their anthropogenic emissions of CO_2' in order to contribute to the EU's own target for the emissions; and the Commission is authorized to monitor the states to check that their targets are met. But the member states set their own targets, in the light of the target for the Union as a whole, and they devise and implement their own policy packages for achieving them.[11] Despite the lack of compulsion, the EU has so far been quite successful in meeting its targets. But in order to achieve the cuts required by the Kyoto Protocol, and the deeper cuts that may well be necessary beyond that, the Union will sooner or later have to strengthen its institutional arrangements in this field, as it has done, through the Maastricht and Amsterdam Treaties, for a wide range of environmental matters.

The Maastricht Treaty built on the Single Act by affirming that sustainable economic progress is a prime objective of the Union, by making financial help for environmental together with transport projects the function of the new Cohesion Fund, and by introducing more decisive procedures for adopting environmental legislation. Although measures that are primarily fiscal, or concern land use, or significantly affect the pattern of a member state's energy supply remain subject to unanimity in the Council, qualified majority voting applies to all other environmental legislation. Maastricht confined the European Parliament's role to consultation for these matters and to the co-operation procedure for almost all the others. But the Amsterdam Treaty accords it the right of co-decision for all other environmental legislation. It was also expected that at Amsterdam, with the change of British government, qualified majority voting would be extended into the fields where the unanimity rule still applied in the Council. But while the British government was ready to accept this, it was blocked by Germany as a result of the quarrel between the federal government and the Länder over jurisdiction in the field of the environment. The Nordic member states, for their part, insisted on somewhat more permissive procedures for opting out of single market regulations that threaten to undermine a member state's high standards. The Amsterdam Treaty sharpened up the references to sustainable development, however, and reinforced the requirement that environmental protection be integrated into other Community policies and activities. Thus the Treaty enhanced the priority for the environment in the making of Union policy as well as making the legislative procedures more democratic.

Taken together, the Union's involvement in industrial, social, employment, and environmental policies has strengthened its positive integration. The three latter have also pointed towards a concept of a 'people's Europe' which was a forerunner of the idea of European citizenship, enunciated in the Maastricht Treaty and consolidated at Amsterdam.

7 From Monetary System to Single Currency

Federal governments have three main fields of economic competence: trade, both external and internal; budget, both tax and expenditure; and currency. With the single market and common commercial policy, the European Union already has as much competence in the field of trade as a federation. It has a half-developed federal budget. Now, in line with the provisions of the Maastricht Treaty for the third stage of economic and monetary union, most of the member states are exchanging their currencies for a single currency, the euro. Federalists have, since the 1950s, repeatedly promoted steps towards a single currency, and such efforts have been supported by people with more specific economic or political motives. But against these efforts stood hard facts of economic divergence among the member states and stubborn defence of national sovereignty. So it was not until four decades after the EEC was founded that the single currency became a reality.

The EEC Treaty itself did not venture far into the fields of monetary or macroeconomic policy. 'Conjunctural policies' and exchange rates were to be seen as 'matters of common concern' (Articles 103, 107). Economic policies were to be co-ordinated (Articles 105, 145). But the Community was given no instruments with which it could ensure that this was done; and the procedures stipulated for taking decisions in these matters were weak. The Council was to vote on them by unanimous agreement; and experience was to show, as could be expected, that in these questions which lie at the centre of member states' politics, the governments could usually agree only on letting each one go its own way. As an experienced participant put it: 'In practice, coordination never went very much beyond polite ritualistic consultation.'[1] The Treaty also provided for a Monetary Committee, comprising two representatives from each member state (so that there could be one from the finance ministry and one from the central bank) and two from the Commission. The Monetary Committee was to give advice to the Council and the Commission; and this advice has served a useful purpose when the governments have been predisposed to act on it.

Why was the EEC Treaty, which was so decisive about tariffs and trade policy, so weak about currency and monetary policy? France, whose accord was the key to the Treaty's success, was disturbed enough by the prospect of opening its long-protected market to competition from German industry, without having to face the loss of monetary sovereignty as well; and the rejection of the European Defence Community by the Assemblée Nationale was a warning against seeking too great a sacrifice of sovereignty for a second time. In the Federal Republic, Chancellor Adenauer had overridden his Economics Minister, Ludwig Erhard, who preferred wider international free trade to a European customs union. Erhard enjoyed much support among German finance and business people, and Adenauer could have seen no advantage in trying to face him down on monetary integration without backing from France. In the mid-1950s, moreover, when the EEC Treaty was conceived and signed, international monetary needs were well served by the Bretton Woods system with the dollar at its centre. There was no pressing practical motive for setting up a new monetary system in the Community.

Nevertheless, federalists thought that monetary union would eventually be required, and soon began to press for steps towards it.

Federalists versus de Gaulle

Directly after the EEC Treaty was signed in March 1957, Jean Monnet asked Professor Robert Triffin and Pierre Uri to design an outline for a European monetary system. Uri was one of Monnet's closest collaborators and the main author of the

Spaak report on which the Treaty had been based. The Spaak report had suggested that monetary unification would perhaps be required.[2] Triffin was an authority on international monetary questions who had been the architect of the European Payments Union, set up at the time of Marshall aid to restore a system of multilateral payments in post-war Europe. Triffin was to recall that when he then met Monnet, in 1948, Monnet judged the payments union proposal too modest in comparison with the monetary union that he believed would be needed. But Triffin shared the aim of monetary union as an essential element in a political union,[3] and was to become Monnet's constant adviser on monetary matters. Triffin's proposals during the first phase of the EEC's development included a single European currency and a European monetary authority as the last step in founding a monetary union for the Community, with a European reserve fund as one of the first steps.[4]

Monnet's Action Committee for the United States of Europe, bringing together the leaders of all the main democratic parties and trade unions of the six EC member states, adopted Triffin's proposal for the reserve fund and promoted it in the Committee's declarations of November 1959 and July 1961.[5] The Committee criticized the EEC Treaty for failing, with its 'very general provisions', to meet the need for the 'common financial policy' that would be a necessary complement to the common market. It proposed a European reserve fund as the first step towards a European currency and common monetary policy, which would enable the Community to exert its due influence in the international monetary system, as the common commercial policy would in the world trading system. The Committee also pointed out that Britain, which in 1961 first sought membership of the Community, would, if its proposals were adopted, be joining an 'economic and political union'. Monnet, in seeing the prospect of British membership as an occasion to strengthen the Community, was the first to enunciate the policy of 'deepening' at the same time as 'widening', which was subsequently to become embedded in Community thinking about enlargement. The fear that the Community might become weakened through the greater number and diversity of its members was to be met by proposals to strengthen its powers and institutions.

Strengthening the Community in view of prospective British membership was also one of the motives for the Commission's first major proposals for monetary integration, put forward in 1962 in the *Action Programme for the Second Stage*. Similarities between these and Monnet's proposals were not surprising since the Commissioner responsible, Robert Marjolin, was another of Monnet's close collaborators—and also one who 'leant towards' the idea of European federation, even though he felt in the 1960s that the time was not ripe for it.[6] The aim of the Action Programme, in addition to offering a framework for prospective British membership, was to set down a path for the Community's development during the second stage of the transitional period on which it was just entering, and through the third stage to the end of that period in 1970. The programme envisaged fixed exchange rates among the member states and a European reserve currency by that date. Meanwhile, some more modest steps should be taken: consultation about monetary policy, mutual assistance to meet balance-of-payments problems, further liberalization of capital movements beyond some measures already decided; and the establishment of committees to facilitate this co-operation, including the Committee of Governors of Central Banks, which was eventually to grow in importance and to play a key role in the economic and monetary union project some three decades later.

The motive of meeting the challenge of future British membership was mainly political: an aspect of a more general federalist desire to develop the Community and to build on its early success by filling out the gaps in the EEC Treaty such as the weakness of its provisions for monetary co-ordination. There were also economic motives. The first strains in the Bretton Woods system had emerged in the late 1950s, with US payments deficits leading to a weak dollar and a crisis in the gold market in 1960. On top of worries about the future of the international monetary system, consequent revaluations of the deutschmark and the Dutch guilder in 1961 caused concern for the stability of exchange rates within the Community. Triffin had pointed out that, with growing trade integration, there would be greater need for the co-ordination of economic and monetary policies in order to maintain equilibrium among the member states; and thinking along such lines had led to the new idea of the optimum currency area, suggesting that for highly interdependent economies the benefits of monetary union would be greater than the costs. The benefits would include the removal of foreign exchange transaction costs, the reduction of reserve requirements, the more efficient use of money and allocation of savings to the most profitable uses, and the business confidence resulting from the elimination of the exchange risk; and these would justify sacrificing the right of each state to conduct a macroeconomic policy tailored to its specific needs. Trends such as inflation or deflation would, moreover, spill over from one of the interdependent group of economies to the others, so that joint control over such trends should be in the general interest.[7] While the theorists of optimum currency area were unable to say whether the Community was in fact such an area, their line of thinking added an economic logic to the more practical economic motives for monetary integration, themselves reinforcing the political motives.

An opposite political motive was to stand in the way of steps towards monetary union in the 1960s. This was de Gaulle's insistence on national sovereignty and its effect on the conduct of Community business. The first outstanding example was his veto that unilaterally cut short the negotiations for British entry into the Community in January 1963. The relations between France and the other member states were upset to the point where much in the Action Programme had to be shelved. In the Federal Republic, moreover, Erhard replaced Adenauer as Chancellor in that year. He was oriented towards the international economic and monetary system and to the United States rather than towards the European Community and France; and unlike Adenauer, he had no rapport whatsoever with de Gaulle. If monetary integration required French leadership and Franco-German understanding, in these circumstances there was little chance of either.

Monetary difficulties pressed on the Community again in

1963 and the following year, with balance-of-payments crises in Italy. Interest in monetary integration was renewed. The Committee of Central Bank Governors was established in 1964; and in 1965 the Commission adopted fixed exchange rates as an objective.[8] In this it had the discreet support of the Monetary Committee and, more significantly, of the Banque de France and of de Gaulle's finance minister, Valéry Giscard d'Estaing.

This did not reflect any change of heart on the part of de Gaulle himself. His opposition to federal elements in the Community remained intransigent. When, having withdrawn his ministers from the Council in July 1965 in order to squash the federalist-inspired proposal for financing the Community budget, he returned them early in 1966 on the understanding that France would not be bound by majority votes on matters that the French government regarded as important, he at the same time replaced Giscard as finance minister by Michel Debré, a militant opponent of all things federal, who was later to lead the opposition in France to the Community's first major monetary union project. Monetary union was not destined to progress while de Gaulle was President of France. The federalists would have to sit it out until his departure.

The first sign that this was impending came with the student revolt of May 1968, followed by workers' militancy that led to wage rises around 20 per cent. Violent speculation against the franc ensued; and it was with a weakened French economy and money that de Gaulle resigned in April 1969.

Giscard was again finance minister in the new French government. Not long before, he had proposed the creation of a common currency, to cure the Community of the instability that resulted from the weakness of the franc, as well as the dollar, and the consequent strength of the mark.[9] By August 1969, the franc was devalued and the mark was allowed to float upwards. Not only did this offend those who valued currency stability, and there were many of them in France. It also led to the imposition of the border taxes, called monetary compensatory amounts, on trade in agricultural products within the Community. Since farm prices were fixed in common in European units of account, they would rise in France when the franc was devalued and would be cut in Germany as the mark appreciated. But the Germans insisted that their farmers should not be paid less in terms of marks; and the French wanted to avoid the inflationary impulse of higher food prices in francs, when they were struggling to get the inflation that followed the events of 1968 under control. So the monetary compensatory amounts were introduced. Although they seemed necessary for France's anti-inflationary policy, this new barrier within the agricultural common market, which had been seen as a principal French interest in the Community, was a heavy blow for the French: another motive for French support for monetary union, which would render any such border taxes unnecessary. On top of this, the prospect of a new British effort to join the Community in the wake of de Gaulle's departure renewed French thoughts about deepening the Community in order to prevent dilution. In short, there were strong reasons to turn French policy round from blocking monetary integration to promoting it.

Emu blocked by economic and political divergence

In 1969 Georges Pompidou became President of France and Willy Brandt Chancellor of the Federal Republic. Both were disposed to relaunch the development of the Community after it had been frozen by de Gaulle. The day after Brandt became Chancellor, Monnet wrote to him suggesting that the time was ripe to transform the Community into a monetary and political union and to enlarge it to include Britain.[10] Brandt was a longstanding supporter of federal ideas. But he also had a more specific motive for wanting to strengthen the Community. He was initiating his Ostpolitik in order to improve relations with the Federal Republic's neighbours to the east and with East Germany in particular, and he knew that this could worry those, particularly in France, who recalled the power games that Germany had played between east and west before World War Two. He therefore wanted to complement his Ostpolitik with a Westpolitik that would strengthen the Federal Republic's relationship with the West, and with France and the Community in particular. Deepening and widening the Community as Monnet proposed would serve this purpose perfectly. Closer ties between France and Germany were also in the Gaullist tradition to which Pompidou adhered; and he was much less averse than de Gaulle to strengthening these ties in the context of the Community.

Pompidou, Brandt, and the other heads of government of the member states met at The Hague in December 1969. Brandt's major proposals were monetary union and enlargement. While enlargement to include Britain was less welcome to France so soon after de Gaulle, Pompidou accepted it provided that it was combined with deepening in the form of monetary union, and completion of some unfinished business of interest to France through a regulation for the joint financing of the common agricultural policy. For monetary union he had the French motives, economic and political, mentioned above; and for finance minister he had Giscard, who was apt to promote the project. Italy and the Benelux countries were also in favour. So the aim of monetary union was adopted by the summit meeting at The Hague.

Meeting soon after, in February 1970, the Council agreed without much difficulty that there should be a common currency at the final stage of monetary integration. But there was sharp division about the steps towards it. The French wanted to move to a permanent fixing of exchange rates without much stress on co-ordinating economic policies beforehand. Once exchange rates were locked in this way, they argued, economic policies of member states would have to be adjusted so as to bring the relationship between their economies into equilibrium. The Germans, on the contrary, saw such definitive monetary integration as the end of a process in which the economies would be brought into equilibrium by the harmonization of economic policies; otherwise the locking of exchange rates would put the relationship between economies under too much strain. With their aversion to inflation, consequent on their two post-war hyper-inflations in this century, they feared in particular that a premature monetary link with more inflationary economies would undermine their ability to prevent it. In order to provide a strong enough framework for an effective monetary union, moreover, Dr Schiller, the German finance minister, affirmed that the EEC Treaty would have to be amended to provide for majority voting on these matters in the Council and, for the sake of democracy, a transfer of powers to the European Parliament.[11] Such federal ideas about institutions had been anathema to de Gaulle; and his successors were not yet ready to accept them. Unable to agree among themselves, the ministers set up a working group to analyse the different suggestions and 'identify the basic issues for a realization by stages of economic and monetary union', as the project had come to be called in deference to the German insistence on coordination of economic policies to accompany the monetary integration.

The group was chaired by Pierre Werner, Prime Minister of Luxembourg, and contained the chairmen of the relevant Community committees, including Bernard Clappier, then Chairman of the Monetary Committee, formerly Robert Schuman's *directeur de cabinet* when Monnet persuaded Schuman to launch the proposal for the European Coal and Steel Community, and since then another of Monnet's close associates. The Werner report, as the document presented by the group to the Council in October 1970 was called, defined economic and monetary union as comprising irrevocable convertibility of the member states' currencies, free movement of capital, and the permanent locking of exchange rates or, which should amount to the same thing, the replacement of the member states' currencies by a single currency. While this was to be achieved no later than 1980, the report was prudent on the subject of institutions, no doubt with the intention of avoiding trouble with the Gaullists. It went no farther than to envisage a 'Community system for the central banks' and a 'centre of decision for economic policy', on the grounds that a 'deeper study of institutional questions' was not in the group's terms of reference. Presumably Clappier, and Giscard with whom he must have been closely in touch, hoped this was vague enough to placate the Gaullists. But Debré was implacable. By the time the Council met to consider the report in November 1970, he had fomented enough opposition in France to the prospective loss of national sovereignty to prevent Giscard from accepting the report's conclusions. The French policy at the Council meeting was to agree to the modest steps assigned to the first stage of the Werner plan and to leave the questions of institutions, powers, and treaty revision until later—a policy closely replicated by the reluctant British when the Delors report on economic and monetary union was presented to the European Council in 1989. France's five partners resisted this line. The Germans and the Dutch wanted to start with steps towards economic policy co-ordination rather than with the narrowing of the margins of exchange rate fluctuation which was the central element of Werner's stage one; and none of the five wanted to limit the agreement to that small step, postponing *sine die* decisions on the larger monetary institutional reforms. But French participation remained essential and French refusal an insuperable obstacle. In March 1971 the Council agreed in principle on the establishment of economic and monetary union by stages; but stage one was to be tried on an experimental basis and there was no commitment to the rest.

The experiment was not a success. The attempt to keep the member states' exchange rates closer together coincided with aggravated turbulence in the international monetary system which again put upward pressure on the mark. By May, the Germans wanted to float again and they suggested that the others float with them—an idea not unlike that which later underlay the Exchange Rate Mechanism of the European Monetary System. But France and Italy refused, both because they wanted to safeguard their exports by keeping their exchange rates down and because of their policy preference for exchange controls rather than floating to deal with turbulence. So the German mark floated without them. By August the dollar, weak and under constant pressure, also floated and the Bretton Woods system, based on a stable dollar at its centre, came to an end.

The Community had a second try in 1972. The Council agreed in March that member states' currencies would stay within a band of 2.25 per cent, or 1.125 per cent on either side of their dollar parity, compared with a band of 4.5 per cent to which other members of the IMF adhered. This was called the 'Snake in the Tunnel', depicting a narrower band moving up and down within a wider one. But speculative pressure was again too strong. The pound, which had joined the Snake in anticipation of British entry into the Community, left it again within a few weeks; and the French franc was floated by January 1974. The Snake was reduced to the currencies of the Federal Republic and half a dozen small neighbours, not all of them members of the Community. France made a third attempt to join in 1975, but this again lasted only a few months.

The ambitious goal of economic and monetary union had been placed in question by politics: divergences of economic philosophy and of attitude towards a federal reform of the Community institutions. The Snake had been seen as a first step towards it; and that was thwarted by the economics of the 1970s. The turbulence of the early 1970s, culminating in the oil shock of 1973–4 when the price of oil more than quadrupled, led to highly divergent performances by the different member states. Germany soon got its inflation under control. At the other extreme Italy, together with Britain, by now a member of the Community, combined high inflation with massive payments deficits. Not only was monetary integration frustrated, but the question was posed whether divergence would impede further integration of any sort within the Community.

One result was a new wave of thinking about optimum currency areas. One view, taken by some neo-classical economists, was that divergent performance was due essentially to differing macroeconomic policies; so the convergence required for economic and monetary union was a matter of political choice, and an optimum currency area would be one in which the governments were ready to decide on policies that would bring stability. Another view was that the divergence was caused by differing economic structures, particularly in the labour markets. Factors such as the strength and behaviour of trade unions built different propensities to inflation into the economies; and so long as this divergence remained significant, monetary integration could not take the form of a permanent locking of exchange rates or single currency.[12]

This thinking led to a proposal to move towards monetary union by developing a parallel currency,[13] which would be launched alongside the member states' currencies both for official use, as a reserve and means of settlement, and for use in the private markets for money and capital. As its importance grew the economies would adapt to it until it could eventually replace the existing currencies as a single Community currency. The idea was taken up by the Commission in 1975;[14] and when the European Monetary System was established in 1979, the European Currency Unit (ecu) began to perform some of these functions. Its further development was among the measures proposed in 1990 for the transitional period in establishing the economic and monetary union; and the Maastricht Treaty assigned this task to the transitional European Monetary Institute.[15] The focus of the next phase of monetary integration which started in the late 1970s with the European Monetary System was, however, not the parallel currency but an exchange rate mechanism.

Jenkins, Schmidt, Giscard, and the EMS

Roy Jenkins, a former British Cabinet minister, became President of the Commission in 1977, when the Community was in a stagnant state and there was much pessimism about its future. He perceived a need to 'break out of the citadel or wither within it', and in order to break out he sought a theme around which he 'could help to move Europe forward'.[16] Inspired by Jean Monnet's example,[17] he sought it among the problems that pressed on the governments of the day, which included unemployment, inflation, and divergence; and his solution was to introduce a bold proposal on to the agenda, in the form of economic and monetary union (Emu).

Jenkins launched the idea publicly in his Jean Monnet Lecture in October 1977, enumerating the expected economic benefits and envisaging that it would 'take Europe over a political threshold'.[18] Reactions from the experts, the media and the politicians were almost uniformly sceptical. A significant exception was the Belgian government, currently taking its turn in the presidency of the Council. The Belgians, instigated by Jenkins, got the European Council in December 1977 to reaffirm its commitment to the objective of Emu and to approve the idea of making progress in that direction. These would have been empty words without the genuine commitment of major member states, and of the Federal Republic, as the Community's leading monetary power, in particular. But Helmut Schmidt, the German Chancellor, who had merely expressed a 'mildly benevolent scepticism' in December, told Jenkins in February that he wanted a major step towards monetary union. He had in mind a European monetary bloc based on a common reserve pool.[19]

Schmidt's conversion was crucial to the establishment of the European Monetary System (EMS), and hence to the drive towards Emu a decade later. The impact of the idea of Emu on his thinking should not be neglected. He had just written the introduction to the German edition of Monnet's *Memoirs,* in which he mentioned the Action Committee's early declarations in favour of it; and he later acknowledged the influence of Jenkins on his thinking about Emu.[20] But the idea would have remained just that without the political and economic grounds in which it could germinate. Politically, Schmidt was much concerned about what he saw as the failure of American leadership under President Carter, whom he regarded as incompetent. This had painful economic consequences for the Federal Republic. Large American payments deficits through 1977 weakened the dollar, which fell by one-tenth between October 1977 and February 1978, and again by another tenth by the autumn of that year. As usual, the weak dollar was reflected in a strong mark, which was bad for German exports; and, to add insult to injury, the US Administration pressed the Germans hard to reflate, so that the German economy would act as a 'locomotive', drawing world demand upwards behind it and thus helping to correct the US payments deficit. The Germans were, as ever, sensitive to the danger of inflation; and Schmidt saw the Americans' pressure as an attempt to shift the responsibility for solving their problem on to the Germans, whose supposed fault was to manage their economy in a prudent manner. In response to this pressure, Schmidt told the Bundestag in January 1978 that Germany could accept the role of locomotive only if it was shared with others. These others would be Europeans and in particular France, whose President, Giscard d'Estaing, Schmidt was wont to call 'my friend', or even 'my only friend'.[21]

Schmidt and Giscard had worked closely together since Schmidt became finance minister in 1972 and both moved from that position to become Chancellor and President respectively in 1974. The political fortunes of both were prospering in 1978, with Giscard in particular being liberated from dependence on Gaullist support following elections in March of that year. When Schmidt then sought Giscard's backing for his proposals for monetary integration it was, given Giscard's long-standing commitment to the idea, readily forthcoming. In April, in the European Council in Copenhagen, they together promoted a project for a reserve pool in a European Monetary Fund, and for greater use of the ecu's forerunner, the European Unit of Account.

The British Prime Minister, James Callaghan, was almost alone in expressing serious reservations about the idea, and work on designing the EMS went ahead. It became clear that consensus would focus on exchange rate stabilization rather than a reserve pool; and the Exchange Rate Mechanism (ERM) was at the centre of the EMS when its structure was agreed by the European Council in Brussels in December 1978.

EMS and Exchange Rate Mechanism

Behind the detail of the ERM was a radical new departure: parities could be changed only by 'mutual agreement' of the states participating in the ERM together with the Commission. Although a member state could pull out of the ERM if it saw fit, so long as it continued to participate this would be an unprecedented transfer of monetary autonomy. Control over the exchange rate had been at the core of monetary sovereignty, and the participants were to take a big step towards sharing it.

The day-to-day management of exchange rates was to be bounded by a 'grid' in which margins of fluctuation were not to exceed plus or minus 2.25 per cent of the central rates, defined in relation to the ecu, which was itself a weighted average of the EMS currencies. From this starting-point, a band was to be calculated for each pair of participating currencies, and if the limits of the band were reached, the authorities responsible for each of the currencies in question were to intervene in the market in order to keep the difference between them within the band. But the governments of states with the weaker currencies, such as France, Italy, and the UK, were averse to this grid system, on the grounds that it favoured the strong currencies, in particular the mark. Intervention on behalf of weak and strong currencies was, they argued, asymmetrical. Intervention by the weaker countries, using foreign currencies to buy their own when it reached the bottom of the band, would be limited by their foreign exchange reserves, and before these were reduced too far they would have to raise interest rates, thus deflating their economies; whereas the stronger countries could continue selling their own currencies and piling up their reserves indefinitely, without being obliged to reciprocate by reducing their interest rates.

The governments with weaker currencies sought alleviation in various forms. One such was the divergence indicator, which was intended to trigger changes in policy by both partners when divergence between a pair of currencies reached three-quarters of the permitted band; those with weaker currencies hoped that this would shift more of the burden of policy adjustment on to the stronger countries, and on to Germany in particular. A second device was the wider band of fluctuation, of plus or minus 6 per cent, secured by Italy, and subsequently, when they entered the ERM, by Spain then Britain, although the Italians applied the normal limits of 2.25 per cent in 1990. Britain, for its part, chose to remain outside the ERM, with the proviso that it could 'enter at a later date'—in the event over a decade later. Credits were also to be available for countries that had to intervene heavily to support their currencies; and loans with interest rate subsidies were to be provided for Italy and Ireland, the two member states which at that time claimed a need for development assistance.

Although the EMS had been strongly promoted by Giscard and Schmidt, and did enter into force in March 1979, it encountered resistance in the most powerful member states. In France the Gaullists, still concerned about sovereignty, and the farmers caused the starting of the system to be delayed for three months, during which the French government sought concessions from its partners regarding the monetary compensatory amounts. But no such concessions being forthcoming, the French demand was dropped.

In Germany, Schmidt faced powerful opposition. The Christian Democrats were hostile. So was the financial sector in general; and Karl Otto Pöhl, Schmidt's own nominee as Vice-President of the Bundesbank, expressed his 'fundamental reservations' about possible inflationary implications. The Bundesbank fought, successfully, to reduce Schmidt's reserve fund idea to a minimalist European Monetary Co-operation Fund, with three-monthly swaps of ecus against one-fifth of the member states' gold and dollar reserves, instead of definitive transfers which could eventually be used for intervention. The European Council did agree that the European Monetary Fund should be established by 1981, with full use of the ecu as a reserve asset and as a means of settlement; but the second oil shock came in 1979, and the resulting instability in the international monetary system intervened to deter the governments from carrying out what they had agreed. But apart from this, Schmidt overcame his opponents in Germany, partly by spending an estimated 200 hours in 1978 persuading people that the EMS was desirable, and partly by keeping his cards very close to his chest until the project was well and truly launched. This he did by ensuring that its development through the spring of 1978 was entrusted to only three people: Dr Schulmann, the economic adviser to his own office; Bernard Clappier, by now Governor of the Banque de France; and Kenneth Couzens, Second Permanent Secretary at the UK Treasury, who, given the cool British attitude to the project, did not participate fully. By the time that what became a Franco-German project was launched, its German opponents, and the Bundesbank in particular, could secure modifications but not prevent it.

One of the British arguments against the EMS at that time was the fear that it would be deflationary and exacerbate the de-industrialization which was already causing concern. This could be compared with the worries expressed in France and Italy, except that when the pound became stronger the British turned the argument on its head and resisted entry into the ERM on the grounds that it would be inflationary. A second argument was that the EMS could upset the wider international monetary system and annoy the Americans. Such also was Callaghan's orientation when he sided with the Americans and against Schmidt about the locomotive role for Germany, rather than working with Schmidt to seek a European response to the Americans' concerns. A third argument, frequently used in Britain regarding initiatives to develop the Community, was that the Continentals would talk about it but not do it. The flavour of this attitude was caught by the unguarded remarks of Couzens to the press after the meeting of the European Council in Bremen at which the proposal prepared by Clappier and Schulmann had been generally approved: 'the Treasury remains sceptical to the point of contempt', he was reported to say, 'of most of the detailed content of the Franco-German scheme', which showed 'the danger of allowing enthusiastic amateurs to dream up schemes for monetary reform'.[22]

Callaghan nevertheless then grasped the political significance of what was happening, and British officials worked hard on the technical preparations for the EMS, though without commitment about eventual participation. Such commitment would have been politically difficult for Callaghan, who was faced with a House of Commons resolution signed by 120 Labour MPs, rejecting 'any attempt by the EEC, its institutions or its member states to assume control of domestic policies through a new monetary system for the Community': an attitude which was later to underlie some of the explanations Mrs Thatcher was to give for keeping the pound out of the ERM through the 1980s.[23] The hostility of those Labour MPs was strongly enough reflected in the Cabinet and the Labour Party to put full membership of the EMS out of court for Callaghan. The most he could achieve was participation in the EMS but not in its key element, the ERM. When the project ran into difficulties at the European Council in Brussels in December 1978, where it was accepted but sidetracked by the issue of the monetary compensatory amounts, Jenkins found British officials 'almost gloating that things had fallen apart'.[24] Once again, they underestimated the forces that have carried the Community forward. The EMS was established three months later, with results that helped during the following decade to transform the prospects for the future of the Community.

The EMS in the 1980s

The Exchange Rate Mechanism of the EMS helped to stabilize the participants' exchange rates in the 1980s. Their variability in the period 1979–85 was half what it had been in 1975–9, and it halved again in 1986–9, both for the nominal rates on which exchange dealings are based and for the real rates that discount the effects of differing rates of inflation. Both exchange rates and interest rates became less volatile, partly because policies became more credible to those dealing in the markets, but partly also because France and Italy damped down potential volatility by retaining exchange controls. Misalignments, that is more durable deviations from exchange rates likely to ensure longer-term equilibrium, also appear to have been reduced.[25] The need for realignments, or changes of parities within the ERM, consequently declined. There were seven realignments between 1979 and 1983, only four from 1983 to 1989.

This new stability would not have been achieved without a convergence of macroeconomic policies. The EMS was launched at a time of growing consensus in western countries that the priority for monetary policy should be to prevent inflation. The participants in the ERM were thus aligning their policies on that of their partner with the strongest economy and currency, the Federal Republic. France was an exception for a couple of years after the arrival of a Socialist government under President Mitterrand. But its expansionary policy led to payments deficits of a size that demanded a response. Two types of policy were proposed. One was to take a step back from European integration by restricting imports and floating the franc out of the ERM. The other, advocated by Jacques Delors, who was then the French finance minister, was to apply a restrictive macroeconomic policy and thus remain within the ERM. President Mitterrand, valuing the relationship with the EC and with the Federal Republic in particular, was persuaded that the franc should stay in the ERM; and French policy too converged on that of the Federal Republic.

The convergence of policy was accompanied by a growing habit of co-operation among the monetary authorities of the participating countries. The central banks worked closely together for their interventions in currency markets in order to keep the exchange rates within the bands. The parities from which the bands were defined were the responsibility of the finance ministers, not the banks; and by 1989 it could be said that parity changes, decided by the finance ministers at weekend meetings in time for the markets to open again on Monday morning, had become 'truly multilateral decisions'.[26] Thus the participants were sharing sovereignty in practice over one of the most fundamental decisions of economic policy.

This did not apply to Britain, which, like Greece and then Portugal, remained outside the ERM throughout the 1980s. Mrs Thatcher had said at an early stage that the time was not right for the pound to enter. The time continued, in her view, not to be right throughout the decade, and it was not until October 1990 that Britain finally participated. The private markets in the City of London were not so hesitant about another product of the EMS, the use of the ecu for private transactions. London was among the leaders in developing such use, which made the ecu one of the most used currencies in certain sectors of the international markets, such as bonds and inter-bank transactions.

But it was the success of the ERM in stabilizing exchange rates and converging policies that offered a basis for the renewed efforts, which began in the late 1980s, to move by stages to a single currency. The other main elements of economic and monetary union, freedom of movement for capital and a single market for financial services, had by then already been set in train by the Single European Act.

The Single Act and a single financial market

The Single Act did something for the exchange rate element in monetary integration. It brought the EMS, which had been set up alongside and not as a part of the Community, within the scope of the treaties, thus consolidating its juridical status; and it made economic and monetary union a formal treaty objective. But its main contribution to Emu was in the freeing of capital movements and the integration of the markets for financial services.

The Single Act, as we saw in Chapter 4, embodied a commitment to complete the single market by the end of 1992, and made it feasible to enact the necessary laws by stipulating qualified majority voting in the Council for most of the measures required. The single market programme also eased the process of legislation by reducing the harmonization of laws and regulations to the minimum needed for health, safety, and consumer protection, and relying beyond that on the mutual recognition by member states of each other's standards and regulations. In the field of financial services the equivalent of mutual recognition is 'home country control', whereby a firm providing such services anywhere in the Community will be subject to the laws of the member state in which it is registered. Community legislation is introduced only to the extent that such laws do not meet the minimum standards deemed essential by the Community institutions.

The legislation necessary to complete the single market for financial services was nevertheless complex and member states defended their own entrenched regulations and institutions. But most of the necessary measures had been adopted by the end of 1992 in the three main fields of banking, insurance, and investment services.

The financial sector could not, however, be seen as integrated if exchange controls were to prevent the transfer of money from one member state to another. The EEC Treaty had established the aim of abolishing obstacles to free movement of capital (Article 3); but the specific provision for this had referred only to the movement of capital 'to the extent necessary to ensure the proper functioning of the common market' (Article 67). The Court of Justice had later ruled that this provision was not 'directly applicable': that is to say, the Court itself could not decide whether the exchange control regulation in question was necessary for the common market; the Council would first have to enact a measure defining the principles on which such necessity should be judged.[27] This the Council had failed to do; and many exchange controls had remained in place, particularly in France and Italy, where they had been seen as a means of damping down pressures for devaluing the exchange rates. The Single Act brought the free movement of capital into the single market programme to be completed by 1992 (Article 13 SEA).

Exchange controls had been regarded as key instruments of macroeconomic policy in France and Italy, as well as in southern member states that had joined the Community in the 1980s, so their removal was widely expected to be one of the hardest tasks confronting the single market programme. But Delors, by now President of the Commission, did not delay in proposing, once the member states had signed the Single Act, that the complete liberalization of capital movements be accelerated. He doubtless sensed that the climate of opinion among French policy-makers was ripe for this, and that the integration of capital markets could be a catalyst for a revival of the Emu project. Directives enacted in 1986 and 1988, together with those agreed in 1960 and 1962 when the Commission made its first attempts to promote monetary integration, did indeed ensure full freedom of capital movements by July 1990, with a delay until mid-1993 for the Community's weaker, peripheral economies.

By the time Delors took the initiative over exchange controls, governments that had previously insisted on the need to maintain them were ready to respond, partly because the balance-of-payments deficits that had worried them in the early 1980s were much reduced and because the new stability within the Exchange Rate Mechanism had made them more relaxed about the risks to their exchange rates. Radical innovations in the financial markets had moreover diminished the effectiveness of such administrative controls and raised the cost of attempting to enforce them; and the more dynamic operators in those markets were eager to be part of the global village which the international financial community was rapidly becoming, and which threatened to leave them on the sidelines if they were hampered by restrictions. Governments gave weight to their interests because a dynamic financial sector was seen as an essential part of a modern economy, owing both to its growing size and to the importance of the services that it provides to the rest of the economy. The Cecchini report estimated the direct savings in the financial sector from the reduction in prices of financial products due to the competition that would follow the opening of markets at ecu 22 billion, or about one-tenth of the total economic gains from completing the single market; and if the effect of the consequently lower interest rates on the rest of the economy was taken into account, this was expected to bring further gain of a similar order of magnitude, comprising some 1.5 per cent of Community gross domestic product in all.[28] These estimates reflected the ample incentive for the more competitive firms in both finance and industry to support the completion of the single market for financial services and the abolition of exchange controls.

Thus the Single Act succeeded in setting the Community on course for the integration of financial markets that is one of the main components of economic and monetary union. The removal of exchange controls also released pressures for the completion of the other element: the single currency or permanent locking of exchange rates. When there is disturbance in the financial markets, capital flows from one member state to another will be bigger if there is no exchange control; and this will put pressure on the exchange rates. Thus the stability achieved in the Exchange Rate Mechanism could be threatened if the participants' macroeconomic policies were not co-ordinated to counteract this risk.

Such co-ordination is another element of Emu; and the integration of capital and other financial markets reduces the autonomy of the member states' policies, so that the gains from joint control may be greater than any loss from the sacrifice of the right to take independent action. With autonomy being thus reduced, the question arose whether it would not be wiser to confront the danger of unstable exchange rates more directly by moving to the permanent renunciation of the right to change them. Exchange rate stability had proved popular among the participants in the ERM. Why not, instead of risking the loss of this advantage as capital markets became integrated, go on to abolish any such risk once and for all? It was economic arguments such as these that, combined once again with political motives, helped to place the Emu project at the top of the Community's agenda by the end of the 1980s.

Emu and the Delors proposals

On top of the general economic arguments for complementing the free movement of capital with the permanent fixing of exchange rates there was an argument that appealed to France in particular. France had, by 1988, got its inflation rate down fairly close to the German level. Having successfully aligned their policies on those of Germany, the French were not inclined to accept that Germany had the right to lead them in co-ordinating macroeconomic policies: they had learnt their lesson and did not want the teacher's tutelage.[29] A single currency would not be managed by the Bundesbank, which, through the strength of the mark, dominated the EMS, but by common Community institutions in which all participants would have their due influence.

The role of the Bundesbank in the EMS was but one aspect of a growth in the Federal Republic's strength and assertiveness that was causing increasing worry in France. The idea of containing German power within a common European framework, rather than attempting to balance it in a system of separate sovereign states, embodied the same political logic as in 1950, when Monnet had initiated the Schuman plan. Now it was the Emu project that seemed apt to integrate Germany more firmly in a Community setting, and doubtless with yet more significant implications for political integration. France became strongly committed to the project, and the more so as the prospect of a united Germany playing a powerful role in Eastern Europe came nearer to realization.

When Delors called in 1986 for early steps to free the movement of capital, he started a process which could lead to monetary union. By 1988 he was ready to launch the Emu project; and he made it increasingly clear that he saw this as a major step towards a federal Community. With firm backing from France and with the consent of Chancellor Kohl, he was able to ensure that it was on the agenda for the meeting of the European Council under German presidency in Hanover in June 1988. That meeting agreed to set up a committee, chaired by Delors and including the central bank governors of the member states, to study and propose 'concrete stages leading towards' the objective of economic and monetary union which had been confirmed 'in adopting the Single Act'. The resulting 'Delors report'[30] proposed the establishment of Emu in three stages, moving from closer co-operation on existing lines to a single currency and European Central Bank.

Agreement was quickly reached to act on the first stage, in which all member states would enter the Exchange Rate Mechanism, and economic and monetary co-operation would be intensified. The European Council in June 1989 decided that this would begin in 1990, and the British government did indeed take the pound into the ERM in that year. But the government did not agree with its partners about further steps towards the single currency; and its proposals for a system of freely competing currencies of member states, managed by their monetary authorities without a European Central Bank, then for the promotion of a hard ecu as a parallel currency that would always be as strong as the strongest among the member states' currencies, were widely seen as attempts to impede progress towards the single currency.

The Delors report's definition of Emu in the third and final stage was a rigorous one, similar to that of Werner: complete liberalization of capital transactions and full integration of financial markets; total and irreversible convertibility of currencies; the elimination of margins of fluctuation and the irrevocable locking of exchange rate parities. The report noted that the locking of parities did not necessarily imply the replacement of the member states' currencies by a single currency, but recommended that it should replace them as soon as possible after parities were locked. With complete liberalization, integration, and convertibility, the member states' currencies would, with permanently locked exchange rates, anyway be no more than the 'non-decimal denominations of a common currency'.[31] In its own document on Emu, published in March 1990, the Commission also came down in favour of the single currency on the grounds that it would be more definitively irrevocable and would eliminate any remaining costs of currency exchange.[32]

The form of Emu proposed in the Delors report was much influenced by the policy of the Bundesbank, as the most powerful of the central banks represented in the committee. That policy was set out clearly by Karl Otto Pöhl, by now President of the Bundesbank, in a paper annexed to the published report.[33] He insisted that the Community should have power to limit the budget deficits of member states in an Emu, because they would, if allowed on the scale that had recently been practised by some states such as Italy, present an inflationary threat to the Community as a whole; and this, like most of his other ideas, was not only adopted in the report but also embodied in the design for Emu that was to become the central element in the Maastricht Treaty.

The concerns of member states with the less-developed economies contrasted with those of the Bundesbank. The governor of the Irish central bank made the case for resource transfers to the less-developed regions in an Emu, analogous to the cohesion policy designed to help the weaker economies to adapt to the single market; and Delors himself also contributed a paper on the subject.[34] This idea too was realized in the enhanced policy of cohesion associated with the Maastricht Treaty.

Following the Delors report, the Emu project had gained momentum by 1990. This owed much to the strength of the French commitment, which was reinforced by German unification. France had seen the single currency not only as a means of regaining some control over monetary policy, but also as a further stage in the great post-war project of anchoring Germany in the Community; and the prospect of a larger and stronger Germany, occupying a central position in Europe and taking full advantage of the opening up of relations with Central and Eastern Europe, added edge and urgency to this aim. The French commitment was shared, for differing mixtures of motives, by a number of other member states, including Germany itself, anxious as ever to pursue the project with France and to continue developing the safe anchorage of the Community in a federal direction. This federalist orientation was also shared by a big majority in the European Parliament, by most of the political party groups represented in it, and by such eminent politicians as Giscard and Schmidt, together with the Commission, whose President played such a notable part in promoting the project.

The Emu project also enjoyed strong support from industry and finance. Business leaders established an Association for the Monetary Union of Europe in order to promote it. In addition to the gains from the liberalization of financial markets, estimated in the Cecchini report at over ecu 40 billion a year, the monetary union was expected to save ecu 13–19 billion, or 0.3–0.4 per cent of Community GDP, in the transaction costs incurred in changing money from one currency to another.[35] Although this saving may not be so welcome to banks, for which those transactions are a significant source of business, they too have been well represented in the Association. More important for industry than the saving of transaction costs is the greater certainty with which longer-term plans could be made for investment and trade within the Union. As with the single market, this 'dynamic effect' is likely to be greater than the more immediate 'static effects'. Industry has also been motivated by fears that currency upsets could disrupt the single market, while monetary union would remove that risk altogether.

For the private financial sector, Emu can be seen as a framework that should enable European firms to be competitive players in the global financial system. At the level of public policy, Emu should give the Union a bargaining power in relation to the dollar and the yen analogous to that which the common tariff secured in the field of trade. American budgetary, exchange rate, and interest rate policies have often caused discomfort to Europeans, and Emu can be expected to give the Union more influence over US policy-making, as well as in the international monetary system and its institutions.

These interests and motives, both economic and political, were enough to account for the momentum of the Emu project. There were also forces that resisted it. There were fears that the weaker economies would lose out if tied so closely to German monetary power, mirrored by Germans' fears that they would catch inflation from their partners. While attuned to the need for more co-operation, finance ministries and central banks contained people who were ill-disposed to part with their powers over macroeconomic policies, and there were those in politics who shared their reluctance. The most outspoken of these was Mrs Thatcher, who reacted as de Gaulle did against the sharing of sovereignty such as Emu requires. But she had less power than de Gaulle to prevent progress towards monetary integration, as the success of the Exchange Rate Mechanism without British participation had demonstrated. Neither she nor her successor, John Major, could stand in the way of the project provided that France and Germany, as well as other member states, were committed to it.

The Bundesbank expressed itself as favourable to Emu in principle, but hesitant about specific steps of monetary integration before the other member states should become as proficient as Germany in preventing inflation. Support in Germany for political union remained solid, however, and the German government stressed its importance for maintaining the stability of the European system in the context of German unification. Chancellor Kohl in particular was strongly committed to political union and saw Emu as essential both for that and to maintain the partnership with France. As both political union and Emu appealed to most member states, the IGC on political union was linked with the IGC on Emu, comprising a more attractive package for Germany than Emu on its own. Whatever the doubts among Germans, the Maastricht Treaty demonstrated the German government's commitment to the project.

From Maastricht Treaty to single currency

The most important words in the Maastricht Treaty were 'the irrevocable fixing of exchange rates leading to the introduction of a single currency', to take place when the participating states entered Stage 3 of Emu, by 1 January 1999 at the latest. The participating states were to exclude those that did not meet the 'convergence criteria', on which Germany insisted as evidence of commitment to the principles of sound money and price stability. The single currency, to be based on the ecu, was to be managed by the European System of Central Banks (ESCB), comprising the European Central Bank (ECB) together with the central banks of the participating states. The ESCB was to be responsible for monetary policy; it was to hold and manage official reserves and conduct foreign exchange operations, and promote the smooth operation of payments systems; and the ECB was to have the exclusive right to authorize the issue of banknotes. The primary aim was to be price stability; without prejudice to that, however, the ESCB was to support the Union's general economic policies. The Governing Council of the ECB comprises the governors of the participating states' central banks, themselves to be independent of governments, together with the President, Vice-President and four other members of the ECB's Executive Board, who were to be appointed for eight-year terms by common accord among the heads of state or government. As a guarantee against political interference that could undermine price stability, they are not allowed to take instructions from any other bodies.

While Stage 1 had already been defined in 1989, with participation by all member states in the Exchange Rate Mechanism as its principal feature, the arrangements for the transition to the single currency through Stage 2 had to be determined in the negotiations leading up to the Maastricht Treaty. There were two sharply opposed views, which echoed the difference between the French and German positions regarding the monetary union project of the early 1970s. France, aiming to lock Germany into the single currency without delay, wanted the transition to be as short as possible, with already a strong role for the ECB. Germany, determined to avoid exchanging the deutschmark for a single currency that might be inflationary, wanted to delay its introduction until strict convergence criteria had been met, and resisted any sharing of power over monetary policy with an ECB in the meantime. Stage 2 as defined in the Treaty was a compromise. Stage 3 was to start in 1997 only if a majority of member states had already satisfied the convergence criteria. Otherwise it was to start in 1999 with those that had, however few they might be. But it would have little substance were it to start without both France and Germany as well as some other states. It was crucial that these should satisfy the criteria; and a great drama was to unfold as the strain of high unemployment, aggravated by the Bundesbank's tight monetary policy following German unification, made it particularly hard to do so. The detail of the criteria became a matter of acute political interest.

In order to qualify, member states were to keep their rates of inflation, measured by the consumer price index, not more than 1.5 per cent above the average of the rates of, at most, the three least inflationary member states during the year, in the event 1997, before the Commission made its examination prior to the decision. Long-term interest rates were not to be more than 2 per cent above the average for those three countries in that year. Exchange rates were to be kept within the 'normal fluctuation margins' of the Exchange Rate Mechanism for two years, without devaluation against any other member state's currency. The government's deficit was not to exceed the 'reference value' of 3 per cent of GDP unless that ratio had 'declined substantially and continuously' and reached a level that came 'close' to it, or there was an excess which was 'only temporary' and the ratio remained 'close' to the 3 per cent. Nor was the ratio of government debt to GDP to exceed 60 per cent, unless it was 'sufficiently diminishing and approaching the reference value at a satisfactory pace'. Not later than the first half of 1998, the European Council was to decide, voting by qualified majority, which member states fulfilled 'the necessary conditions for the adoption of the single currency'. It was to make its decision on the basis of a recommendation from the Council. Reports by the Commission and by the European Monetary Institute, set up by the Maastricht Treaty as a more elaborate reincarnation of the Committee of Governors of Central Banks to pave the way for the single currency, were to be taken into account. The representatives of the participating states were to fix the exchange rates of their currencies with the new currency by unanimous agreement, to apply 'irrevocably' from 1 January 1999 when it was to 'become a currency in its own right', followed by its 'rapid introduction' as their single currency.

The states that did not satisfy these conditions were to have temporary 'derogations' from participation in the single currency, to be withdrawn when it was accepted by the Council, voting by qualified majority on a proposal from the Commission, that the conditions had been met. Meanwhile, they would not have a vote in decisions regarding the single currency. Since Britain and Denmark made it clear that they would not sign the Treaty if it committed them to move to Stage 3, both obtained protocols exempting them unless they should notify their intentions to do so. Denmark went farther and notified, even before ratifying, that it had already chosen not to move to Stage 3, in order to secure a positive vote from sceptical citizens in its second referendum on Maastricht.

Stage 2 began, in January 1994, in unfavourable circumstances. After the European Council had agreed on the Treaty in December 1991, the money markets had assumed that the single currency would be established. But the rejection of the Treaty in the first Danish referendum in June 1992 broke their confidence in the Emu project. The pound and lira, which had already been seen as overvalued, became suspect. In September vast sales by speculators forced them through the floor of the ERM. They then joined the Greek drachma in floating outside it. The other member states continued to hold their currencies within their ERM bands. But there were no fewer than four realignments of central rates in the next five months. The system remained under pressure, in part because of doubts whether some states would resist the temptation to devalue in order to relieve their unemployment. This led speculators to attack the French franc, and in August 1993 it too was forced through its ERM floor. Bowing to the inevitable, the governments agreed to widen the margins to 15 per cent on either side of the central rates.

British opinion, expecting that recession and unemployment would make the criteria for government deficits and debts, together with exchange rates, impossible to meet, tended once again to discount the will of the founder member states to press on with the project of unification. But the political will remained strong, particularly in Germany, where Chancellor Kohl remained resolute, and France, where the new Socialist Prime Minister, Lionel Jospin, after a few weeks of hesitation, in June 1997 espoused the traditional French commitment to the single currency as an integral part of the European project. Apart from Britain and Denmark, joined now by Sweden, the other member states were also determined, some through federalist conviction and all through desire to be part of the mainstream, to qualify for participation in the euro, as it had by now been named; and the three sceptical states too wanted to meet the criteria, to which the Maastricht Treaty had committed all the member states and which were, moreover, seen to represent good economic housekeeping.

By the first half of 1998, when it had to be decided which states had sufficiently met the criteria in 1997, a substantial majority appeared to have done so. Inflation in the Union had averaged 2 per cent, with only Greece beyond the limit of 1.5 per cent above the average of the three with the lowest rates. Interest rates were correspondingly in line. So were exchange rates, though Britain did not participate in the ERM. The government deficits of all save Greece were less than 3 per cent, reduced in most cases, despite the intervening recession, from over 3 per cent in 1991. Greece itself had made a great effort in reducing its deficit from 12 per cent of GDP in 1991 to 4 per cent in 1997, while Italy had met the criterion through its yet more impressive reduction from more than 10 per cent to just over 2 per cent.

It was only on government debts that most of the member states were adrift. These had risen through the high unemployment in the 1990s and by 1997 those of only Britain, Finland, France, and Luxembourg were clearly below 60 per cent of GDP. For Germany, still carrying the burden of unification, the figure was fractionally above. Austria, Denmark, Ireland, and Portugal were not far above, the two latter having reduced their ratios during the 1990s, as had the Netherlands, whose ratio, like those of Spain and Sweden, was in the range of 68–77 per cent. But the ratios for Belgium, Greece, and Italy were each over 100 per cent.

The decision on fulfilment of the criteria was to be taken by a qualified majority and the Treaty contained words such as 'close', 'satisfactory', 'substantial', 'sufficiently', and 'temporary', which were subject to a political rather than a judicial interpretation. The case of Greece was clear: a derogation was inevitable. Denmark's opt-out too was clear. The Swedish government had announced that it did not want to participate in the first wave and there was not going to be a qualified majority to compel it to do so. The position of the British government had changed since Labour came to power. The new government underlined the obstacles to joining in the first wave. Britain was in a period of economic upswing, and hence of high interest rates, while the Continent was still in recession with low interest rates, so that early participation in the euro would cause a sharp inflationary shock. Nor could the government be sure of securing the voters' assent in the promised referendum, until there had been time to reverse the scepticism about the single currency induced by the previous government's negative attitude. But the government did indicate its intention of holding a referendum following the next elections, probably in 2001 or 2002. The grant of operational independence to the

Bank of England immediately after the elections of May 1997 had been a signal of support for the Emu project; and the budgetary as well as the monetary policy continued in line with the criteria. Given the disastrous impact of the pound's ejection from the ERM in 1991 on the fortunes of the previous government, ERM membership was still seen as politically risky; but it was argued on the British side that, while the Treaty required exchange rates to remain within the 'normal fluctuation margins' of the ERM, it did not specify ERM membership as such. This was, however, an argument for the future, as in 1998 the British government still maintained its opt-out.

For the others, apart from Luxembourg and Finland which clearly met all the criteria, the critical question concerned the government debts. A rigorous adherence to the criterion of 60 per cent was not required by the Treaty; and the German government, the chief advocate of rigour, itself had a debt above that figure and was also strongly committed to the Emu project, which could evidently not proceed without some flexibility on this. Italy's heroic cutting of its deficit had recently begun to reduce its debt of over 120 per cent and the Italian government demonstrated its determination to continue the process. France was eager to include Spain and Portugal as well as Italy, as a counterweight to German influence in the euro area; and if they were in, it would follow that Austria, Ireland and the Netherlands, whose debt ratios were declining and not far from 60 per cent, would also be included, as well as Belgium, which had begun to reduce its debt of over 120 per cent sooner than Italy. Thus Austria, Belgium, Finland, France, Germany, Ireland, Italy, Luxembourg, the Netherlands, Portgal, and Spain would comprise a wide 'euroland' of eleven founder states. Germany was constrained not only by its own principles of monetary rectitude but also by some facts of German political life: in particular forthcoming federal elections against the background of a public reluctant to lose the deutschmark. But the German government, impressed by the performance of Italy in particular, finally accepted that the eleven should participate; and the European Council, meeting on 2–3 May 1998, agreed that the euro should start with all of them. Only four remained outside: Greece because it did not meet the criteria; Britain, Denmark and Sweden of their own volition. The appointment of the ECB's President was not agreed so smoothly. All member states save France eventually accepted this, only on the understanding that Duisenberg would step down in mid-term to make way for Jean-Claude Trichet, the governor of the Banque de France.

The ECB and the EU Institutions

The ECB, while it takes its decisions independently, is accountable to the EU institutions. It has to make an annual report to the Commission, Council, and Parliament, and there is provision for the members of the ECB's Executive Board to be heard by the Parliament's relevant committees. There is to be liaison with the Council and the Commission, with the President of the Council and a member of the Commission having the right to participate, though not to vote, in meetings of the ECB's Governing Council, and the President of the ECB being invited to appropriate meetings of the Council. But that does not ensure co-ordination between the two main instruments of macroeconomic policy: money and the budget balances.

Emu confronts a structural problem. While the ESCB is responsible for money, the bulk of taxation and budget expenditure is in the hands of the member states. Yet the effect of a state's level of borrowing to cover a deficit will have its impact on the financial market, and hence on the interest rate, of the euro area as a whole. States will therefore be tempted to higher borrowing than is optimal for the whole area, and to offset this, interest rates will be above the optimum, building in a bias towards low investment and growth. Co-ordination of decisions on the size of budget balances is therefore desirable.

The Treaty lays down strict rules about government deficits. There is to be no printing of money to cover them, or bailing out of governments with unmanageable debts: that is to say, member states' governments or public bodies are to receive no form of official credits or privileged access to EU or member states' institutions, neither is the Union nor another member state to undertake responsibility for their commitments. Nor are governments to have budget deficits or public debts that exceed the levels defined in the convergence criteria. Sanctions against an offending government may be decided by the Council, by a qualified majority excluding the vote of the government in question; the Council may publish its recommendations to that government, so influencing its borrowing power in the markets, and may require specific information to be published before the government issues bonds or securities; the Council can ask the European Investment Bank to reconsider its lending policy to that member state; and it may require a non-interest-bearing deposit, or impose fines. In short, the Treaty provided for laxity in public finance to be severely discouraged; and the Stability and Growth Pact, concluded at Amsterdam in June 1997, underlined this point.

The Pact reaffirmed the Maastricht Treaty's principle of budgetary discipline and, building on the deficit criterion, adopted the aim of budgets 'close to balance or in surplus', so that governments can deal with normal cyclical fluctuations while keeping the deficit within 3 per cent of GDP. Two Regulations formed part of the Pact, one on surveillance of budgetary positions and of economic policies and the other on the excessive deficit procedure. Prompt action is required of the Commission in reporting on deficits that threaten to become excessive and of the Council in making its recommendations to the member states in question; and the member states are, barring special circumstances such as a fall of 0.75 per cent or more of real GDP from one year to the next, to correct any excessive deficits no later than the year following their identification. The Council is also 'invited' always to impose sanctions if a member state fails to respond as recommended.

One objection to the rules is that, in times of recession, deficits of more than 3 per cent of GDP may be desirable, so they should not be forbidden by treaty. Rather than considering the scope for flexibility that the wording of the Treaty provides, however, the European Council responded to concern about employment, expressed with particular force by the new

French government, by underlining the importance of employment policy in the formation of economic policy and by adding the new employment chapter to the Amsterdam Treaty.

Another objection to the focus on the 3 per cent criterion is that, to secure an optimal mix of monetary and budget policies, there should be a more effective system for co-ordination within that limit. The Treaty does provide for co-ordination. The Economic and Finance (Ecofin) Council is to recommend broad guidelines for the economic policies of the member states. It is to do this by qualified majority on a proposal from the Commission and with the advice of an Economic and Finance Committee which replaces the Monetary Committee. The Council is then to monitor the consistency of the states' policies with the guidelines and may, again by a qualified majority, make recommendations to them, and may if it sees fit make them public. This could well influence the markets, and hence the policy of the state in question, if a stricter budgetary policy is recommended. But if the recommendation were to be a more expansionary policy, it is not likely to carry such weight. In either case, the arrangements for co-ordination are rather weak; and this has given rise to calls for the Ecofin Council to be made into an 'economic government'. But, for reasons given in Chapter 3, a Council of representatives of member states' governments is not likely itself to be capable of becoming an effective government. Nor does the Treaty give it the powers that would be required.

As the inauguration of the euro approached, the matter became urgent for those governments likely to participate. They wanted at least to discuss questions of policy co-ordination among themselves. The British objected, on the grounds that the treaty provisions for co-ordination applied to all member states, and all could be affected by agreements reached by the euro group. In December 1997 the European Council reaffirmed the responsibility of the Ecofin Council for the policy guidelines, but also decided that the ministers of the euro group 'may meet informally among themselves to discuss issues connected with their shared specific responsibilities for the single currency'.[36] This Euro-x Committee, as it was named before the number of founder members of the group was known, will certainly consider policies regarding budget balances, and may well cast the net wider across economic and fiscal policies, presenting the conclusions to the others who comprise a minority in the Ecofin Council.

Another field in which the Council may not be up to the task entrusted to it is in the relationships of the euro in the international monetary system. Although the Commission has proved a successful representative of the Union in the field of trade, the governments took advantage of the IMF's rule that only states can be members, to make it clear that the Commission would not have that role in the IMF. The Council is to use the unwieldy unanimity procedure to conclude formal agreements on any exchange rate mechanism with non-Community currencies. In the absence of such a system, the Treaty provides for it to decide by qualified majority on 'general orientations' for exchange-rate policy in relation to those currencies. But the European Council affirmed that exchange rates 'should be seen as the outcome of all other economic policies', in effect leaving exchange rate policy as such, save 'in exceptional circumstances', to the foreign exchange operations of the ECB.

In its relations with the currencies of other EU member states, however, the euro group pursues a more active policy. In view of the possible impact of exchange-rate volatility in the single market, there was pressure for the remaining member states to be required to join an 'ERM2'. France in particular was concerned that the 'outs' might use exchange-rate depreciation to compete unfairly with the 'ins'. The European Council in Amsterdam in June 1997 decided that the ERM2 was to start, concurrently with the third stage of Emu, on 1 January 1999. The central rates are linked, not as before through a grid of bilateral rates, but to the euro, which is the centre of the mechanism. The bands of 15 per cent on either side of the central rates remain, but narrower bands may be accepted for non-euro states that request them. The states with a derogation will anyway have to achieve such stability in practice if they are to qualify to join the euro. The British government too intends to maintain exchange rate stability, although, being reluctant to embark on a second ERM experience, it secured the proviso that participation in ERM 2 would be voluntary.

The EU with the euro

The establishment of the ECB and the euro is a climactic event. It gives the Union the most powerful instrument of economic policy and provides definitively for the sharing of sovereignty in the field of the economy. It will have a powerful impact on the economics and politics of Europe and the world.

Advocates of the euro have argued that the economic effect will be dynamic. Cutting out the transaction costs is the least of it. The euro will provide the monetary framework required for investment in the economy of the twenty-first century. There will be a vast capital market, to the benefit of both lenders and borrowers. The euro will give a lift to competition and efficiency; and it will be particularly helpful to small and medium enterprises, which are the principal providers of jobs but find it hard to take advantage of a single market fragmented by currency frontiers. Politically, the ESCB and ECB provide the institutions of a federal central banking system; the euro completes the array of economic instruments required by a federal system; the Union is thereby strengthened, anchoring Germany together with the other member states yet more firmly in a system that guarantees peace and security among them; and it is apt to play a constructive part in a multipolar world. The euro will be a counterweight to the dollar and hence to American monetary power, as was the common external tariff in the field of trade; and it can provide the basis for a more equal partnership within the international monetary organizations.

The arguments of opponents have been the mirror-image of these. The euro would not bring prosperity because the member states lack the means of adjustment that enable other single currency areas such as the USA to dispense with adjustment through the exchange rate, in particular labour mobility across state borders and inter-regional transfers resulting from central taxation and expenditure. These are present in the EU only to a small extent. Nor is there the flexibility of labour markets in the EU that might facilitate adjustment in response to differing movements of real productivity and nominal earned incomes. Thus countries or regions that become uncompetitive will lack the means to deal with the resulting unemployment. The ECB will, as we have seen, be inclined to pursue a restrictive monetary policy, causing high interest rates and euro exchange rate and thus aggravating unemployment throughout the Union. This will not be acceptable to the citizens and will result in political conflicts both within and between the member states. With none of this will the EU institutions, not firmly rooted like those of the member states, be strong enough to cope, so it will lead to disintegration of the Union's principal achievement, the single market, and to a decline, not an enhancement, of security.[37]

Federalists may accept that the opponents have some points about the euro's potential downside. But their reaction is the opposite, proposing that the Union adopt the policy instruments and institutional reforms designed to ensure the outcome envisaged by the advocates: instruments required for sufficiently effective policies in fields such as education, training, infrastructure, and research and technological development, together with co-ordination of economic policies; and reforms making qualified majority voting and co-decision the general rules in these matters and giving the Commission the necessary executive competences. Such, federalists may argue, is the action that the Union will have to take if the euro is to result in fusion, not fission.

8 European Budget and Public Finance Union

The Community's budget has been at the centre of conflicts that have accompanied the development of the Community, for two highly political reasons.

First, the budget has been an arena for struggles about the distribution of gains from integration. France saw the expenditure on agriculture as a way of ensuring that the French agricultural interest was satisfied, offsetting that of German industry. Then Britain fought to secure refunds to compensate its heavy net payment into the agricultural part of the budget. Then the Community's weaker, peripheral economies sought aid through the budget to help them meet the competition of the stronger economies in the single market and again for the single currency. These distributional motives played a big part in giving the budget its significant economic weight, reaching some ecu 82.4 billion, 1.2 per cent of GNP in the Community, by 1997.

Secondly, the budget has been a focus for conflict over the powers of the different institutions: over who controls the size, pattern, and management of the expenditure. Here the issue has been the relative power of the member states and of the Community institutions. Some, in what has been termed the 'nationalist approach', have wanted to keep power in the hands of the governments. Others, preferring the federalist approach, have held rather that 'new forms of representation and legitimation should be built up alongside the national governments and parliaments', and that the role of the European Parliament over against that of the Council should therefore be enhanced.[1] It is with respect to the budget that the federalist approach first came close to realization.

Own resources, Monnet, and de Gaulle

Jean Monnet had concluded from his experience of international organizations that the Community would be hamstrung if it depended on the financial contributions of the member states, which they might unilaterally reduce or withhold from one year to the next. As the architect of the ECSC Treaty he insisted that it should have its own resources of revenue; and the Community was empowered to levy a tax directly on the value of the production of coal and steel. The Treaty set a limit of 1 per cent of that value, which could however be exceeded if the Council accepted by a qualified majority a proposal by the High Authority for a higher rate.

Monnet, in his speech at the inauguration of the High Authority in August 1952, underlined that the Community obtained its financial resources 'not from the contributions of states', but from 'levies directly imposed' on production, citing this as one of the characteristics that made the institutions 'federal'.[2] Altiero Spinelli, who helped him draft the speech, doubtless sharpened this point with his knowledge of the origins of the US constitution, which was given federal taxing powers precisely because the preceding confederal system was being bankrupted by the failure of the states to pay their contributions. The underlying idea was later to be formalized by the theory of fiscal federalism, in its principle of congruence, which stipulates that each level of government should have its own sources of revenue, whether separate taxes or parts of shared taxes, sufficient to match its expenditure responsibilities.[3] Like many aspects of the ECSC, 'own resources' have remained a basic principle for the Community ever since, underlying the process of developing its budget.

The ECSC Treaty also kept the control of the administrative budget out of the hands of the governments. The budget was to be agreed among the Presidents of the four main institutions: the High Authority, the Parliamentary Assembly, the Council, and the Court of Justice. Thus the governments were represented in the process of approving the budget by the President of the Council; but the Commission and the Parliament were likewise represented, foreshadowing the co-legislation by Council and Parliament on a budget proposed by the Commission, which was later to govern the adoption of part of the EC's budget—with the Court's role becoming a more normal one of ultimate judicial authority.

The EEC Treaty of 1957 gave the Commission, for the execution of the budget, the strong independent status that had in general belonged to the High Authority in the ECSC. Thus Article 205 EEC (205/274 ECT) provided that 'The Commission shall implement the budget . . . on its own responsibility'. But in adopting the EEC budget, the Parliament's role was only consultative. Adoption was to be the sole responsibility of the member states' representatives in the Council, even if it was to be done by qualified majority thus avoiding the blockage of a single government's veto (Article 203 EEC, 203/272 ECT). While own resources were envisaged, moreover, they could not be introduced until the member states had unanimously ratified the arrangements for levying them (Article 201 EEC, 201/269 ECT); meanwhile, the Community would have to get by with contributions from the member states.

This mixture of intergovernmental and federal elements was to prove explosive. Eventually, in the 1970s, the own resources were introduced and the European Parliament's role strengthened, but not before the Community had endured a severe crisis over these matters in the mid-1960s.

The budget to pay for the common agricultural policy was seen by de Gaulle as an important French national interest, and by the Commission and the federalists as a significant step towards a federal Community. Both wanted it to be introduced as soon as possible. In December 1964 the common price for wheat was agreed; and since this was the key decision in constructing the agricultural policy, the Commission proposed that the own resources to finance the price support should come into effect at the same time as the common wheat price, in July 1967,[4] and tabled a financial regulation to govern the expenditure of such resources on agriculture from that date. At the same time the Germans, following the logic of the original Franco-German bargain on agriculture and industry, claimed that the establishment of the agricultural common market should be balanced by equivalent progress on industrial trade, which would be completion of the customs union by the same date. The Commission proposed that this be reflected in the allocation of both agricultural import levies and customs duties as own resources from July 1967. Since these own resources of the Community would no longer pass through member states' budgets and would thus escape control by their parliaments, the Commission also proposed that the Parliamentary Assembly, as the European Parliament was still called, should exercise some control over the EC's budget.

This federalist proposal was a direct challenge to de Gaulle's concept of national sovereignty. Until then the Commission had avoided provoking him. But the majority of Commissioners felt this was the time to take a stand. French policy had been so negative about almost everything other than the agricultural policy and the finance for it, that they feared de Gaulle would put the Community on ice once these had been agreed; and they believed that the French interest in the agricultural policy was so strong that he would swallow the pill of parliamentary powers if linked with the agricultural and financial decisions. The Commission was firmly backed in this by the Dutch parliament, with its refusal to accept any proposal for EC own resources that did not provide for control by elected representatives. So the Commission put the parliamentary powers into its package.

De Gaulle's counter-attack has been described in Chapter 1. He was not going to accept any building up of federal institutions, infringing what he saw as the exclusive legitimacy of member states and their governments. The Commission and the other governments had to accept that the agricultural policy would be financed by member states' contributions, which member states' parliaments could approve, until he had left the scene. They would just have to wait until then.

Own resources and European Parliament's powers

In 1969 de Gaulle resigned and the Commission revived its proposals for own resources and for the strengthening of the European Parliament's control over the budget. The French still saw the own resources of the Community as a major French interest, so Georges Pompidou, de Gaulle's successor as French President, went to the Community's Summit meeting in The Hague in December of that year determined to secure 'completion' of the Community's programme in this respect. Such completion was agreed, along with widening to include Britain and other applicants, and deepening in the form of economic and monetary union. The arrangements for own resources were rapidly determined and set down in a Treaty signed in April 1970.[5] The Community was to have the agricultural levies and customs duties as proposed in 1965. But the cost of the agricultural policy had grown so that these were no longer enough to pay for it, and the Community was also allocated a share in the value-added tax (VAT) that was levied in all the member states. The Community's share was up to 1 per cent of the value added by businesses producing or trading in the goods and services that were included in the VAT's 'base'. Defining the base was a most complex matter, since it differed from country to country in the Community and many thousands of products were involved. In order to allow time for the agreement on this and its administrative consequences, the Community's share of VAT was to be paid only at the end of a transitional period lasting until the start of 1978—which was eventually stretched to 1980. Thus member states were continuing to pay national contributions to the Community budget for over two decades after the EEC Treaty, stipulating that own resources should be introduced, had come into force.

The political choice of own resources had nevertheless been quickly made in the first months of 1970. But the question of who was to control their expenditure was not so easily resolved. The French government, in this early post-de Gaulle period, was still reluctant to give powers to the European Parliament, while France's partners wanted it to have such powers and the Dutch were particularly insistent. The French, less intransigent without de Gaulle, were ready to concede something for the Parliament, provided that the bulk of the expenditure, most notably that on agriculture, remained under the control of the governments. This they secured through the device of dividing expenditure into two categories: compulsory and non-compulsory expenditure (NCE). The compulsory expenditure was to be that 'necessarily resulting from this Treaty or from acts adopted in accordance therewith' (amendment to Article 203 EEC). The argument was that when, for instance, the ministers in the Agriculture Council decided on agricultural prices, these prices became part of Community law and must be supported as such, whatever the cost to the budget might be. So the Parliament could have no right to alter the budget for agriculture. The French foreign minister defended this idea in the Assemblée Nationale as a means of preserving the sovereignty of the Council and preventing change in the allocation of powers among the Community institutions—arguments repeated in the 1980s by the British government in resisting greater powers for the European Parliament. Since agriculture then accounted for some nine-tenths of Community expenditure, and this was seen in France as an important national interest, the definition of agricultural expenditure as compulsory was the French ministers' central demand. But they also sought to include a number of other headings under the 'compulsory' part of the budget.

The Dutch and the European Parliament wanted, on the contrary, to reduce the scope of compulsory expenditure. It amounted, after all, to a licence for ministers from spending departments to take decisions regardless of the budgetary consequences; and the uncontrolled expansion of agricultural expenditure was subsequently to show the danger of such licence. The scope of compulsory expenditure was later reduced. It now comprises spending for agriculture and for fulfilling the Community's international obligations. But the Parliament sought further to gain leverage over the compulsory as well as non-compulsory expenditure, through a right to reject the budget as a whole.

The European Parliament, although it then had few formal powers, was not lacking in influence over the arrangements the Community was making for the budget. The Council's proposals for giving the Community own resources and amending the budgetary procedures laid down in the treaties would have to be ratified by all the member states; and ratification was not likely to be forthcoming from the Dutch and some other parliaments if the principle of parliamentary control over resources which belonged to the Community, and thus escaped the control of member states' parliaments, was too blatantly ignored. Faced with this sanction, and with the Dutch government itself strongly supporting the grant of powers to the European Parliament, the governments agreed in April 1970 to provide for the Parliament to share power with the Council in approving the non-compulsory part of the budget. For the compulsory expenditure, the Parliament could propose 'modifications' but the Council could normally overrule them; and for the final approval of the budget, the Parliament was to be consulted and, if the text of the treaty amendment was liberally interpreted, might be construed to have the right to reject the budget as a whole. The Parliament held that this was not good enough, and the President of the Council, who was in the first half of 1970 Belgian and sympathetic to the Parliament's case, declared that the Council would consider proposals about it from the Commission, which the Commission undertook to submit within two years.

The Commission set up an expert group with Georges Vedel, a distinguished French lawyer, as its chairman, to study the constitutional implications of greater powers for the European Parliament. The Vedel report proposed a general right for the Parliament of co-legislation with the Council, and likewise a share in the nomination of the Commission's President.[6] Following the Commission's proposals, a second Treaty on the budgetary procedures was adopted in 1975, sharpening up the Parliament's powers to amend the budget and strengthening its claim to be able to reject it as a whole. The Parliament's capacity to supervise the process of Community spending was also enhanced. It was given the power to grant the Commission a Discharge for the implementation of the budget, i.e. to approve the way in which the Commission had spent the money—giving rise to the budget Commissioner's suggestion that the Commission might be obliged to resign if Discharge was refused.[7] At the least, the Commission was required to take action on the comments with which the Parliament accompanied its grant of Discharge.

The 1975 Treaty also established the Court of Auditors, responsible not only for ensuring propriety but also for judging whether 'the financial management has been sound' (Article 206a EEC, Article 188c/248 ECT). This followed the revelation by the Parliament's Budget Committee in 1973 that some 100 million units of account (precursors of ecus) of expenditure could not be accounted for. The annual reports of the Court of Auditors were to provide much material that would assist parliamentary scrutiny of Community spending.

The Treaties of 1970 and 1975 have been considered in some detail, not only because they ensured that the Community would have its own resources, or, in plain words, its own tax revenue. These treaties, together with the EEC's founding treaty, resulted in what amounts to a federal relationship among the institutions for the enactment of the Community budget, as far as the non-compulsory expenditure is concerned. For this, the European Parliament has the right of co-legislation with the Council: this part of the budget cannot be enacted without the Parliament's approval, and the Parliament has the edge over the Council in case of disagreement. For decisions on the budget, the Council has always used the procedure of voting by qualified majority, even when, following de Gaulle's *démarche* at Luxembourg, all Councils save those dealing with the budget were proceeding only by unanimity. The Commission has the sole right to propose the draft budget and to execute the budget once approved: it acts, in fact, like a government. Questions of lawfulness are referred to the Court. This is how legislature, executive, and judiciary interact in a federal system of government; and, since 1975, the non-compulsory expenditure has grown to the point where it is around one-half of the total budget.

This system for the non-compulsory expenditure has on the whole worked well. But the procedures for the part of the budget designated as compulsory expenditure remained severely defective. There was no proper parliamentary control; and the doctrine of expenditure 'necessarily' resulting from acts adopted in accordance with the Treaty was to give the Agriculture Council scope for the unchecked spending that nearly brought the Community to grief in the 1980s. Nor did the legislative branch of the institutions—Parliament and Council—have any authoritative way of treating the budget as a coherent whole, with the various spending Councils having autonomous legislative competence, and the Parliament lacking powers over tax and compulsory expenditure. The Community was to come closer to achieving some coherence. But it had to suffer grave budgetary crises before it brought itself to the point of doing so.

The idea of a federal budget

In the mid-1970s, the Commission had cause to be concerned about the future of the Community. The project for economic and monetary union had been shelved and its offshoot, the Snake in the Tunnel, had been reduced to an exchange rate club of Germany and a few small countries. Sharply differing inflation and deficits, following the oil shock of 1973–4, raised the question how integration could proceed among such divergent economies; and Britain, reopening the issue of membership through the referendum organized for mid-1975, posed an additional question of political divergence. The Commission wanted to know how the budget could help to make the Community more cohesive and capable again of contemplating a project such as Emu. It asked Sir Donald MacDougall, a much-respected British economist, to chair a group to 'examine the future role of public finance at the Community level in the general context of European economic integration'. The group started work late in 1974 and its report was published in April 1977.

The report considered the budget in the light of the principles of fiscal federalism.[8] It examined the criteria for assigning functions to the different levels of a multi-tier system of government: in the Community's case, EC, member states, regions, and local government. One criterion for assigning functions to a higher level was externality, when the costs or benefits of an activity spill over from one area of the body politic to another. Thus wind or rivers may carry pollution across frontiers, so there is a cross-frontier function of pollution control and perhaps of compensation to perform. Another criterion is indivisibility, or economies of scale: nuclear fusion research facilities are too costly for any member state and cannot be divided into smaller units, so the Community itself finances one. A third criterion is the desire to provide citizens with a minimum standard of services or of prosperity, which is reflected in the Community's 'cohesion' policy of resource transfers to the regions with weaker economies. Against these criteria for transferring functions to a higher level are those that favour keeping them closer to the citizens: democratic control and flexibility; innovation, comparison, and competition among different units of government; and the advantages of political homogeneity within the smaller communities. The Maastricht Treaty employed the term subsidiarity for this principle of keeping functions with the smaller units of government unless they would be better performed by bigger ones.

The report applied these principles to the three main aims of economic policy: stabilization, or the use of macroeconomic policy to secure price stability and high rates of economic activity and employment; allocation, or the use of microeconomic policy instruments to favour the efficient use of resources; and redistribution.

The Community budget would not play much part in stabilization so long as it remained small and, complying with the Treaty, balanced. This would be the function, rather, of Emu, with its monetary policy together with any co-ordination of member states' budget policies.

Allocation, in the market economy, is mainly the function of the market. But some public expenditure is required to ensure a level playing field, for example, through competition policy; and the Community has allocated money in fields such as technological research, infrastructure, and training, for reasons relating to the efficient use of resources. Such reasons pertain to some of the expenditure on agriculture, but the bulk of it stems from distributional motives.

It was, indeed, in redistribution that the MacDougall group saw the main purpose of the Community's budget, as a condition for enabling the weaker economies to participate fully in economic integration and eventually in an economic and monetary union. It envisaged expenditure on structural, employment, and regional policies to help the weaker regions, and transfers to offset the impact of cyclical fluctuations on particular regions. The report estimated that ecu 10 billion, or 0.7 per cent of Community GDP at that time, should reduce the difference of incomes between richer and poorer regions by some 10 per cent, which 'might be judged an acceptable start'. This compared with a reduction of about one-third in the difference between the regions within five existing federations studied by the group. But there were reasons why the Community should be less ambitious, at least at first: there was less propensity to migrate between the member states and hence less pressure to harmonize income levels; and, without direct taxes and benefits to individuals, the Community lacked some of the most powerful instruments of redistribution of incomes among the regions of federal states.[9]

Following its analysis, the group considered budgets of three orders of magnitude. A budget of the size in fully developed federal states such as the United States or the Federal Republic of Germany, amounting to 20–25 per cent of GDP, was not considered. With the existing budget of 0.7 per cent of GDP in the Community in the mid-1970s as the starting-point, the group defined first a 'pre-federal' budget for a community with a single market and further steps towards monetary union. This could amount to 2–2.5 per cent of GDP. The next type of budget considered would be for a 'small public sector federation', with monetary union but without defence responsibilities; and this might be 5–7 per cent of GDP. By the early 1990s, however, when the Emu project had been incorporated into the Maastricht Treaty, a subsequent study group took the view that Emu would require a more modest budget than the MacDougall report had defined as pre-federal. Finally, the report estimated that defence competences could add some 3 per cent of GDP, bringing the total to 7.5–10 per cent.[10]

As a source of finance for an expanded budget, the group was attracted by a share of VAT with a progressive key, which would cause the richer member states to pay a higher percentage of VAT than the poorer ones.[11]

While few of the group's recommendations were accorded early implementation, the report's thinking has influenced the later development of the budget. First, however, there were some tough problems to be overcome.

The British budget question

The British budget question took up unduly much time and political energy from the mid-1970s to the mid-1980s.[12] With their large imports of foodstuffs, the British paid heavily for the common agricultural policy, through levies on their imports from outside the Community and high prices for imports from within it; and British agriculture, as a small though efficient sector, brought in less benefit from the price supports than the agricultural sectors in the other member states. The net budgetary cost of the agricultural policy to Britain was estimated at about 0.75 per cent of GDP when studies were done before Britain joined the Community.[13] This was one reason why the Treaty of Accession provided for seven years of transition before the EC's budgetary system would apply in full to Britain. It was hoped that, by 1980, the share of agriculture in the budget would have been reduced and the bias against the British thus alleviated. But in case this should not be sufficient, the British during the entry negotiations secured the declaration from the Community that if unacceptable situations should arise, 'the very survival of the Community would demand that the institutions find equitable solutions'.[14]

In line with the thinking that was to inform the MacDougall report, Edward Heath, who as Prime Minister had driven the entry negotiations through to a successful conclusion, persuaded the Community's Paris Summit in October 1972 to agree to the idea of a regional development fund, hoping that it would be big enough to go a good way towards solving the problem of the bias in the agricultural budget through payments to Britain's economically weaker regions. But while the establishment of the fund was being negotiated, the Community ran into difficulties. The oil shock evoked defensive attitudes. The Germans became weary of their role as 'paymaster' of the Community, stemming from the original Franco-German bargain on agriculture, followed by the rise of the German economy to be the richest in the Community and hence the biggest contributor of VAT. The British themselves, after Heath's government had been replaced by a Labour government early in 1974, turned their attention to 'renegotiating the terms of entry' rather than to securing a large regional fund. So the fund started on a small scale, with 300 million units of account in 1975 rising to 500 million in 1976 and in 1977; and although, after the European Parliament had succeeded in getting it declared non-compulsory, the fund's budget rose to ecu 2.4 billion in 1984 and ecu 11.1 billion by 1997, the net benefit was destined to go to the poorer member states, Greece, Portugal, Spain, and Ireland, rather than to Britain. By 1975, then, Britain was set for a decade of conflict over special refunds to deal with the British budget question.

The Labour government's 'renegotiation' was not effective, except in securing a 'yes' vote in the referendum. The Community did agree in March 1975 to refund any excess gross contributions to the budget. But the complicated formula that was agreed brought no significant results. Then, with full incorporation in the budget system looming close ahead, the Labour government sought to use the negotiations for the European Monetary System in 1978 to reopen the budget question. The Commission was asked to carry out concurrent studies of such matters alongside the establishment of the EMS, with the result that a paper on the subject was presented to the first meeting of the European Council attended by Mrs Thatcher as the new Conservative Prime Minister, held in Dublin in December 1979.

Valéry Giscard d'Estaing and Helmut Schmidt, who between them were leading the Community at that time, came to the meeting with a low offer which Mrs Thatcher could hardly accept. She, for her part, gave a foretaste of the posture she was to adopt in the Community by repeatedly asserting that she wanted 'our money back'. Britain had just cause to seek redress, because the net contribution to the budget was as big as had been foreseen before entry, while agricultural spending continued to dominate the budget and the regional fund was a puny counterweight. Nor, with the bad economic conditions of the 1970s, was there a clear benefit from membership for British industry. But instead of winning allies by working constructively in the Community, the British government preferred to block decisions until its budgetary demands were satisfied. With curbing public expenditure at home a priority, the government could hardly have been expected to pursue an expansionary policy for the Community's budget; but that need not have precluded a more positive policy in other areas. As it was, many in the other member states felt that Britain wanted to reduce the Community to little more than a free trade area; and that discouraged them from striving to find solutions for Britain's problem.[15] At the same time the other member states were disappointingly reluctant to act on their commitment to respond adequately to an 'unacceptable situation'. The result was five years of patched-up arrangements for refunds accompanied by serious impediment of the Community's development.

It was not until the Community was faced with financial necessity that the logjam was broken, during the French presidency in the first half of 1984. Agricultural expenditure had expanded through the 1970s and early 1980s until the 1 per cent of VAT, together with the customs duties and import levies, did not suffice to finance the Community's budget. By 1983 the money was running out, and it was clear that the limit to the Community's share of VAT would have to be raised if the commitments under the agricultural policy were to be met. But once again, ratification by all the member states was required if the scope of own resources was to be enlarged. British assent was necessary, and would not be forthcoming without a satisfactory answer to the British budget question. Behind that necessity, moreover, lay a perception that the Community would not recover its dynamism unless an answer was found. The bargain that was reached was an increase of the VAT limit to 1.4 per cent, together with a refund for Britain of about two-thirds of its net contribution, based in fact on the difference between the percentage of the Community's total VAT receipts provided by Britain and the percentage of expenditure allocations that Britain received. The European Council at which this deal was approved, at Fontainebleau in June 1984, also undertook to ensure that the growth of agricultural expenditure would be controlled in future. But instead, the spending rose faster than ever; and, with the net contribution from VAT at no more than 1.25 per cent when the refund to Britain was deducted from the 1.4 per cent limit, the budget was again deep in crisis by 1987. Own resources had to be increased again in 1988, accompanied by a renewal of the mechanism agreed for Britain at Fontainebleau and, this time, a more thorough reform of the Community's budgetary arrangements. But the British refund will not remain permanently unchallenged; it is likely eventually to be subsumed in a more general system of burden-sharing. Meanwhile, the beginnings of such a system were initiated as part of the reform in 1988, to deal with the problem of the weaker economies on the Community's periphery.

Cohesion

The agricultural policy demanded by France and the refunds demanded by Britain were somewhat peculiar forms of redistribution, which generated fierce conflicts around the Community's budget. The Community has also developed forms of redistribution that fit more readily into the pattern found by the MacDougall report to be typical of federal systems; and these have caused less aggravation in the Community's politics.

Already in the EEC Treaty, the European Investment Bank and the Social Fund were established in order to meet the demands of Italy, which, as the weakest economy in the Community at that time, wanted the opening of its market to competition from stronger economies to be accompanied by some help for its development. The European Development Fund, included at the same time in the Implementing Convention for the association of overseas countries and territories, was designed to secure the help of other member states in sharing the cost of development aid for French colonies, as they then were, in Africa; and it may thus be said that this too was a form of redistributional policy. When the EMS was founded in 1979, low-interest loans, subsidized from the Community budget, were provided for Ireland and Italy, on the grounds of their monetary weakness and development needs. Then when Greece entered the Community, in 1981, its Treaty of Accession included a provision for 'unacceptable situations' such as Britain had secured less formally in its entry negotiations; and the Greeks took advantage of the negotiations for Iberian enlargement, which would have to be ratified by all member states including Greece, to ensure agreement that the Community budget would finance the Integrated Mediterranean Programmes for the benefit of development in the Mediterranean parts of the Community.

The accession of Spain and Portugal, in January 1986, coincided with the conclusion of the negotiations for the Single European Act, with the single market programme at its centre. With strong support from Spain, Portugal, Ireland, and Greece, President Delors argued that the Single Act should include a commitment to accompany the completion of the single market with a policy of 'economic and social cohesion' designed to reduce disparities between regions, and the backwardness of least-favoured regions, in order to help the weaker economies face the challenge of open competition. The Single Act required the Commission to submit to the Council proposals for the future of the structural funds: the Social Fund, the Regional Development Fund, and the Guidance Section of the European Agricultural Guidance and Guarantee Fund. This the

Commission did; and, in connection with the reform of the budget in the first half of 1988, it proposed the doubling of the structural funds in order to fulfil the obligations undertaken in the Single Act. The European Council, under German presidency, agreed to double the budget for the funds, increasing it progressively to that level by 1993.

The Maastricht Treaty was the occasion for the same four countries to press for a bigger cohesion budget to help them adapt to the requirements of economic and monetary union. The Treaty added the Cohesion Fund to the existing structural funds, to assist the adjustment of poorer countries to Emu; and in 1992 the Commission proposed another big increase as part of a further package of budgetary reform. In December 1992 the European Council, this time under British presidency, agreed to raise the allocation for cohesion again, this time by about two-fifths over the period 1993–9, bringing it to almost half of 1 per cent of the Community's GDP. This compares with some two-thirds of one per cent of GDP envisaged by the MacDougall report for a Community in a pre-federal stage, before monetary union. But the structural funds are more closely tailored to the promotion of development than, for example, the unemployment assistance that MacDougall recommended as a major item of expenditure. The net receipts from structural funds in 1992, before this new expansion, amounted to 2.4–2.8 per cent of the GDP of Greece, Ireland, and Portugal, compared with the 3–10 per cent of gross regional product going, according to MacDougall, to the receiving regions of existing states. For Spain, with its more developed economy, the net receipts were 0.46 per cent of GDP. A successor to the MacDougall report, produced for the Commission in 1993, found the economic case for a high level of inter-regional redistribution within the Community weaker than MacDougall had done, citing the evidence that the countries with lower incomes had anyway been catching up on the Community's average.[16]

Agreement to such a substantial cohesion policy was far from easy to achieve. The British government in particular, with its scepticism about public expenditure and about many aspects of Community development, was strongly inclined to resist. But in the Single Act, the principle of cohesion was linked with the completion of the single market to which Britain was strongly committed; and in the budgetary reforms of 1988 and 1992, the British government was concerned not to lose support for the payment of its refunds. The allocation for cohesion was an element in comprehensive packages which each member state had some reason to approve.

The budgetary reform of 1988

With world prices for agricultural products low and surplus production in the Community continuing unchecked, the cost of storage and of export subsidies soared and the extra revenue from the 1.4 per cent VAT limit agreed in 1984 was quickly spent. By 1987 no less than 1.9 per cent VAT would have been needed to balance the budget without resort to devices that pushed the costs into future years. Advances paid to member states to cover their costs in implementing the agricultural policy were paid two months later than previously; and even if this practice was to be continued, it brought the budget only a once-for-all gain. Stocks in store which had halved or more in value were still accounted at the original price, and no provision was made for the day of reckoning when they would have to be disposed of. More revenue was required and, this time, agricultural spending really did have to be brought under control. The mechanism for the British refund was due to lapse, five years after it was agreed at Fontainebleau in 1984; and the commitment to the policy of cohesion also had to be respected. A comprehensive reform of the budget, bringing these elements together and, because of their importance, having implications for the relationship between the institutions, was clearly required. It was undertaken, on a proposal from the Commission and under German presidency in the European Council, in the first half of 1988.[17]

The trigger for the reform was, once again, the interest of France and other agricultural exporters in securing more own resources for the Community to pay for the agricultural policy.

This time Spain and the other states with less-developed economies were also pressing for more resources to finance the policy of cohesion. Britain was intent on a bargain that would include the renewal of its refunds. Germany, having its turn in the presidency of the Council, wanted to succeed in dispatching the Community's business and maintaining its dynamism. President Delors likewise sought success in problem-solving, as well as an opportunity to move the Community in a federal direction. He was moreover determined to put an end to the series of annual quarrels over the budget that had sapped the Community's political energy, by securing firm agreement on a 'financial perspective' that would fix the main components of expenditure for five years ahead. The reform was based on Commission proposals which became known as the Delors package. The mix of motives among the governments and the Commission was powerful enough to ensure significant improvements in each of the three dimensions of Community budgetary policy: revenue, expenditure, and control.

The Community's existing sources of revenue had two drawbacks: they were slower-growing than GNP; and they were regressive. The yield from customs duties had fallen as tariffs were cut through international trade negotiations. Agricultural imports had fallen as the agricultural policy induced self-sufficiency for the Community, reducing the scope for import levies. The base of goods and services on which VAT was calculated declined as a proportion of GNP as member states grew richer and a bigger share of national incomes was saved or applied to purposes such as education and health, largely outside the VAT base. Thus the Community budget was squeezed by the relatively slow growth of its own resources. Secondly, these indirect taxes bore harder on the poor than on the rich. Tariffs and levies are highest on items such as food and clothing, which take a larger part of the spending of those with lower incomes; and, just as VAT contributions hit the poorer countries harder, so they do the poorer people. The Commission wanted to move towards a less restrictive and regressive revenue system.

As a moderately progressive new tax, the Commission proposed the logical complement to VAT: a tax on the difference between the gross national product and the VAT base, which would reverse the incidence of VAT and bear more heavily on the rich than on the poor. This was too much for some among the richer, however, and in particular for Italy, where a new calculation of gross product, including an estimate of the informal economy which escapes the tax man and the national statistics, showed the average Italian to be richer than the average Briton. The European Council decided, therefore, that the 'fourth resource', as it was called, should be neutral in relation to incomes, and related it direct to GNP (though as a concession to the poorer, any part of the VAT base which exceeded 55 per cent of GNP, which does not apply in any of the richer countries, was to be excluded from the calculation).

In order to escape from the constraint of revenue growing slower than gross product, the Commission proposed and the European Council agreed that the total revenue could rise so as to finance expenditure of 1.2 per cent of Community GNP by 1992, while commitments, which are bigger than appropriations for payments because they include the budgets for some multi-year programmes, could in that year be as much as 1.3 per cent of GNP. Thus while the VAT limit was kept at 1.4 per cent, no such limit was applied to the fourth resource, which could be levied at whatever percentage was needed to finance the balance of expenditure beyond what the other three taxes could afford, provided that the global limit of 1.2 per cent of GNP was respected for the four taxes combined.

The European Development Fund and the British refund are not included in the budget, and together amounted to about one-tenth of one per cent of GNP. Total Community expenditure was, therefore, to reach about 1.3 per cent of GNP by 1992. Although borrowing and lending are, moreover, generally included in the budgets of states, the loan transactions of the European Investment Bank, the ECSC, Euratom, and the New Community Instrument, which was introduced in 1979 to support policies against unemployment, low investment, and divergence, are not included in the Community's budget. While the budget still fell short of the 2 per cent or so of gross product envisaged by MacDougall for a pre-federal Community, and by the successor report for a Community with economic and monetary union,[18] the difference between that and the limit set for total expenditure in the financial perspective had narrowed significantly.

The revenue agreed by the European Council allowed for Community expenditure to increase by over 14 per cent a year from 1988 to 1992. Within that total, agricultural expenditure was to rise much less fast, its growth being limited to not more than 74 per cent of that of Community GNP, and hence to some 2–3 per cent a year.

The rapid expansion of the budget was no longer to be mainly for agriculture, but rather for the structural funds, which, together with the still predominant agriculture, were to take up over four-fifths of the total budget in 1992. But there was also some scope for expansion in new policies as well as in the other existing policies, which included, in the 1988 budget, items such as regional and social policies, energy, environment, transport, innovation and the internal market, research and investment, information and culture, development (other than European Development Fund), and administration.

As a firm framework for the containment of agricultural expenditure and the expansion of the structural funds, the European Council agreed the financial perspective which set out the allocations under six major headings for each year from 1988 to 1992. With the cost of agriculture contained as intended, non-compulsory expenditure would rise to one-third of the total budget by 1992. Aware of the past failures, the European Council made a serious effort to provide the Community with a proper system of budgetary control.

Agricultural spending was to be checked by the system of stabilizers, reducing prices if production exceeds an agreed threshold. Member states undertook to supply the Commission with regular and up-to-date information about their expenditure, product by product. If the Commission perceived a danger of overspending, it was to ask the Agriculture Council to strengthen the stabilizers; and if that Council failed to take strong enough action, the Commission was to call a joint meeting of the Agriculture and Finance Councils, where the finance ministers' interest in budgetary discipline should be brought to bear. If that too was not enough, the Commission was to use its own management powers. This reinforcement of the Commission's budgetary powers was strongly backed by the British government, which had usually looked askance at the strengthening of the Commission, but favoured rigorous control over expenditure. The control was moreover reinforced by a new role for the European Parliament that ensued from the budgetary reform.

With the decision to double the structural funds taken, and the member governments obliged to ensure that it was realized, the Council had to make sure that the Parliament would not use its power to amend the budget for non-compulsory expenditure in a way that could upset the arrangement. Not that the Parliament had been hostile to the cohesion policy or the structural funds: on the contrary, it had strongly supported them. But in case the Parliament should be tempted to transfer funds from structural to other headings, either because of any unexpected shortage of revenue to finance all items of non-compulsory expenditure or in a trial of strength with the Council, the Council sought a firm commitment that the Parliament would accept the allocation for the structural funds. The Parliament in turn demanded a commitment from the Council that the allocations for agricultural support would not exceed the amounts foreseen in the financial perspective. The result was that an Inter-Institutional Agreement, concluded between the Parliament, Council, and Commission to regulate their relationship with respect to the new budgetary arrangements, committed the Parliament to accept the allocations in the financial perspective while the Council accepted the Parliament's control over the total of compulsory expenditure: neither Parliament nor Council could alter the objectives of the perspective without the agreement of the other. Thus the Council accepted that the Parliament could veto any proposal for expenditure on agriculture beyond the allocations then agreed: a significant step towards parliamentary control over the compulsory expenditure. The Council, moreover, agreed that payments beyond the appropriations were not to be made until the budget or financial estimates had already been properly amended.[19]

The reform as a whole was the result of a serious display of resolution by the Community institutions. The outcome during the period 1988–92 was, moreover, blessed by favourable circumstances. Economic growth was stronger than had been expected; with higher world prices, agricultural expenditure increased only moderately; and the ceilings of the financial perspective had been set fairly generously. So the new procedures for control did not encounter difficult problems. On the contrary there was money available to spend on new policies, the outstanding example being the response to an entirely new challenge, in the movement of Central and East European countries towards market economies and pluralist democracies. The first allocations for helping this process were for aid for Hungary and Poland. The Parliament raised the sum agreed by the Commission and Council in the second half of 1989 from ecu 200 million to ecu 300 million; and the Council accepted the corresponding adjustment in the financial perspective. In June 1990, both Parliament and Council went farther, agreeing to reserve ecu 850 million in 1991 and ecu 1 billion in 1992 for co-operation with Central and Eastern Europe. Thus the budgetary reform of 1988 worked quite well. It did, moreover, shift the budget in modest but significant ways towards a more federal system, with respect to revenue, expenditure, and institutional procedures. But the new financial perspective, to start in 1993, had to take account of some new circumstances, including the Maastricht Treaty.

Beyond Maastricht: towards a public finance union?

During the negotiations for the Maastricht Treaty, Spain led the lower income countries in pressing for more resources for the cohesion policy, to ease the adjustments required to prepare for economic and monetary union. The Treaty provided for the new Cohesion Fund, to help finance environmental projects and investment in trans-European transport networks (TENs) in member states with less than 90 per cent of the average Community GNP. It also provided for financial contributions from the Community for TENs with respect to energy and telecommunications as well as transport. The potential scale of such projects, which may extend not only throughout the Union but also beyond it into Central and Eastern Europe, and which should be of particular value to the more peripheral member states, is enormous: the Commission estimated that the cost of twenty six of these projects could amount to ecu 82 billion, and suggested that the Community budget might contribute ecu 3 billion a year.[20] Responding to complaints about the inequity of the budget, a Protocol on Economic and Social Cohesion also expressed the intention of 'correcting, for the less prosperous Member States, regressive elements' in the existing revenue system. The Protocol also affirmed the 'need to review' the size of the structural funds.

Soon after the agreement on the Maastricht Treaty, Delors presented the Commission's proposals for a financial perspective for the following five years, taking into account the needs stemming from the Treaty.[21] He proposed that the total budget rise by 5 per cent a year in real terms, from ecu 66.5 billion in 1992 to ecu 83.2 billion (in 1992 prices) in 1997. The expenditure on structural funds, including the new Cohesion Fund, would increase by nearly three-fifths, and more would also go to external aid, research and development, and TENs. The correction of regressive elements on the revenue side would take the form of a substantial shift from VAT to the 'fourth resource', based on GNP and therefore neutral as between the richer and poorer member states.

The European Council, meeting in Edinburgh in December 1992, adopted a financial perspective fairly close to the Delors proposals.[22] The main difference was the stretching of the period from five to seven years, 1993–9. The total for the final year was trimmed to ecu 80.1 billion and the increase in structural funds reduced to two-fifths, which would nevertheless bring them, taken together, to as much as 0.45 per cent of the Union's GNP. The distribution by country of the funds was, moreover, so arranged that the receipts of Spain, Portugal, Ireland, and Greece would again be doubled—and hence quadrupled since 1988. Expenditure on external policies was to rise from ecu 3.95 billion in 1993 to ecu 5.6 billion in 1999, and on internal policies from ecu 3.9 billion to ecu 5.1 billion, the latter considerably less than the Commission had wanted. The decision on revenue was almost exactly as Delors had proposed, with the VAT contributions reduced from 1.4 per cent to 1 per cent of the member states' VAT bases, which were capped at 50 per cent of GNP for those with incomes per head less than 90 per cent of the average. The ceiling for the budget total was to rise from 1.2 per cent of the Union's GNP to 1.27 per cent in 1999. With the take from VAT reduced, the GNP-related fourth resource was to provide a larger part of this; but the European Council agreed that the Commission should examine candidates for a fifth resource. Suggestions for this have included corporate taxes, and an energy and carbon tax, already proposed by the Commission in order to reduce the damage caused to the environment by too much consumption of energy, particularly carbon fuels.[23] Finally, the European Council noted that a new Inter-Institutional Agreement would be needed for this financial perspective; and one was subsequently agreed which consolidated the role of the Parliament in relation to the 'compulsory expenditure'.

While the financial perspective 1993–9 offered a plausible framework for the budget during the 1990s, it was shaped by the political pressures of the time; and the Commission judged that, a decade and a half after the MacDougall report, and with economic and monetary union in prospect, a new perspective for the longer term would be useful. The result was *Stable Money—Sound Finances*, the report of a successor study group, published in 1993.[24] This 1993 report envisaged a smaller budget than MacDougall had done for the time when the single currency would be in place: its figure was 1.75–2.1 per cent of GDP for the limit over the following fifteen years,[25] compared with MacDougall's 5–7 per cent for a Community with monetary union. Three main reasons were given for the change of view: a rigorous application of subsidiarity; declining conviction in the economic case for inter-regional redistribution; and absence of a role for the Union's budget in macroeconomic stabilization.

The principle of subsidiarity was strongly emphasized following the Maastricht Treaty. The view that redistribution need not be as expensive as MacDougall believed had already been expressed in the annex signed by Delors in his *Report on Economic and Monetary Union*.[26] New technologies, it was argued, produced goods for which transport costs were lower, reducing one of the disadvantages of the periphery, while telecommunications and capital mobility were eroding the advantages of the centre. The results could be seen in the troubles besetting some central regions such as North-East France, Wallonia, and the Ruhr, and the dynamism of outlying regions such as Bavaria, Puglia, the Rhone Valley, and parts of South Wales and Scotland. While cohesion would still cost money, it would be better spent on infrastructure that helps economic development than on straight financial transfers among member states. The Delors report itself noted that structural policies might have to be strengthened in the process of creating the economic and monetary union;[27] and the 1993 report likewise held that the cohesion budget should be increased, but stressed the importance of improving the performance of the funds.[28] However reasonable these arguments may be, it should nevertheless be recognized that we cannot be sure how the peripheral economies will perform over the next decade, let alone the Central and East European countries due to join the Union during the period considered by the study group.

As regards the study group's third reason for envisaging a more modest budget, the starting point must be Article 199 of the EC Treaty, which stipulates that the revenue and expenditure shown in the budget shall be in balance. Without treaty amendment, therefore, the budget balance cannot be used as a policy instrument. So long as the ceiling for the Union's expenditure does not rise far above the present 1.27 per cent of GDP, it is in any case the member states' budgets and public sector borrowing requirements that will play the main part, alongside monetary policy, in macroeconomic policy within the Union. But it is possible for the Community to use its borrowing powers to stimulate investment, and thus make a public finance contribution to economic policy. This was already done when the New Community Instrument was launched in 1979 to borrow money from the international capital market in order to promote investment and employment as well as convergence. Even if without the same intention, the Community's borrowing under its powers relating to the ECSC, Euratom, and the European Investment Bank has had similar effects. The Albert–Ball report to the European Parliament in 1983 suggested that the EC could stimulate investment and hence the dynamism and competitiveness of the Community economy by increasing its expenditure on investment in such things as infrastructure and regional development, financed by money raised in these ways.[29] The Commission, in its document on Emu in March 1990, likewise noted that the Community could borrow for investment projects in such a way as to support 'a desired thrust of the concerted economic policies of member states'.[30] The ambitious proposals for TENs in the 1994 White Paper on *Growth, Competitiveness, Employment* can be seen in this light.[31] Such investments are financed mainly by the private sector; the Community's contribution comes mainly from the European Investment Bank, whose lending reached the impressive sum of ecu 20.9 billion in 1996; and the cost to the Community's budget for such items as interest rate subsidies can come mainly from the existing allocations for structural funds.

A further reason for the 1993 report's modest perspective for the total budget was its expectation that, by shifting from price to income support, the agricultural budget could be reduced over the longer term. Against that, the report foresaw higher spending on the environment, research and development, TENs, higher education, and development aid; and in addition to some increase in the expenditure on cohesion, it saw the need to put money by for an inter-regional stabilization mechanism, to deal with macroeconomic shocks that might hit particular regions hard, after the single currency has deprived them of the use of the exchange rate as an adjustment mechanism.

Along with lower spending on agriculture, the report saw a more neutral system of revenue for the budget as the principal means of making it more equitable. MacDougall had been bolder, suggesting that VAT contributions be adjusted by a key which would increase the percentage contributed by the rich and reduce that contributed by the poor, thus turning it into a progressive tax; and one of its authors later proposed a surcharge on member states' income tax, which would leave them free to fix their own tax rates while ensuring that they contribute to the EC budget in progressive proportion to their citizens' incomes.[32] But when the Commission, as we saw, tried to introduce a mildly progressive tax in 1988, it was resisted by at least one of the richer member states. In the less buoyant atmosphere after Maastricht, the report did not venture to recommend trying again. The same applied to its view of the problem of a member state such as Britain, with a particular case of inequity in relation to the Community budget. A proposal had been made, in the Padoa–Schioppa report of 1987, for transfers among the member states which would ensure that each state's net balance with respect to the budget would be inversely related to its income per head, so that the richer states would become net contributors and the poorer ones net recipients.[33] But the 1993 report judged it more practical to deal with special cases by negotiating special arrangements.

A Financial Framework for 2000–2006

The Commission continued to be chary of disturbing the status quo regarding the British rebate. In 1997, in its 'Agenda 2000' document, it pointed out merely that some adjustment of the technical details would be required as a consequence of the first wave of enlargement. But it went farther than the 1993 report in suggesting that the British problem might eventually be addressed by what it called 'a generalized system of corrections', which could be considered if and when the ceiling for expenditure should be lifted beyond 1.27 per cent.[34] While the Commission understandably preferred to let the sleeping dog lie for what was likely to be a long time, there were signs that Germany, no longer, since unification, being the rich man of Europe, would soon press hard for change, in order to get some of its own 'money back'.

The Commission in its 'Agenda 2000' foreshadowed its proposals for a new financial 'framework', as it was now called, for 2000–6, to follow that for 1993–9.[35] Here it was more modest than the 1993 study group's report, indicating that the introduction of the single currency would not need to be accompanied by a rise in the expenditure ceiling of 1.27 per cent of GNP and that the initial costs of the first wave of enlargement could be accommodated as well. One reason was that underspending, including on agriculture, in the period 1993–9 would anyway leave a margin for some expansion. But the main reason was that the Commission did not foresee a need for major additional spending. The further phase of reform of agricultural policy, also put forward in 'Agenda 2000', would not cut expenditure, with savings on lower price supports outweighed by compensation for farmers and with some spending in the new member states towards the end of the period; but the rate of growth of the total cost would remain within the guideline, set in 1988, of 74 per cent of the rate of growth of GNP. The Commission proposed to keep the proportion of GNP allocated to the structural funds steady at 0.46 per cent, amounting to ecu 275 billion over the whole period, with spending in the EU15 focused more sharply on the regions in greater need and with 30 per cent of the total in 2006 going to the new member states. The allocations for 'other internal policies' would rise approximately in line with the rate of growth of GNP until the first wave of enlargement, expected around halfway through the period, when higher spending on items such as education and training, and programmes to ensure proper functioning of the single market, would contribute to a somewhat faster rise. Throughout the period, policies relevant to growth, employment, and new technologies, e.g. trans-European networks, research, environment-friendly technologies, education and training, and small and medium enterprises, would likewise be accorded a faster rate of growth. Allocations to 'external action' would rise in step with GNP, with the increase going to bolster pre-accession programmes and enhanced co-operation with the Union's eastern and southern neighbours. As regards the budget for administration, the Commission hoped that gains in efficiency would offset the costs associated with the first wave of enlargement.

The Commission proposed that, with expenditure contained beneath the existing ceiling, there was no need to change the system of own resources which had been put in place in 1993. That reform had made the system more equitable: the share of the regressive VAT resource would have fallen from 62 per cent in 1992 to 33 per cent in 1999, and that of the neutral GNP-related resource risen to about half. Although there is no progressive element, the system has proved distinctly less regressive than it was before. The Commission noted, however, that there had been demands for new resources, partly on the grounds that member states saw the VAT and GNP contributions 'as transfers from national exchequers and not as real own resources of the Community'.[36] Underlying these demands is the fear that a Euro-sceptic government might decide to withhold such contributions and thus undermine the fiscal autonomy which is one of the principles that have made the Union's finances so much more solid than, for example, those of the United Nations. But the Commission argued that problems associated with member states' views of the VAT and GNP contributions would remain unless there was a reform replacing them entirely by autonomous resources, 'which would have little chance of being countenanced by all Member States in the present phase of the integration process', and that there was not 'a strong case for a rapid modification of the present arrangements'.[37] Laws to reform the system, whether by raising the ceiling or changing the resources, have to be ratified by all the member states, and the Commission's caution is doubtless conditioned by that obstacle.

This raises the question whether the present system is adequate for a Union that is introducing the euro and on the threshold of enlargement to the East. Would it be able to cope with crises that may arise? Suppose, for example, that unemployment in one or more member states provokes political tensions that threaten the euro, or that a new entrant from Central Europe finds its citizens unable to take the strain of membership. Higher expenditure from the budget might be urgently required in order to save the Union. But given the need for unanimity to raise the ceiling, would it be forthcoming in time? Perhaps, moreover, unanimity might be too hard to reach on the future of the British rebate, or on a reform of the own resources in order to avert a perceived danger that Euro-sceptic governments would be tempted to withhold their VAT or GNP contributions. The unanimity rule might be incompatible with the timely taking of decisions required to keep the Union viable. Failure to grasp the nettle of reform in anticipation of such potential crises could expose the Union to such risks.

Relevant to such questions was the 1993 study group's radical view on institutional reform. Their report suggested that an enlarged Community with a single currency and a somewhat bigger budget would need more democratic and effective institutions, including a Parliament with full legislative powers, to which a European government would be responsible, within the framework of a constitution that would have 'the principle of subsidiarity as its cornerstone'.[38] Such institutions would be able to deal more efficiently and equitably with what has been called the 'public finance union' aspect of the European Union.[39]

9 From Common Tariff to Great Civilian Power

The economy of the EU is equivalent to that of the USA in its production and somewhat greater in its external trade. It is much greater than the economy of any other country in both. But if it is to bring its weight to bear in defending its interests or shaping the international economic system, the Union must have an external policy; and the experience of its external relations shows that this common policy becomes truly effective when it disposes of a common policy instrument.[1]

The original Community, the ECSC, designed as the framework for a new Franco-German relationship, was not given the main tool of external trade policy, that is a common external tariff. The project for a European Defence Community, responding to the challenge of Soviet military power, was on the contrary intended to integrate the basic instrument of the member states' security policy by creating a European Army. But after years of indecision French politicians decided they would not go so far, and the project was shelved in 1954. The Community's first effective instrument of external policy was, then, the common tariff of the EEC, which was within a few years to make the Community a power in the international trading system equivalent to the United States.

The common external tariff

It was not inevitable that the EEC should have a common external tariff. Following the example of the ECSC, there was no mention of it in the memorandum from the Benelux governments which was the starting-point for the negotiations to create the EEC; and the German Minister of Economics, Ludwig Erhard, backed by German industry, would have wished that the Federal Republic keep its own low tariff for its trade outside the Community.[2] But the French preferred a customs union complete with common tariff. They feared, with their long protectionist tradition, that their own protection would be undermined by competition coming through Germany and Benelux which had lower tariffs. They also began to see the common tariff as cement to bind the member states together politically, providing a base within which France could recover the influence it had lost during World War Two.

The federalists who composed the Spaak report on which the EEC Treaty was based also had their reasons for preferring a customs union, with common tariff, to a free trade area in which each member state would keep its own tariff.[3] They wanted a level playing field, in which competition would not be affected by differing tariffs among the member states; and they saw the common tariff as an instrument that would give the Community bargaining power in international trade negotiations. Such power could be used for liberal or protectionist ends. Their inclination was liberal. They proposed, in conformity with the Gatt rules, that the common tariff was to be no higher than the average of the member states' tariffs (there were four, not six of these, since the Benelux countries already had their own common tariff); and the EEC Treaty duly provided for a tariff along these lines, to be introduced by aligning the member states' tariffs on it in three steps during the 12–15 year transitional period. They also envisaged that the bargaining power would be used as a means of getting the tariffs of the Community's trading partners down; and this too was to occur in the event. Over a century earlier, Friedrich List, promoting the project for a German customs union, wrote that 'without a common tariff system . . . political nationality was robbed of its most solid foundation'.[4] While the authors of the Spaak report did not express themselves in such terms, their idea of making the Community an actor in the world trading system can nevertheless be seen as a step in the direction of political union.

For the French government, the common tariff became a weapon in the rivalry with the British for European leadership. The British were faced by a dilemma. Outside the customs union, their exports to the Continent would be threatened; inside it, their imports from the Commonwealth might decline. Because they resisted union with the Continent at the expense of Commonwealth ties, they devised the proposal for a European free trade area that would enable them to get the best of both worlds: free trade with the Europeans, but without a common external tariff that would interfere with the free entry to the British market that most exports from the Commonwealth to Britain then enjoyed under the system of Commonwealth preference. Politically, the dilemma would be neatly circumvented. The economic effects were also expected to be favourable. According to the anglo-saxon economics of the time, the choice between customs union and free trade area revolved around the concepts of trade creation and trade diversion. Trade creation was the replacement of high-cost domestic production by lower-cost imports when a tariff was removed, and would thus raise efficiency and welfare. Trade diversion, on the contrary, replaced low-cost imports from the rest of the world by higher-cost production from another country within the area where tariffs were being removed. At least for the member states with the lower tariffs, a free trade area would cause less diversion than a customs union that forced them to raise their tariffs against the rest of the world.[5] So the customs union acquired a protectionist connotation, reinforcing for the British the political arguments against it. Econometric calculations were later to show that trade creation within the Community in the 1960s was about ten times as large as trade diversion.[6] Doubtless liberal pressure for lower tariffs was one significant reason. But meanwhile, the British attempt to breach the Community's common tariff by means of a free trade area was thwarted. The French feared that if the British were allowed free trade without the commitment to a common agricultural policy, the German commitment to that crucial part of their bargain with France would be weakened; and the federalists feared that the wider and looser scheme would undermine the Community's common institutions and instruments. The return to power of General de Gaulle during the course of the free trade area negotiations brought a new edge to

French reluctance to give Britain a privileged relationship with the Community, and he broke off the negotiations in November 1958. When Britain approached the Community in 1961 in order to seek full membership, the common tariff was already evoking a reappraisal of US–EC relations.

Towards the end of June 1962, Jean Monnet's Action Committee for the United States of Europe called for a partnership of equals between a united Europe and the United States.[7] A week later, on 4 July, President Kennedy, making a 'Declaration of Interdependence' at Philadelphia, said 'We do not regard a strong and united Europe as a rival but as a partner'. The first embodiment of this idea was his proposal for trade negotiations in which the EC and the USA would be the principal parties. His Trade Expansion Act, enacted by Congress in October 1962 with the main purpose of securing cuts in the Community's external tariff, gave the President power to negotiate tariff cuts of up to 50 per cent, setting a time limit at mid-1967. The Kennedy round of trade negotiations in the Gatt ensued.

Such negotiations involve complicated conflicts of interest, and the Kennedy round was no exception. The Americans wanted tariffs to be cut by a given percentage across the board, while the Community wanted the highest tariffs, of which the USA had more than the EC, to be cut more deeply than the rest. The Americans wanted concessions on agriculture from the Europeans, who in turn objected to the Americans' protectionist treatment of their chemical industry. With all the Gatt participants and several thousand tariff positions involved, these conflicts would anyway take time to resolve; but they were further complicated by sharp differences within the Community itself.[8]

Gaullist France was contesting American leadership while France's five EC partners were inclined to support American policy. Germany and Benelux were liberal whereas France and Italy were more protectionist. The Germans saw their interest in industrial trade while the French wanted to secure the markets for their agriculture. Conflict over the Community's institutions and de Gaulle's tactic of the empty chair blocked the Community's decision-taking capacity for half a year in the middle of the Kennedy round. But the negotiations were nevertheless concluded just before the deadline of mid-1967 with the unprecedented success of cuts in the tariffs of industrialized countries by an average of about one-third. The Community was evidently too important to its members for them to risk failure in what was, with the common agricultural policy, one of its two main projects of the 1960s. The Americans were determined to keep the Atlantic relationship in working order. Behind these political motives, the stronger industries on both sides of the Atlantic saw their future in wider open markets, beyond the confines of the EC or the USA; so they were demanding success from their politicians.

Had the Kennedy round failed, the world might have slid back to the protectionism that had blighted the international economy in the 1930s. Instead, the way was cleared for continued expansion of world trade, with the prospect of some immediate economic benefits and of more significant longer-term dynamic effects.[9] Politically, the success of the Kennedy round helped the Community to come through the 1960s in a condition that made its further development possible; and the Commission's reputation was enhanced. Although the Council acted to keep it on a tight rein, the Commission was able, by exploring appropriate compromises with the negotiating partners, to make it hard for the Council to renege on them. Given the satisfactory conclusion, the merit of the Commission's measure of independence was demonstrated. Above all, the Kennedy round vindicated the decision to give the Community its common external tariff by showing that the idea of EC–US partnership was feasible, despite considerable difficulties. One of these was what was seen on both sides of the Atlantic as de Gaulle's anti-American policy. Another was the process of a change in relative power, painful for the country whose superiority is being reduced, and clearly recognized by an American observer at the time:[10]

> The dominant position of the United States in Gatt evaporated with the implementation of the Rome Treaty . . . The Common Market is now the most important member of Gatt, and can determine in large measure the success or failure of any attempt to liberalize trade. When Europeans instruct Americans in the realities of the new inter-

national economic situation they are demonstrating the change in relative power that has taken place.

While EC–US relations were later to suffer from an American reaction to changes in relative power, in the form of a harder-nosed diplomacy, the Kennedy round nevertheless had a lasting effect. The process of tariff cutting was to continue through successive Gatt rounds, until tariffs were far below their original levels; and the concept of partnership, embodied in this practical demonstration, can still be seen as a valid option in the 1990s. For the Community itself, this use of the common tariff had established its position as an equal of the United States in the world trading system, causing it, as an emergent union without security competences, to be visualized as 'the first of the world's civilian centres of power'.[11]

Non-tariff distortions

Although the Kennedy round went far to establish a low-tariff international trading system, many forms of protection with instruments other than tariffs remained. For trade among the advanced industrial countries of the Organization for Economic Co-operation and Development (OECD), agricultural protection was the most important. We have seen in Chapter 5 how the Community, with massive protection for its farmers through import levies and support through export subsidies, turned from being a big net importer of key agricultural products to being one of the world's largest exporters; and this disrupted the trade of OECD countries such as Australia, Canada, New Zealand, and the USA, as well as of some less-developed countries. Some other European countries have been even more protectionist in the field of agriculture, and the USA has also protected its farmers heavily. The Uruguay round of Gatt negotiations was the first to bring agricultural protection under a form of international control.

The Swedish economist Gunnar Myrdal, writing in the mid-1950s, predicted that international integration would be prevented by what he called national integration: the efforts of governments to improve their citizens' welfare by intervention in the economy.[12] Such measures would, he thought, disrupt or distort international trade, even if unintentionally. If he was right, the regional integration within the EC would have the same effect on wider international economic relations. But the experience of the Kennedy round and of the opening of markets to trade in manufactures among the advanced industrial countries proved him wrong. The interest of the more dynamic sectors of the economy in wider markets that would give them space to develop new technologies was strong enough to overcome the pressures for protection, whether on the part of the EC or of other advanced industrial economies. But with respect to agriculture, where intervention is much heavier, his idea has proved abundantly justified, not least as far as the EC is concerned.

Myrdal's idea has also found some justification in the treatment by advanced industrial countries of their imports from other parts of the world. Imports from less-developed countries of many products, such as textiles and shoes, in which they have a comparative advantage, have been tightly restricted by quotas. The same applied to the Community's imports from Central and Eastern Europe, though this began to change rapidly in 1990 as the reforms there gathered momentum. Within the OECD group, Japan's success in exporting a wide range of manufactures was met by the demand that the Japanese apply voluntary export restrictions, with the threat that other action would be taken if they failed to do so. With the recessions and stagflation of the 1970s, such instruments of protection multiplied.

While quotas restricting mutual trade among the EC member states had been abolished, other forms of protection such as subsidies, preferential public procurement, and divergent standards or regulations were distorting and obstructing the Community's internal trade: hence the single market programme, to complete the necessary legislation by the end of 1992. But this programme raised the question whether it would, like the common tariff on manufactures, lead to a wider liberalization of international trade, or whether, like the agricultural levies and subsidies, it would instead provoke international disintegration.

The general interest in liberal trade is harder to bring to bear against protectionist pressures in the case of non-tariff distortions than of tariffs, because there is no formula for liberalization as simple as that of cutting tariffs by up to one-half. Even that formula led to a highly complex negotiation. When standards, regulations, or state aids in a variety of forms are involved, the complexity, and hence the scope for lobbies to secure special treatment, is yet greater. But there are principles that can help in resisting them. For services such as banking and insurance, home-country treatment is such a principle: that services supplied by third-country firms are treated in the same way as those of local suppliers. The EC's Second Banking Directive of 1989 applies this principle to banks, provided that their country of origin applies the same principle in its treatment of Community banks. Since the Community's rules give banks more scope than do those of the other two major financial powers, the USA and Japan, this Directive helped to allay fears that the single market would become a pretext for the building of a highly protected 'Fortress Europe'. Insulation from the world market would harm the more dynamic elements in financial services as well as in industry, so it is in their interests to resist the pressures for protection.

Since the Community's single market is backed by Community law enforced by the courts, it is more solidly based than the results of wider international negotiations. It has been suggested that 'the Community provides an example of effective international law-making that at some point might be replicated at the global level',[13] but meanwhile, the Gatt has been the best available framework. In its Tokyo round of negotiations, completed in 1979, codes were drawn up to guide behaviour with respect to subsidies and public procurement. In the Uruguay round, non-tariff distortions moved to the centre of the stage. Thus in addition to tariff cuts, the agenda included rules for trade in agriculture, services, and textiles; anti-dumping duties and safeguards against 'disruptive' imports; investment; intellectual property; methods of resolving disputes; and the establishment of the World Trade Organization, more comprehensive and stronger than the Gatt had been, though still without the legislative, judicial, and executive capacity of the Community.

It was the conflict over agriculture that proved the most intractable. But although it was hard to close the gap between the positions of the EC and the US in this field, the Community's own decision to shift its agricultural protection away from price support removed a major obstacle to agreement in the Gatt, and a programme was eventually designed for limiting export subsidies and reducing import protection. So the Community and the US were finally able to lead the way to the conclusion of an accord, signed by all the contracting parties in April 1994. France, reluctant to accept the agricultural liberalization, had insisted in return on making the Community's anti-dumping duties easier to apply. Despite some weaknesses, however, the Uruguay round can be accounted a major step in liberalizing world trade and a success for the Community, and in particular for the Commission and for Sir Leon Brittan, the Commissioner responsible for negotiating the accord.

The Union has continued to play a leading part within the newly established WTO, for example in negotiating the Telecommunications Agreement and the IT Agreement providing for tariff-free trade in IT equipment. It also took the lead in securing the agreement in 1997 on liberalization of trade in financial services with, eventually, full US participation and over a hundred signatories in all, accounting for some 97 per cent of world trade in that sector.

Lome Convention

The tariff-cutting in Gatt negotiations is based on the most-favoured nation (mfn) principle: reductions accorded to one participant are extended to all. The aim was to establish a generally liberal system rather than to proliferate bilateral deals. The Americans, who had been much irked by the Commonwealth preferences introduced between the two world wars, were insistent on this principle, which underlay the Gatt rounds in which the Community demonstrated its equality with the USA as a trading power. But the EC, from the starting-point of French imperial preferences, was to use its common external tariff to develop a network of preferences that included the big majority of its trading partners. The full mfn tariff is levied only on imports from the USA, Australia, Canada, New Zealand, and Japan, the CIS states and five remaining state-trading countries. Most-favoured nation has become least-favoured nation; and the EC has used its tariff in this way as a powerful instrument of policy towards the rest of Europe and the Third World.

When it was agreed that the EEC would be a customs union, the French and their five partners were faced with a trilemma. The tariff-free entry into France from the French empire (as it then was) could have remained as an exception, as was indeed agreed for imports from East Germany into the Federal Republic; but France wanted a better deal for its colonies. Or the common tariff could have been imposed on the imports into France, as was later to be the fate of imports into Britain from Australia, Canada, and New Zealand when Britain joined the Community. But this was unacceptable to France. The French insisted, instead, on extending the preference in favour of their colonies to imports into the whole of the Community. The Germans and Dutch, more concerned about trade with other less-developed countries and reluctant to become involved in supporting French colonies, resisted this idea. But Guy Mollet, the French Prime Minister, told them that the Assemblée Nationale would not ratify the EEC Treaty unless these preferences were agreed.[14] Without France, the EEC could not have been established. So France's five partners accepted, and Part IV was added to the EEC Treaty, providing for favours to 'Overseas Countries and Territories', mainly French colonies and mainly in Africa, though there were also a few such associates of Belgium, Italy, and the Netherlands, and a few in the Atlantic and the Pacific as well as Africa.

Part IV provided that no tariffs would be imposed on imports from these associates into the whole of the Community. Exports to them from the Community would at the same time enjoy 'reverse preferences', that is to say any preferences that were already granted to such exports from France, Belgium, Italy, or the Netherlands would be extended to exports from all the Community countries. France also persuaded its partners that the Community should create a European Development Fund (EDF), with a budget of $581.25 million for aid to the associates in the first five years, to be renewed for subsequent periods. Thus the Community put together a package of trade preferences and aid for these associated countries.

With the coming of independence for the French colonies, the package was renewed in the form of the Yaounde Convention for successive periods, until this was replaced by the Lome Convention in 1975, following the accession of Britain to the Community. The Yaounde associates were joined, under the Lome Convention, by the Commonwealth countries in Africa, the Caribbean, and the Pacific (hence the term ACP used for the Community's partners in this Convention); and the remaining countries of Africa south of the Sahara have since acceded to it (though not all the provisions apply to South Africa), as have also others from the Caribbean, bringing the number of the Union's partners to over seventy.

The provisions of Part IV were extended during the course of the Yaounde and Lome Conventions. First, a joint Council of Ministers and Committee of Ambassadors and Joint Assembly were established, reflecting the independence secured by most of the Community's associates in the 1960s. Then the Lome Convention removed the reverse preferences, which most of the ACP countries regarded as a relic of the imperial order that caused them to buy more expensive goods from the Community rather than cheaper goods elsewhere. In view of the importance of sugar exports for a number of small Commonwealth countries in the Caribbean and the Pacific, the Community agreed to import 1.3 million tonnes of sugar from them at the high prices guaranteed to EC farmers. There is by now preferential access to the EC market for most of the ACP exports of products that are subject to levies under the common tariffs and agricultural policy. The Convention has been renewed, with the agreement of all the partners, at five-year intervals, up to the fourth renewal ('Lome IV') for a ten-year period starting in 1990. The aid has been increased with each renewal, and has reached ecu 14.6 billion for the second half of Lome IV, of which ecu 13.3 billion comprises grants from the EDF and ecu 1.3 billion loans from the European Investment Bank. There are five funds for particular purposes. Two of these, Stabex and Sysmin, provide compensation for countries that lose significantly from falls in commodity earnings (Sysmin for minerals, Stabex for other commodities); and there is structural adjustment aid, refugee aid, and emergency aid for disaster relief. Since debt became such a heavy burden for many ACP countries in the 1980s, over 90 per cent of the aid under Lome IV takes the form of grants.

Thus Part IV of the EEC Treaty, designed originally mainly to resolve the problem of preferential entry into France from a dozen of its colonies, has developed incrementally into a complex structure of trade and aid support for almost the whole of Africa and a score of small countries, mostly islands, in the Caribbean and the Pacific. A new political element was also introduced in Lome IV, which affirmed that respect for human rights is a basic goal of development; and in 1995 it was agreed that co-operation could be partly or entirely suspended with a partner state that violates democratic principles and the rule of law. But although many have seen the Lome Convention as a model for relations between advanced industrial and less-developed countries, its effectiveness in stimulating development has been far from clear. Imports into the Community from ACP countries of tropical products such as cocoa, coffee, and tropical hardwoods have certainly benefited, but largely through diversion of trade from other less-developed countries, in Asia and Latin America. The aid has surely been helpful and some sugar exporters would have suffered severely without the guaranteed sale of sugar at high prices. Yet the response of the ACP countries to the tariff-free entry for manufactures into the EC has been disappointing. It seems that the lack of an industrial culture has prevented most of them from taking advantage of this opportunity. Rather than an engine of development, the Lome Convention appears to have acted as a system of life-support. Politically, however, it has eased the post-imperial transition to a new relationship between ACP countries and Europeans, which could have been more difficult if preferences had remained tied only to the former imperial powers.

The effects of the Yaounde and Lome Conventions on Asians and Latin Americans were negative. Trade diverted towards the ACP countries was diverted away from them; and they include some that remain among the world's poorest, such as Cambodia and Bangladesh. The Asian countries of the Commonwealth were excluded from the Lome Convention when the ACP Commonwealth countries were able to adhere to it, evidently because some of the EC member states were not willing to accept the competition from developing countries that could export manufactures, giving the impression that the Europeans preferred to associate with suppliers of primary products in a form of neo-colonial relationship rather than with countries that showed a capacity for industrial development. The Community was also discriminating against almost all the large countries of the Third World which could be expected to become great industrial powers in the next century: Brazil, China, India, Indonesia, Mexico. All this added up to a case for extending preferences beyond the ACP countries to the developing countries of Asia and Latin America: hence, for the Generalized System of Preferences (GSP). While this has benefited Asians and Latin Americans, it has eroded the tariff advantage of the ACP partners, as have the Union's Mediterranean preferences and arrangements for free trade in Europe, together with the tariff cuts in successive Gatt rounds. Lome IV comes to an end in February 2000 and it will not be easy to devise a meaningful successor.

The Generalized System of Preferences

It was soon after the signature of the first Yaounde Convention that Third World countries began to propose that the advanced industrial countries should grant them generalized preferences, without discrimination in favour of one or other group in the Third World. There were arguments in favour of a positive response by the Community. Such preferences should promote prosperity and stability in the Third World, and hence its potential as a growing market and a reliable source of primary products. While industries in the Community would resist imports of manufactures like clothing and footwear produced with cheap labour, such imports would improve life for many of the poorer consumers. The Community would gain friends that would be useful for a new and politically still developing organization. For the Dutch and Germans, generalized preferences would be a move towards the wider concept of relations with the Third World that had caused them to resist Part IV of the EEC Treaty. The British, when approaching membership of the Community in the early 1970s, had strong grounds to support the GSP proposal, because it would help to ease the problem posed by the common external tariff for imports that had hitherto entered the UK market tariff-free from the Asian members of the Commonwealth.

A small group of officials in the Commission skilfully exploited the potential support for the GSP in the member states. As had been done in the Kennedy round, they discussed possible solutions with their negotiating partners which the EC member governments then found it hard to repudiate.[15] They used the window of opportunity offered by the negotiations for British accession to promote the GSP as a solution to the problem of the Asian Commonwealth; and the EC decided to adopt its GSP just as those negotiations were completed. So it was that the EC, despite the handicap of its cumbersome decision-making process, introduced its GSP before the USA or Japan. The system was installed initially for a decade beginning 1971 and was renewed for a further decade, each time with a break half-way for reconsideration of the rules. It was renewed annually from 1991 to 1994, pending conclusion of the Uruguay round, whereupon it was renewed for the four years up to 1998.

The GSP has provided for tariff-free entry into the Community for manufactures and semi-manufactures from less-developed countries, but with limits imposed for products described as 'sensitive'. For each of these products, where competition based on low wages is painful for European industry, the tariff reductions were applied only to those imports within a quota fixed by the Community. With quotas subdivided by product and country, the system was extremely complicated, and in 1995 the quotas were replaced by a scale of tariff reductions. 'Very sensitive' products, mainly textiles, incur 85 per cent of the full tariff rate; 'sensitive' products, such as shoes, cars, and consumer electronics, incur 70 per cent, and some 'semi-sensitive' ones 35 per cent, while the rest are exempt. As a further line of defence, 'safeguard' quotas can still be applied if imports cause or threaten serious damage to industry in the Union. Quotas also remain for textiles, under the Multi-Fibre Arrangement (MFA) negotiated in the Gatt. But following an agreement in the Uruguay round, the MFA is being phased out over a ten-year period under the supervision of the WTO, though here again protection by 'safeguards' is held in reserve. Some agricultural products are included in the GSP, although, in order to soften the impact on farmers, the tariffs are not eliminated but, as is now the case for sensitive manufactures, imposed at reduced rates. Least-developed countries are completely exempted from duties on industrial products and a range of agricultural products. A number of Latin American countries receive similar benefits to help them finance their action against drug production and trafficking; and the Central Americans are also accorded benefits for their agricultural products. As with the Lome Convention, the EU's GSP partners are not required to grant reverse preferences; and there is a general aid programme for less-developed countries, though less generous than under Lome.

Not surprisingly, it is the newly industrializing countries, along with the consumers in the Union who have been able to buy their cheap manufactures, that have benefited the most from the GSP; and the Union's system for 1995–8 started a process of winding it down for sectors or whole countries that no longer need special treatment. States with average incomes above $6000 in 1991, namely South Korea, Hong Kong, Singapore, and some oil-rich countries, have been excluded in two steps during the period, the first cutting the margin of preference by half and the second eliminating it. For others, sectors deemed sufficiently developed to dispense with the GSP are excluded through a similar two-step procedure.

The Union has introduced incentives for respect of human rights, as with Lome, and also for environmental protection. Preferential margins can be increased to help partners pay for measures aiming at compliance with the International Labour Office's Conventions on child labour and trade union freedoms, and with international standards of sustainable forest management; and the preferences can be withdrawn in case of practices such as slave or forced labour, exporting prison-manufactured products, and inadequate controls of drug-trafficking.

In recognition of their importance, the Community has negotiated co-operation agreements with some of the larger Asian and Latin American countries, such as China, India, Brazil, and Mexico, as well as agreements with some regional groups such as the South-East Asian ASEAN, the Gulf States, the Central Americans, and the Union's neighbours around the Mediterranean. There are regular meetings to discuss problems of their relations with the Community. These have been particularly useful in the case of Central America, where the Community facilitated the peace process and the Union continues to support the economic integration; and, faced with the dangers of political instability in the Mediterranean region, the Union has come to give a high priority to what it calls the 'Euro-Mediterranean' process.

Euro-Mediterranean process

Just as, from the modest start with Part IV of the EEC Treaty, the Community developed preferential systems for almost the whole of Africa, Asia, and Latin America, so it has evolved preferential arrangements for almost all the countries around the Mediterranean.

It started with Greece. The Greeks wanted access to the newly established EEC and applied for association with it in mid-1959, soon after the negotiations for a free trade area had been terminated. The EC for its part, wanting to strengthen its position in relation to the British-led Efta group and to establish itself as an actor in international economic relations, was keen to conclude such an agreement, which was therefore done in time for the association to come into force in 1962. While the details have varied, the form of association has been followed in a number of subsequent agreements with European states, including the Europe Agreements with Central and East Europeans. The aim was a customs union between Greece and the Community, with a transitional period of twelve years for the EC but a longer period for Greek tariffs that protected sensitive products. Some Greek agricultural products were to receive intra-Community treatment at once, others later. Financial assistance was to be provided for Greece. A Council of Association, comprising representatives of the Commission and of the governments of EC member states and Greece, could decide by unanimity on anything required to fulfil the aims of the agreement. The ultimate aim was Greek accession to the Community, which was in fact achieved in 1981, after a period in which it had been precluded because Greece succumbed to a military dictatorship.

The Turks, whose exports to the Community were competitive with those of Greece, followed the Greeks in seeking a similar form of association. Here again an agreement was concluded and association came into force in 1964. It was largely similar to that with Greece, although there was no clear commitment to eventual membership, and the transitional period to complete a customs union was still more extended, being set at 22 years in a protocol to the agreement in 1970. Some aspects of the agreement were suspended during a period of military rule. But with a democratic government again functioning, Turkey applied in 1987 for accession to the Community, which delayed until 1990 before making clear its view that the application was premature. The customs union did, however, reach its final stage in 1996, with Turkey aligning its external tariffs and quotas on those of the Community. But in 1997 the Union still deemed Turkey not ready for accession negotiations, although it was decided to adopt a strategy to bring Turkey closer to the EU, and to invite it to participate in the European

Conference of heads of state or government of all the member states and candidates for membership.

At the other end of the Mediterranean, the door was opened for Morocco and Tunisia by a Declaration of Intent attached to the EEC Treaty to negotiate for association with 'independent countries of the franc area'. Both countries took advantage of this to negotiate free access to the EC market for industrial products and tariff preferences for agricultural products; and by 1972 they had been followed by almost all other countries bordering on or close to the Mediterranean. The other Arab countries included Algeria, Egypt, Jordan, Lebanon, and Syria. With the inclusion of Arabs, the Community could hardly refuse Israel. As European countries, Cyprus and Malta obtained association. The then Yugoslavia, European but Communist, was accorded a co-operation agreement because of its political choice of separation from the Soviet bloc. Spain, while still under Franco's dictatorship, was not eligible for EC membership, but negotiated an agreement for preferences reducing tariffs on manufactures by 60 per cent. Thus only Albania and Libya remained, by their own self-exclusion, as Mediterranean countries without a preferential agreement with the Community.

This web of agreements had grown incrementally and *ad hoc* through the 1960s, with the Community finding it hard to refuse each new applicant what its neighbours had received. By 1972, the Commission was pressing for a 'global approach' to provide an orderly framework for the agreements; and although no formal global framework such as the Lome Convention was established, by the end of the 1970s they had much in common. All provided tariff-free entry for manufactures into the EC market, though there were ceilings for some products beyond which tariffs would be imposed. Tariffs were at reduced rates for most agricultural products, from which the Community's partners derived benefit, though the potential for this was reduced when Spain, with its large competitive production, joined the Community. There was no reciprocation through reverse preferences, except for Cyprus, Malta, Turkey, and Israel which had agreed to a free trade area; and these were also the countries with the capacity to benefit from the free trade in manufactures. There was in all cases an element of financial aid and other co-operation, in the fields of science and technology, problems of migrant labour, and the environment in particular. In short, apart from the absence of a global framework, the Mediterranean agreements were not so different from the Lome Convention.

In the 1990s the case for such a framework grew stronger. The pressure of population on resources in countries to the south of the Mediterranean, together with instability in parts of North Africa and the Middle East, caused mounting concern in the Union, particularly among southern member states. After the programme of aid and trade liberalization for Central and Eastern Europe got under way in 1990, it was France that led the demand for a better deal for the Union's southern neighbours; and it became clear that agreement on a full development of the eastern relationship would depend on a complementary effort towards the south. Once again, France and Germany led the Union to agree on a package acceptable to both. In addition to the eastern policy, the Union decided to initiate a global framework for what became known as a Euro-Mediterranean process, together with a substantial aid budget. The process was launched at a conference of foreign ministers of the member states and the Mediterranean partners in Barcelona in 1995. It includes the aim of establishing a free trade area among the participants by the year 2010 and provision for wide-ranging economic, social, cultural, and political co-operation meanwhile. There were to be regular meetings of foreign ministers and of senior officials, together with representatives of the Commission. The Union allocated ecu 4.7 billion for grants from its budget for the period 1995–9, together with loans from the European Investment Bank of up to ecu 2.3 billion for 1997–9. Development of the Euro-Mediterranean process has, however, been hampered by political difficulties, including those connected with the Middle East peace process.

Efta

When the EEC was founded many in Britain saw it as a protectionist grouping that would split the European economy. But it has in the event not only more than doubled its membership, but also been the catalyst for extending free trade throughout Western Europe.

When negotiations for a free trade area of all the OEEC members were brought to a halt in 1958, a truncated free trade area was set up by seven countries: Britain, Denmark, Norway, Sweden, Austria, Switzerland, and Portugal. Finland and Iceland later became members of the European Free Trade Association (Efta), as it was called; and Britain, Denmark, and Portugal left it when they joined the Community in the 1970s and 1980s. The six remaining members of Efta (it was only in 1991 that Liechtenstein joined, making seven) stood aside from the Community for motives that included fears about dilution of neutrality or of long-standing democracy and insistence on national sovereignty.

When Britain negotiated accession to the Community, it posed the condition that all the Efta countries should secure industrial free trade with the Community when the accession took place. Otherwise, the British government explained, the House of Commons would not accept the accession treaty. Although the British negotiating position was weaker than that of France when it posed a similar condition with respect to the French colonies, since France was essential to the Community, which had, however, proved itself capable of doing without Britain, the British nevertheless had cards to play. France's five partners wanted Britain to join, so the Community would have suffered difficult times if the negotiations had broken down; and the Federal Republic in particular wanted to restore its trade links with Efta countries. These were traditionally strong with the Scandinavians, Austrians, and Swiss, and Efta had succeeded in diverting some of their trade with Germany to Efta members, particularly Britain. Contrary to the Community's experience, where trade creation was ten times trade diversion, it was estimated that not far short of half the increase of trade within Efta due to the removal of tariffs was trade diversion, much of it from Germany.[16] Thus for economic as well as political reasons, the Community agreed to the principle of industrial free trade with Efta countries.

Here again, the Commission made good use of the window of opportunity between mid-1971, when the enlargement negotiations were concluded, and the end of 1972 when Britain, Denmark, and Ireland entered the Community. Some of the EC member states wanted to insist on a measure of harmonization of Efta countries' policies with those of the EC before free trade would be allowed. But this would have made the negotiations complex and long, risking delay beyond the target date of end-1972 and, worse still, the onset of economic and political disruption caused by the oil shock at the end of 1973. The Commission managed to persuade the member states to confine the agreements to relatively straightforward free trade areas with each Efta country, thus ensuring that free trade would extend over the whole of Western Europe: within the EC; within Efta; and between the EC and each Efta country under the six free trade agreements.

Although the EC, enlarged to twelve members, accounted for nine-tenths of the population of Western Europe and Efta for only one-tenth, the Efta countries were rich and together comprised the EC's biggest trading partner. Both sides gained from the trade creation that followed this widening of the market; and political relations within Western Europe were better than they would have been had no such economic accommodation been reached. The EC's single market programme, however, disturbed the equilibrium that held through most of the 1970s and 1980s. Efta countries feared their trade would be damaged unless they participated with the Community in the removal of non-tariff distortions. Austria applied for full membership in 1989 and other Efta countries followed. The EC, worried lest accession negotiations might disrupt the 1992 programme, sought negotiations with them collectively to deal with their concerns about the single market by creating a European Economic Area (EEA) that would enable them to participate in it as far as possible.

The wheel had come full circle and harmonization was seen as necessary now that the focus was on non-tariff distortions rather than tariffs. The problem for the Community was to give the Efta countries enough say in the EC legislative process relating to the single market without undermining the Community's autonomy; the problem for Efta was that the Community's single market requires the enactment of laws, and then their enforcement, in ways that are not compatible with the national sovereignty on which Efta countries had insisted hitherto. Political agreement on the EEA was reached in October 1991, but the Court of Justice challenged the legitimacy of the arrangement whereby disputes were to be settled by a tribunal comprising three of its members and two judges from Efta states, thus pre-empting the ultimate authority of the Court in interpreting Community laws. The problem was solved by creating a joint Surveillance Authority whose decisions are subject to review by the Court of Justice and by the Efta associates.

The EEA came into being in January 1994, with Austria, Finland, Iceland, Norway, and Sweden as the European Union's partners in it. The Swiss had voted against participation in their referendum in December 1992; and Liechtenstein had to settle some issues regarding its relationship with Switzerland before it could take part. The four freedoms of movement, for goods, services, capital, and people going about their business, apply with some qualifications. Because the EEA is a free trade area, not a customs union, border controls remain in order to prevent deflections of trade. The Efta participants are consulted about new single market legislation, but the responsibility for enacting it remains that of the Community alone. The right to participate fully in the processes of decision-taking and legislation was one of the motives for Finland, Norway, Sweden, and Switzerland to follow Austria in applying for membership of the EC. After the accession of Austria, Finland, and Sweden in 1995, the EEA is the means of access to the Union's market for only Norway, Iceland, and Liechtenstein, with Switzerland still relying on its bilateral free trade agreement.

Central and Eastern Europe

Soon after the end of World War Two, the Soviet Union came to be seen in Western Europe as a hostile superpower, dominating its smaller neighbours in Central and Eastern Europe and preventing western countries from having a normal relationship with them. The EC's six founder members reacted to Stalin's use of force by negotiating the treaty for a European Defence Community, which as we have seen was shelved in 1954. For some time Soviet policy was aimed at preventing further development of the Community; and this resulted in a refusal to accord the Community diplomatic recognition until the late 1980s. Through the Gaullist and early post-Gaullist periods, the EC member states kept commercial policy towards the East as far as possible in their own hands, preferring to negotiate direct with the eastern countries rather than conduct a common Community policy. But the EEC Treaty provided for the common commercial policy to be completed after the end of the transitional period, and late in 1974 the Commission was authorized to offer the negotiation of trade agreements to all the state-trading countries.

It was fifteen years before an agreement was finally reached between the EC and the Soviet Union in 1989. The Soviet refusal to recognize the Community's institutions was one reason. The bad relations caused by the Soviet intervention in Afghanistan in 1979 and repression in Poland in 1981 were another. The Soviet attempt to give the Council for Mutual Economic Assistance (Comecon) a big role in the negotiations was yet another, because this would have given the Soviet Union added leverage over Comecon's other members in Central and Eastern Europe and was thus unacceptable to the Community, which wished rather that they should have more autonomy.

Behind these political motives lay the economic fact that neither the EC nor the Soviet Union had much to gain from trade negotiations with each other. The trade itself was considerable. But the Community imposed no tariffs or quotas on most of its imports, largely oil, gas, and raw materials, from the Soviet Union, which thus had little significant to demand of Community commercial policy; and the Community's negotiators, accustomed to seeking tariff reductions from other market economies, found nothing of comparable significance to demand of a command economy. Thus trade negotiations offered neither the EC nor the Soviet Union enough economic incentive to overcome the political obstacles.

Until the Soviet policy was changed by Mikhail Gorbachev, the relations of the other European members of Comecon with the Community were constrained by Soviet power, with serious implications for countries such as Czechoslovakia, Hungary, Poland, Bulgaria, and Romania, which depended much less than the Soviet Union on exports of energy and raw materials to the Community, and more on agricultural products competitive with those of the Community and on low-technology manufactures, competing with EC industries that were already hard-pressed by imports from the newly industrializing countries. East Germany's situation was easier, because it had free access to the market of the Federal Republic under a Protocol to the EEC Treaty. But the other Central and East Europeans were hard hit by the Community's protection of its sensitive sectors. They were allowed to negotiate with the EC about its protection of particular sectors such as agriculture, steel, and textiles; but Soviet policy prevented them from embarking on general trade negotiations until Comecon as a whole should reach an agreement with the EC.

Under Gorbachev the deadlock was broken. The EC reached trade and co-operation agreements with Hungary, Poland, and the Soviet Union in 1989, and after that with most of the other Central and East Europeans. These were at first limited by the difficulty that the EC still found in dealing with command economies, but this began to disappear as, one after another, the countries of the former Soviet bloc embarked on the transformation of their economic and political systems.

The Community responded rapidly to the radical changes in Central Europe. It accepted that the accession of East Germany to the Federal Republic would bring the whole united Germany into the EC without the need for prior changes in the treaties, although some transitional measures were required to ease the accommodation of the new Länder with certain Community laws and policies. When the Poles and Hungarians decided to establish pluralist democracies and market economies, the Community gave them GSP treatment from the start of 1990, removed most of the remaining quotas restricting its imports from them, and allocated substantial sums of aid in its PHARE programme; and these benefits were extended to other Central and East European countries as they too embarked on their reforms. In April 1990, the Community declared itself ready to negotiate association with those that were taking steps towards pluralist democracy and market economy; and by 1996 Europe Agreements had been concluded with ten Central and East European states: in Central Europe, the Czech Republic, Hungary, Poland, Slovenia, and Slovakia; with Bulgaria and Romania in South-East Europe; and with Estonia, Latvia, and Lithuania. These provided for a phased programme to industrial free trade, to be reached within five years by the Community and ten years by the associates. There was liberalization in the fields of trade in services, establishment of businesses, and the movement of capital, together with some reduction in agricultural protection. Co-operation is organized in the economic, financial and cultural fields, although much of its significance depends on funding by the PHARE programme. There is a set of joint institutions with each associate state for supervision of the agreement and for political dialogue: a Council of Association at the level of ministers and Commissioners; a Committee of Association for high officials; and a Parliamentary Association Committee in which members of parliament of the associated state meet members of the European Parliament.

The Community's response to the process of transformation among its eastern neighbours was swift and comprehensive, partly because of the strong political motive to support these new democracies, but also because its long experience with preferential and association agreements gave it many precedents on which such action could be based. Finance of the PHARE programme from the Community budget was soon increased to some ecu 1 billion a year. But the Community's 'sensitive sectors' remained heavily protected, in particular agriculture, steel, and textiles, where Central and East Europeans were well placed to increase their exports. It was not until June 1993 that the European Council decided on an accelerated liberalization under the Europe Agreements, and, as we saw in Chapter 3, declared that these associated states could, if they wished, in due course become members of the Union.

Step by somewhat ponderous step over the next four years the Union moved towards negotiations for accession. There was a 'structured dialogue' on political matters between the Union and the associates at the level of ministers and Commissioners. In December 1994 the European Council agreed on the 'route plan' specifying what the associates had to do to prepare themselves for accession. They filled in the Commission's exhaustive questionnaire regarding the progress they had made, providing material for the Commission's assessment as to how far they had met the conditions for membership. The Union's member states for their part sought to agree on specific reforms to prepare the Union's institutions for enlargement but, as we saw in Chapter 2, failed to reach agreement at Amsterdam in June 1997, postponing the matter to a subsequent IGC, while the Commission's 'Agenda 2000' document set the stage for the doubtless tough negotiations on the necessary reforms of the Union's policies, in particular regarding agriculture and the structural funds.[17] The final step towards the opening of accession negotiations was taken in December 1997 at Luxembourg when the European Council considered the Commission's Opinions on the readiness of the associates for membership and accepted its recommendation that negotiations be started with five of them, the Czech Republic, Estonia, Hungary, Poland, and Slovenia, as well as with Cyprus. In order to maintain movement towards accession for the other five, the concept of pre-accession strategies was launched, with a substantial increase in aid for their transformation processes, as was the series of annual 'European Conferences' of heads of state or government of the member and applicant states.

The response to the disintegration of Yugoslavia and the Soviet

Union was harder to devise. While Slovenia was before long ready to negotiate its Europe Agreement, the political situation of the other states of former Yugoslavia and the war in Bosnia impeded the development of the Union's relations with them.

The new Russia's reforms were launched in the face of enormous economic and political difficulties, in the context of conversion of the highly centralized Soviet Union into a loose association of states; and most of the others were even worse placed. Estonia, Latvia, and Lithuania were exceptions, whose incorporation into the Soviet Union following World War Two had never been recognized as legitimate by most western governments, and with which the European Union concluded the Europe Agreements. In 1991 the Community launched the programme of technical assistance which, after the dissolution of the Soviet Union towards the end of the year, was called Technical Assistance to the Commonwealth of Independent States (TACIS). The budget for this was ecu 2 billion for 1996–9, similar to that for the preceding five years. The programme's aim is to provide know-how and advice to help the CIS states develop effective market economies and pluralist democracies. The Union also concluded Partnership and Co-operation Agreements with Russia and the other CIS states. For industrial trade, these provide for mfn treatment and for the removal, by the Union, of quotas, save those on steel and textiles and any that might be invoked as safeguards. There is also provision for moving eventually to free trade, as well as for economic, financial, and cultural co-operation, and for regular political dialogue at ministerial level. There are joint institutions with each partner analogous to those of the Europe Agreements: Co-operation Council, Co-operation Committee, and Parliamentary Co-operation Commission.

It is very important that the Union conduct a constructive policy towards Russia in particular. The economic element is fundamental. But given the political and security aspects of the relationship, much will depend on how effectively the Union combines its economic policy with the other elements of its foreign and security policy.

Foreign policy co-operation or common foreign policy

No sooner were the negotiations to found the first Community, the ECSC, under way than the proposal for a European Defence Community, and hence for a common foreign and security policy, was made. With the USA insisting on a German contribution to the defence of the West, following the Communist aggression in Korea, Monnet applied the same logic to military as he had to industrial power: Germany and France, with other European countries, should be contained together within a Community framework. But much more than coal and steel, armed forces were at the heart of national sovereignty: hence Monnet's conclusion that federation would have to become an immediate objective.[18] But that federal project failed, partly because of fierce Gaullist opposition. After de Gaulle came to power, inheriting a Community whose federal characteristics he abhorred, he attempted to initiate co-operation in foreign policy among the member states on an intergovernmental basis. But the Fouchet plan, as the proposal was called, likewise foundered after negotiations in 1961–2, having provoked sharp opposition among France's five partners: partly because of a cleavage between de Gaulle's policy towards the USA and theirs; partly because federalists objected to the stress on intergovernmental at the expense of Community institutions. So it was not until after de Gaulle's departure that the member states started to organize foreign policy co-operation.

The Community's Hague Summit in December 1969, which launched the process of enlargement and the project of monetary union, also asked the foreign ministers to report on how to achieve 'political unification', in the sense of foreign policy co-operation. The result was the Davignon report,[19] on the basis of which the Council decided in October 1970 to hold regular meetings of foreign ministers and senior foreign affairs ministry officials, calling the procedure European Political Co-operation (EPC). The EPC had an early success in the first round of the Conference on Security and Co-operation in Europe (CSCE), concluding with the Helsinki Final Act in

1975. Among other things, the EPC put human rights on the agenda, thus contributing to the ferment that eventually led to the political changes in Central and Eastern Europe. But differences over matters such as sanctions against South Africa stood in the way of common policies; France and Britain in particular resisted co-operation in certain areas where they felt they had special interests; and Greece, in the first years after joining the Community in 1981, was responsible for no less than three-quarters of all the cases of unilateral action. Yet the intensive exchange of information, constant meetings, and efforts to harmonize views exercised a drip effect, and by the time the Single European Act was negotiated the member states found it worthwhile to formalize the EPC procedures in the treaty and to create a small EPC secretariat in Brussels. When the Single Act came into force in 1987, it also provided that the EPC could include the 'political and economic aspects of security', and that the European Parliament should be 'closely associated' with the EPC, as well as gaining its new power to grant or withhold its assent before association agreements can come into effect and before the Council can act on an application for membership.

With these modest institutional arrangements, the flow of information among the member states' foreign ministries attained a considerable volume. The annual programme of EPC meetings included four for the foreign ministers, twelve for the foreign ministries' political directors, and some hundred working groups on particular subjects. Outside the Community, the ambassadors of the Twelve in each capital had meetings; the President for the time being of the Council, or the troika of present, preceding, and succeeding Presidents, made visits where discussions were thought to be useful; and there were regular contacts with a score of countries and groups, including Central and East European countries; China, India, and Japan; ASEAN, and the Central American and Gulf groups of states. Common positions or declarations were produced at a rate of more than one a week.[20] But beyond the exchange of information and the expression of common views, common action requires common instruments to be effective.

These exist in the Community's instruments of external economic policy, and have sometimes been used in co-ordination with the EPC's positions, for example with respect to the trade and aid instruments in the relationship with ASEAN or Central America. Most importantly, the Community responded to the great changes that began in Central and Eastern Europe in 1989 with its powerful common policy towards that area, using the instruments of external economic policy available to it in a comprehensive way in order to promote the establishment of market economies and pluralist democracies. It was the Community institutions and instruments that made this possible, not the intergovernmental mechanism of the EPC.

With the notable exception of its policy towards Central Europe, indeed, the Community could hardly be said to have established 'a common foreign policy', which the Single Act had committed the member states to do. The EPC became 'a major procedure for foreign policy-making', but it was not likely that, without a change in its form, it could evolve as a 'federal foreign policy'.[21] Various proposals had been made to move it in that direction. The Tindemans report on European Union, presented to the European Council in 1975, proposed that the Council should vote by majority in this field;[22] and the European Parliament, in its Draft Treaty on European Union in 1984, wanted the Commission to be responsible for the preparation of foreign policies, as it is in other fields of Community competence. But it was not until the Maastricht Treaty that there was further significant development of the foreign policy system.

The addition of 'political union' to the Emu project as the basis for the Maastricht Treaty was, as we have seen, a consequence of the determination of both France and Germany, supported by other member states, to strengthen the Community framework following German unification; and the common foreign and security policy (CFSP) was, together with institutional reform, intended to be a principal element of political union. Most of the member states, led by Germany, supported the idea that the Community institutions should be responsible for the CFSP, with a progressive introduction of majority voting. But Britain, along with France, insisted that the institutions be separate. The outcome was the so-called second pillar of the Union, almost entirely lacking the federal elements of the Community institutions.

Not satisfied with this result, the more federalist governments insisted that the provisions for the CFSP be reviewed in the IGC to be convened in 1996. The performance of the CFSP, meanwhile, did not dispel their scepticism about its efficacy, since despite the more elaborate arrangements little had been accomplished that could not have been done under the EPC; and public confidence in the Union had been damaged by the failure of these arrangements to achieve results with respect to Bosnia that might be expected under the grander title of Common Foreign and Security Policy. So the Amsterdam Treaty provided for some development of the Maastricht arrangements.[23]

Maastricht had enjoined the European Council to lay down 'the principles and general guidelines' for the CFSP, and the Council to take the decisions for 'defining and implementing' it by adopting common positions and joint actions. All this was to be done by unanimous agreement, though, as a gesture to the federalists, there was the somewhat implausible provision for unanimous agreement to vote by qualified majority on implementation of a joint action, and a Declaration suggested that dissenting governments abstain rather than veto measures supported by a qualified majority. Amsterdam added some precision, supplementing the principles and guidelines to be decided by the European Council with common strategies, and giving definitions of strategies, actions, and positions. The new treaty also conceded something to the pressure for movement towards majority voting by accepting qualified majority voting for the Council when adopting joint actions or common positions, though only on the basis of a unanimously agreed common strategy, or decisions implementing them in the absence of such a strategy; but at the same time a member of the Council is allowed, 'for important and stated reasons of national policy', to prevent a vote from being taken, whereupon the Council 'may, acting by a qualified majority, request that the matter be referred to the European Council for decision by unanimity'. Those who want majority voting may hope that this complicated procedure will result in sparing use of the veto, but may also fear that there will not be much change in the culture of unanimity among diplomats and ministers, or that the opting out for which special provisions also exist will become a habit that will inhibit the development of a truly common foreign and security policy. The new treaty also included some provisions on the preparation and implementation of CFSP decisions. The EU is to be represented for CFSP matters by the Presidency, assisted by the Secretary-General of the Council, who is to have international standing as the Union's 'High Representative' for CFSP. The Secretary-General is also to contribute to preparing and implementing the decisions, and is to be responsible for a policy planning and early warning unit in the Council Secretariat which is, among other things, to prepare papers on policy options for the Council.

The Maastricht Treaty provided that the European Parliament was to be 'consulted' and Amsterdam specified that the Parliament's agreement was to be required for any increase in operational expenditure on the CFSP from one year to the next. This for the first time gives the Parliament some real power in the field of CFSP, even if member states have the option of themselves paying for the increase direct in proportion to their GNPs. It is provided that the Commission be 'fully associated' with the work, which can mean anything or nothing, as can the Amsterdam Treaty's provision that the Commission may be asked by the Council to submit proposals for implementing a joint action. But these vague formulations scarcely reflect the Commission's central role in the external economic relations, where the Union has its only common external policy instruments, and which is thus more effective than other aspects of external policy. The Commission responded to Maastricht by setting up a new Directorate-General to deal with CFSP matters, but, while it has had some influence, there are also fears that the unwieldy intergovernmental CFSP is tending to encroach on the conduct of external economic relations. There has certainly been little movement in the opposite direction. The Commission's proposal that the Amsterdam Treaty extend to trade in services and intellectual property the institutional arrangements that had proved their worth in the common commercial policy for goods was not accepted. The procedure for agreements in the field of the CFSP with states or international organizations is, moreover, to be purely intergovernmental: negotiation by the Presidency and conclusion by the Council's unanimous vote. The Amsterdam Treaty offers some new scope for developing a more effective CFSP; but how far the member states will make use of it remains to be seen.

The Maastricht Treaty also moved tentatively towards competence for the Union in the field of defence. Since the failure of the EDC in the mid-1950s, the Community had been excluded from this field. But international events have been pressing member states towards closer European co-operation on security. With arms reduction and the disintegration of the Soviet Union, American expenditure on defence in Europe began to decline rapidly, raising the question of how Europeans would take more responsibility for their defence in a continent and a world where many uncertainties remain. Thus most member states have felt the need for a more integrated system centred on Western Europe. This feeling lay behind the move towards Franco-German co-operation in, for example, the Eurocorps, which Belgium, Luxembourg, and Spain subsequently joined; and former Chancellor Helmut Schmidt proposed reviving the concept of a European Army.[24] When the Maastricht Treaty was being negotiated, there was pressure for the inclusion of competences in the field of defence.

The Maastricht Treaty was tentative in its approach to defence because the British resisted the pressure of the French, backed by the Germans and some others, to give the Union a defence competence based on the incorporation of the WEU. The British government's resistance stemmed partly from its scepticism about political union in general and partly, joined here by the Dutch, from its anxiety lest the primacy of Nato might be challenged by any new arrangement. Thus the treaty left the matter open, providing that the CFSP was to include all questions of security, including 'the eventual framing of a common defence policy, which might in time lead to a common defence'. While the new British government remained reluctant to involve the Union in defence matters, it accepted that the Amsterdam Treaty authorize the Council to move to a common defence policy or a common defence, without the need for further Treaty amendment. Where, moreover, Maastricht had provided that the WEU was to be 'an integral part of the development of the Union', which may request it to carry out decisions and actions with defence implications, Amsterdam added that the Union should 'foster closer institutional relations with the WEU with a view to the possibility of the integration of the WEU into the Union, should the European Council so decide': again, no need for treaty amendment. Both treaties also affirmed, however, that the Union's policy would respect member states' Nato obligations and be compatible with Nato policies.

The membership of WEU comprises the member states of the Union save the former neutrals, Austria, Finland, Ireland, and Sweden, together with Denmark, which opted out of all defence commitments arising from the Maastricht Treaty. The WEU members agreed at Maastricht to make military units 'answerable' to WEU, to co-operate in planning and logistics, and perhaps to establish a European armaments agency. The Amsterdam Treaty specified as potential operations humanitarian, rescue, peacekeeping, and crisis-management tasks including the use of combat forces in peacemaking; and a bridge was provided between the WEU members and the rest, with the latter entitled to participate in such tasks and in the WEU's relative planning and decision-taking. Thus Amsterdam showed a modest rapprochement between the British and French, as well as between the neutrals and the others. Maastricht had produced few results in the field of defence, although the British and French had co-operated bilaterally with considerable success in Bosnia. Nor, for all the careful drafting, are the defence provisions of the Amsterdam Treaty likely to enable the Union to develop an effective defence policy until the British and French in particular can come closer to agreement on the Union's role in this field. Meanwhile, it is to be expected that the instruments of external economic policy, to which the single currency is now being added, will provide the basis for the effective core of the Union's external policy.

The EC has used what at first appeared to be a modest set of instruments to create a dense network of relationships with all parts of the world. It was the catalyst for the series of Gatt negotiations that have reduced the tariffs on trade among industrialized countries to very low levels and led to the establishment of the World Trade Organization. The relationship with the USA is punctuated by disputes over trade in specific products, but there is a process of organized collaboration, with biannual meetings between the Commission and the US Administration and joint meetings of representatives of the European Parliament and the US Congress. A combination of tariff preferences and economic aid has given the Community a strong relationship with less-developed countries. The success in transforming the relations with most Central and East European countries has been impressive. The Union's inability to measure up to challenges such as that of Bosnia has diverted attention from these achievements; and unless the weaknesses of the CFSP can be overcome, any expectation of major achievements in the field of defence will be disappointed. But even if it acquires growing defence capability, the Union's multinational character and international situation are likely to prevent it from becoming a military superpower. Thus the Union may remain a great civilian power. Building on the Community's own experience as an emergent multinational polity, it may fulfil Jean Monnet's hope that, endowed with federal institutions, it could be 'a useful example to the world' of how to establish prosperity and peace.[25]

10 The Building of the Union

Steps

This book has shown how a score of substantial steps have taken the Community from its first manifestation in the ECSC up to the Union of today. In the 1950s the big steps were the founding of the three Communities: the ECSC, establishing the Community institutions to govern the coal and steel industries of the six founder states; the EEC, giving the institutions responsibility for the customs union and common market; and Euratom. In the 1960s the customs union was completed ahead of timetable, the common agricultural policy was put in place, and the Kennedy round negotiated. The 1970s brought in Britain, Denmark, and Ireland; and despite the problems that ensued from this and from the stagflation that began in 1974, the Community's institutions and policies were significantly strengthened. The amending treaties of 1970 and 1975 gave the Community its own tax revenue and the European Parliament power over non-compulsory expenditure, making the institutions in effect federal for that corner of Community activity; direct elections were introduced; the foreign policy co-operation (EPC) and the European Council were established. The European Monetary System was created and industrial policies were developed. New relationships were initiated in Europe, with the association with Efta countries, and in the wider world, with the Lome Convention and the generalized and Mediterranean preferences.

Although the 1980s started on a low note, with the Community hamstrung by the British budget question, major steps were taken in the second half of the decade. Following the European Parliament's Draft Treaty on European Union and the Commission's single market proposals, the Single European Act committed the member states to complete the vast programme of legislation for the single market by 1992, gave the Community some additional competences, and strengthened the institutions, making the Council more decisive and giving the Parliament more influence, particularly with respect to the single market legislation. The entry of Spain and Portugal in 1986 was followed by the doubling of the structural funds; and budgetary reform sharpened control over the agricultural expenditure. The collapse of the Soviet system in Central and Eastern Europe gave a new impulse to the Community's external policy, and it entered the 1990s enlarged through German unification. The Maastricht Treaty on European Union followed, providing for economic and monetary union as well as some other new competences; giving the Parliament powers of legislative co-decision, assent, and approval over the appointment of the Commission; and bringing external and internal security within the scope of the treaties through the common foreign and security policy (CFSP) and the co-operation in justice and home affairs (CJHA). Austria, Finland, and Sweden acceded, bringing the number of member states to fifteen, containing nine-tenths of the population of Western Europe; and the way was opened for ten associated Central and East European states, as well as Cyprus, to join the Union. The Amsterdam Treaty extends the Parliament's power of co-decision to perhaps one-half of Union legislation and its power of approval to the appointment of the Commission's President; gives the President power to decide, with the governments, on the nominations of the other Commissioners; improves the guarantee of citizens' rights; and provides for better functioning of the Union in a number of significant ways.

These, together with numerous smaller steps, have brought the Community far towards becoming a federal European Union. Over trade, it has most of the powers of a federation: externally, the common policy for trade and aid; internally, responsibility for the single market, along with the common agricultural and transport policies, together with the competition and other industrial policies. There are the powers that go with the single currency and European Central Bank, though these do not as yet apply to all member states. The Union's budgetary expenditure, at some 1¼ per cent of GNP, is substantial, accompanied by the power to obtain the tax resources to finance it. There are significant powers over environmental and social legislation. But the Union does not dispose of its own instruments for the defence-related aspects of foreign policy, which remain with the member states. Without control over armed forces, the Union will not become a federal state. But it may become appropriate to call the Community federal, if its federal powers over the economy are controlled by federal institutions.

The institutions that exercise the Community's powers have, apart from the Council, the federal characteristic of a direct relationship with citizens of member states. The juridical system is broadly federal. The Commission is an executive accountable to the Parliament and Council, and independent of the several member states' governments. It is empowered to 'implement the budget . . . on its own responsibility' (Art. 205/274 ECT), though in implementing many other measures the Commission is closely circumscribed by the Council together with its network of supervisory committees. The Commission also has the right to propose laws, as governments do, to the legislature; and it has a capacity of political initiative, which it has used in launching the single market programme, the agricultural and budgetary reforms, and the single currency project. The Parliament and Council comprise a two-chamber legislature: the Parliament as the directly elected house of the people, the Council as the house of the states. The Parliament has equal power with the Council over around half of the budget and of the legislation, together with influence over most of the rest; it has the power of assent over accession, association, some other international agreements, and some internal matters; it has the power to approve the appointment of the Commission's President, then of the Commission itself, backed by powers of dismissal and scrutiny of expenditure and administration. So it goes a good way towards fulfilling the principal functions of representative government, namely, the enactment of legislation and control of the executive. In the Council, a procedure of majority voting now applies to the bulk of legislation. But unanimity remains the rule for some important decisions and, like a diplomatic conference rather than a legislative chamber, its meetings are not open to the public nor is a proper account of its legislative proceedings published. These features, together with its persisting predominance over the Parliament in legislation and detailed control over the Commission in execution, are not appropriate for a house of states in a federal union; and the arrangements for security co-operation remain more intergovernmental.

Three principal reforms would be required to complete the process of making the Community's institutions federal. The principle of majority voting would have to apply to the Council's decisions generally; co-decision would have to apply to legislation generally; and the executive competence accorded by the Treaty to the Commission would have to be extended from the budget to those matters where implementation is still effectively controlled by the Council and its committees. Given these reforms and with the existing powers in the economic and environmental fields, the Community might be called federal. But there is a major obstacle to such reforms. Each requires the states' governments to transfer some more power to the Community: for the majority voting, from the governments severally to their representatives in the Council jointly; for co-decision and executive competence, from the Council to the Parliament and the Commission.

The member states have already gone far in transferring such powers to the Community. But further steps come closer to the core of their sovereignty: most forcibly as regards the Union's 'pillars' relating to external and internal security, but also in reforming the institutional arrangements of the Community itself. With the challenges relating to the single currency and the coming enlargement, there will be pressure for such reforms and, as in the past, also resistance to them. In order to understand the process of development and reform of the Community and the Union, and to form a reasoned view of the prospects that the process will continue, it is necessary to assess the forces that promote it and those that resist it. Here we bring together evidence about these forces that has emerged in the course of the events recorded in this book.

Linkages and neofunctionalism

We have seen how the establishment of the ECSC was followed by a development of the Community's powers and institutions that has continued for nearly half-a-century. The most elaborate explanation by political scientists remains that devised in the early period by the neofunctionalists, who held that, because of the mutual interdependence of economic problems, there would, from the starting-point of 'a real delegation of decision-making to a supranational agency', be a 'cumulative and expansive process whereby the supranational agency slowly extends its authority so as to progressively undermine the independence of the nation-state'; and as this proceeded, 'relevant interest groups would shift their attention and ultimately their loyalties from the nation-state'.[1] While this explanation of what they called 'spillover' has been found seriously incomplete, and hence in some ways misleading, such linkages have played an important part in some significant developments.

French insistence on the common agricultural policy to counterbalance the gains to German industry from the common market was the first, classic example. The British demand for the Regional Development Fund was intended, in turn, to counterweigh the effect on Britain of the agricultural policy. But the long struggle, first by the Labour government then by Mrs Thatcher, to secure compensation through the budget had a powerful negative impact on the Community's development, as decision-taking was frustrated by the conflict. The British insistence on effective Community controls over agricultural expenditure, embodied in the agri-budgetary reform, was more positive. The member states with less-developed economies, fearing the effect of more intense competition as a result of the single market, exacted a doubling of the structural funds as a condition for accepting it, and another big increase for their agreement to the Emu project. Most significantly, France sought to redress the loss of control over its monetary policy to the Bundesbank, which had been accentuated by the integration of financial markets; and this, combined with the determination to anchor Germany yet more securely in the Union, motivated the French drive to secure the single currency and European Central Bank.

While linkages can come from the desire to redress a disadvantage, they can also result from determination to consolidate a gain. The French insisted that the Community have its own tax resources in order to safeguard their gains from the agricultural policy. Acceleration of the customs union was supported in order to make the common external tariff and the internal free trade irreversible. One motive for the single market programme was fear that the internal free trade would be negated by the proliferation of non-tariff barriers; and the single currency project was motivated partly by fear that the free movement of capital resulting from the single market programme would undermine the currency stability that had been achieved through the Exchange Rate Mechanism unless the participants took the further step to a single currency.

Although spillover as defined by the neofunctionalists was an influence in these developments, it was not the only influence nor, in crucial cases, the most important. They were forced to recognize this when de Gaulle demonstrated how their spillover could be frustrated by the power of the nation-state. Writing in the 1970s, two of them maintained the emphasis on linkages, but accepted that these could move the Community either forward or back. There was a new focus on leadership as distinct from automatic process, but this was not held likely to promote 'important new tasks or powers for the Community system'. The result would be a Community in equilibrium, conserving a balance between forces for and against further integration.[2] Thus while belatedly recognizing the exogenous forces that could frustrate spillover, they failed to appreciate those that had already driven the creation of the EEC and were to provide the motive power for such seminal developments as the single market and the single currency: most particularly, the need of economic interests for a large market that would not be fragmented by the borders between member states, and the political will to secure and then consolidate peace based on Franco-German reconciliation and partnership. But before we examine those forces, which are fundamental for an understanding of the process of integration, we should be aware of the contrary forces, also originally ignored by the neofunctionalists: nationalism and defence of the sovereignty of the nation-state.

Forces against federal Union

The experience recounted in preceding chapters shows how nation-states can powerfully resist moves towards federation. France led by de Gaulle was the prime example, with his defence of the 'Europe of states' against the federalists' 'myths, fictions and pageants'.[3] Among academics, this approach has been reflected in the 'realist' school, with their view of the immutable status of the nation-state and the unreality of proposals to transfer sovereignty to common institutions, and hence their stress on intergovernmental co-operation. The Gaullist policy succeeded in blocking, first the project for a European Defence Community, then the practice of majority voting in the EC Council; and it continued to influence French policy after de Gaulle's demise.

While France remained sensitive about sovereignty, it was the British who became the most stubborn champions of the sovereign nation-state. Harold Macmillan, in attempting to negotiate entry, assured the House of Commons in 1961 that he accepted de Gaulle's view of sovereignty.[4] A decade later Edward Heath was moved to reaffirm, in the White Paper on the terms of accession, that 'There is no question of any erosion of essential national sovereignty'.[5] But what national sovereignty was 'essential'? The Labour government that followed Heath in 1974, and Mrs Thatcher, who followed them in 1979, proved more jealous of Britain's sovereignty than Heath would probably have been. All member states behaved defensively during the economic troubles of the 1970s. But the Labour government was more insistent on sovereignty, more inclined to block Community action, than most of its partners. The Labour Party, by then in opposition, went so far as to campaign in the 1983 elections for British withdrawal from the Community, causing many social democrats to leave the party in order to create, with the Liberals, a pro-European Alliance, later to become the Liberal Democrats. Mrs Thatcher was a strong proponent of free trade, and hence of the single market programme. But her attitude towards sovereignty became yet more intransigent than that of the Labour government had been. In a speech at Bruges in 1988, she asserted that 'some in the European Community seem to want . . . a European super-state exercising a new dominance from Brussels', which would 'suppress nationhood' and lead to an 'identikit European personality'.[6] Specific targets of this general anathema were monetary union and stronger powers for the European Parliament; and in place of such sharing of sovereignty, she proposed 'cooperation between independent sovereign states'. Unlike most political leaders in the Community, she saw German union as another argument against further integration, preferring to rely on more traditional inter-state relationships rather than on more federal links as the framework for containing German power. John Major, after succeeding her as Prime Minister in 1990, likewise resisted federal developments and proclaimed a need to 'reassert the authority of national governments'.[7]

In the debate on the Maastricht Treaty in the House of Commons, parliamentary sovereignty was emphasized, in the sense of unlimited legislative authority for the Westminster parliament, contrasting with legislative authority in federal systems which is distributed among legislatures at different levels of government within the framework of a constitution. The referendum in Denmark in 1992 underlined the Danes' attachment to national sovereignty; and the French referendum soon after demonstrated the strength of such feelings in France. But while the Labour government that replaced the Conservatives in May 1997 continued to insist on sovereignty in the fields of external and internal security, its attitude to reform of the Community was closer to that of the majority of member states, accepting more co-decision and majority voting, and looking more favourably than its predecessor on participation in the single currency. It is no longer so certain that Britain will be opposed to further federal steps.

Nationalist opposition was not so strong in other member states. But German citizens have been concerned about the prospect of the single currency replacing the deutschmark, reflecting fears that Germany could catch inflation from its neighbours if it did not resist the sharing of monetary sovereignty. While there were rational grounds for these fears, such resistance was also an example of a more general inertia that works against the transfer of powers to the Community. It was, after all, the governments and bureaucracies of all the member states that appeared content with the practice of unanimous voting in the Council for two whole decades, during which its inefficiency became increasingly evident; and the Council's network of committees of member states' officials remains an impediment to efficient executive action by the Commission. Official inertia is backed by protectionist pressure from the less dynamic parts of the economy.

Periods such as 1965–85, when this combination of hostility and inertia stunted the development of the Community, and a somewhat similar phase in the mid-1990s, lent credibility to theorists who saw it as not essentially different from other international organizations or groups. One such view, playing down formal international institutions in favour of 'clusters of intergovernmental and transnational networks' associated with them, concluded that 'very little in the record [of the three first post-war decades] suggests that international organizations such as . . . the European Community will become increasingly autonomous and powerful in world politics'.[8] The period from the Single Act to the Maastricht Treaty showed this to have been a misjudgement of the Community's potential. To place the Community in the category of international 'regimes', defined as 'sets of implicit or explicit principles, norms, rules, and decision-making procedures around which actor expectations converge in a given area of international relations',[9] also fails to give due weight to the significance of the rule of law, of common instruments such as the external tariff and the single currency, and of the federal elements in the institutions. So too does the 'liberal intergovernmentalist' focus on the politics and governments of the member states, which sees the Community as 'a regime for policy co-ordination' that serves 'to strengthen the power of governments'.[10] The working of the legal system is, however, not a matter of policy co-ordination but of the rule of law which applies to governments as well as citizens over a wide field of competence. The common commercial policy is not a matter of co-ordination of governments' policies but of formation and execution of a common policy based on common instruments, in which the Commission plays a prominent part. Nor is the single currency managed through the co-ordination of governments' policies, but by monetary institutions of federal form.

The power of independent European governments has been eroded by forces of interdependence that have reduced their capacity for separate action. In areas where the Union has been given competence, their influence in the making of more effective, common policies, and in that sense their power, has been strengthened. But while it is necessary to give full weight to the role of governments in policy formation, attention should not be deflected from the common policy instruments that enable the common policies to be more effective than co-ordinated policies based on member states' own instruments would be, nor from the federal elements in the institutions that provide the context in which the member states' representatives can perform effectively in the legislative and policy-making process. Individual governments can block legislation or policy-making in fields where unanimity applies, and prevent common action where they retain control of their own policy instruments. But from the ECSC to the single currency, the arsenal of common policy instruments has continued to be augmented, as have the scope for majority voting and the European Parliament's powers, though these reforms required unanimity. Thus the forces favouring federal development have been no less influential than those opposed to it.

Forces favouring federal steps

The Community was founded because it was felt that 'co-operation between independent sovereign states' would not satisfy vital national interests. France, in order to establish permanent peace with Germany, wanted to contain the resurgent Germans within a strong framework that would satisfy them because it did not hold them down, but bound the member states equally. The Germans sought, first, to recover equal status after their defeat in war, then a stable base in the West from which they could conduct an Ostpolitik and finally their unification, without endangering their security. Such motives led France and Germany to found the Community in the 1950s, to relaunch it in 1969, and to promote the projects of Emu and political union that led to the Maastricht Treaty.

Specific political motives such as these have been generalized into a critique of the nation-state as inadequate to deal with the contemporary economic and security problems that transcend its borders. This caused Italians, reacting against their experiences of fascism and of World War Two, and inspired by the thinking of Altiero Spinelli, to promote the idea of a federal Europe, from the project for a European Political Community associated with the European Defence Community in the 1950s to the European Parliament's Draft Treaty in the 1980s. The Benelux countries, smaller and hence yet more conscious of interdependence, have generally shared this approach; and it has been widely accepted by Community citizens.

Thus political motives for founding and developing the Community, largely absent in Britain with its different wartime experience and its insular and imperial tradition, have been prevalent on the Continent, and have been powerful forces when the political conjuncture allowed. Politics did not allow to the extent that Monnet and others had hoped, however, when the Assemblée Nationale declined to ratify the EDC Treaty because resolute Gaullists and Communists and nervous Centrists refused to accept the radical sharing of sovereignty. The Community steered well clear of the field of defence until the Maastricht Treaty. But because it was seen to have fostered the Franco-German reconciliation and thus to have consolidated the post-war peace, there was a powerful motive for continuing the Community's development, though in the economic rather than the security field.

While this political motive was more or less federalist, less for France but more for the other five, the development of the Community in the economic field was also promoted by economic interests, both business and non-communist trade unions. From the start the Dutch and Germans, then increasingly the others, became strong supporters of the common market. One cannot be sure how far economic integration was a cause of the economic success of the Community in the 1960s. But it was seen as the framework for the unprecedented growth of prosperity. So when the single market was proposed in 1985, the programme again secured powerful business support; and this too being seen as successful, there was again strong support, from both finance and industry, for the single currency project. The institutional reforms that accompanied the installation of these powers and instruments were initiated by federalists such as Monnet, Delors, and Kohl, but they would not have been achieved without the support of business for the economic parts of the packages. Although the integration was not in the field of security as such, the combination of economic integration with the Community's institutions and rule of law was seen as making a decisive contribution to the solidity of the peace in Western Europe; and this reinforced the political motive for federal steps, just as the success of the common market and the single market programme bolstered the economic motive for developing the Community's powers and policy instruments.

These motives have been reinforced by the desire of European countries to improve their standing and influence in the wider world. Already in 1950, the six founder members of the Community saw clearly how Europeans, weakened by their divisions that had led to two great fratricidal wars, had forfeited their capacity to defend their interests, let alone apply their full weight to shaping the course of world politics. To combine their strength to deal with external challenges was another motive for integration. While the British, less conscious of their reduced circumstances, held back, French diplomacy seized the opportunity to lead the Continent and thus reverse Britain's post-war superiority: a more traditional aim than that of Monnet, but the two combined were a powerful force for creating and defending the Community and its customs union.

Bargaining power in international trade negotiations, particularly in relation to the United States, was a motive for establishing the common external tariff. Greater autonomy in relation to the dollar was a reason for the determination of Schmidt and Giscard to establish the EMS. The need to meet Japanese and American competition was the prime mover behind the single market programme. While Europeans have thus sought to redress the balance of power with respect to the United States and later Japan by developing the Community, the Americans have significantly helped them to do so. US support was a powerful force in favour of building the Community in its earlier days, though later there was more ambivalence.

The Community's preferential arrangements were a response to pressures from developing countries and from European neighbours for access to the EC market. The readiness to respond was motivated partly by French, then British desire to secure Community support for French Union and Commonwealth countries, partly by the European interest in stability around the Mediterranean, and partly in order to strengthen economic and political links with other West European and developing countries. Having established the customs union, the member states could no longer conduct separate trade policies and were obliged to develop relationships, and hence the Community itself, in these ways; and this experience enabled the Community to respond strongly to the emergence of pluralist democracies in Central and Eastern Europe, thus adding to its capacity to conduct a common external policy. The desire to redress the balance of power with the Soviet Union had motivated the project for a European Defence Community in the 1950s. Then the Community sought to use its economic strength to secure more autonomy for Central and East Europeans. Following the disintegration of the Soviet Union, the European Union has used its collective weight to promote stability among its eastern neighbours in order to enhance European security.

In short, the increasingly interdependent world presses on the member states to defend their interests through the Union, in particular in relation to the United States, Japan, and the emerging industrial powers, but also in the promotion of a safe and prosperous international order.

These various pressures, political and economic, external and internal, have impelled the member states to give the Union considerable power. While federalists have constantly sought reforms of the institutions to make them more federal, specific political interests have also supported such reforms for more particular reasons. Thus the Dutch parliament, standing firm on the principle that public expenditure must be subject to parliamentary control, insisted that the European Parliament be given powers to control the Community budget. The German Constitutional Court, for its part, judged that the single currency would be incompatible with the German constitution unless the Union's institutions were made more democratic. Desire for efficiency in controlling agricultural expenditure and policing the single market led Britain's Conservative government, usually among the most insistent on keeping the Commission under the Council's control, to support greater powers for the Commission to prevent excess agri-budgetary expenditure, and an expanded role for it in getting member states to comply with Community laws. Britain agreed that the Court of Justice should have the power to fine member states if it finds that they have contravened Community law; and Mrs Thatcher accepted that qualified majority voting was desirable in order to complete the legislation for the single market, although she hoped to achieve that through an informal arrangement rather than by treaty amendment.

Thus federalists have joined forces with specific interests not only to give the Community and Union its powers and policy instruments, but also to provide it with institutions capable of being reformed in a federal direction, in order to make them more democratic and effective, and to ensure an effective rule of law.

Federalists

Unlike the neofunctionalists, federalists have had a clear idea about the problems common to nation-states that would require common action to resolve, and about the form of institutions that would be needed to undertake it: common problems in the fields of trade, money, security, and the environment; and institutions of democratic constitutional government to deal with the common affairs, leaving the member states to manage their own affairs with their own democratic institutions. The problems have been identified through observation and analysis of how far states are able to deal with them independently; and it has been assumed that democracies would not for long accept that important functions of government be entrusted to institutions other than those of representative government, in a framework of the rule of law.

Federalists have adopted two main approaches to the achievement of such a federal system. One, pioneered in post-war Europe by Altiero Spinelli, was that of a constituent assembly of people's representatives drawing up a federal constitution for ratification by the member states. With the direct election of the European Parliament in 1979, the people's representatives were in place; and Spinelli, as one of their number, persuaded them to design and approve the Draft Treaty on European Union. Without going so far as a federal state with integrated armed forces, this did propose a reform that would have made the Community's institutions federal; and although the immediate result was not a federal Community, but an impulse towards the more modest Single Act, the Draft Treaty remained a benchmark against which federalists could measure subsequent proposals for Community reform.

The other approach, of steps towards federation, was developed by Jean Monnet. While he was often not explicit about a federal aim, he did insert it in his draft of the Schuman Declaration and in the statutes of his Action Committee for the United States of Europe, as well as expressing it on various other occasions. His close advisers, such as Etienne Hirsch, Pierre Uri, and Robert Triffin, were also federalists. While his pragmatic nature and his commitment to the art of the possible were indispensable for his achievements, it may be doubted whether he would have been able to initiate the creation of institutions with such scope for development in a federal direction had he not seen them as part of a process that would lead to federation.

Paul-Henri Spaak, the architect of the Rome Treaties, was also a federalist. So was Walter Hallstein, the President of the dynamic initial EEC Commission, and, in their different ways, Sicco Mansholt, Robert Marjolin, and Jean Rey, his colleagues in that Commission who shared the credit for its performance. The Community's successes in the 1970s owed much to statesmen who, if not at the time explicitly federalist, have shown a commitment to important elements of the federalist programme: Willy Brandt, Valéry Giscard d'Estaing, Edward Heath, Roy Jenkins, and Helmut Schmidt. More recently Jacques Delors, who has initiated key steps towards Union, has been explicit about his federal aim; and the same may be said of Helmut Kohl.

Thus most of the steps towards Union have been promoted by people for whom a federal Union itself was an objective. The steps have also been supported by institutions that generally shared the aim: in particular the Commission and European Parliament, but also the parliaments of certain member states, including in various ways the Italian, Belgian, and Dutch parliaments and the German Bundestag. There has also been much support from European party groups, interest groups, and federalist movements.

These federalist statesmen and bodies have been central to the Community's foundation and development by steps towards a federal system. But they would not have succeeded had they not allied themselves with forces that had a particular interest in a given step rather than in the federal system towards which it could lead. Industrial and financial interests supported the acceleration of the customs union, the single market programme, and the single currency. Monnet harnessed the specific interests of France and West Germany to the creation of the ECSC. The Commission had French and Dutch support for the establishment of the common agricultural policy, and that of the Dutch parliament for control of the budget by the European Parliament, of Spain for the cohesion policy, of Britain for the agri-budgetary controls, and of France for the single currency. The European Parliament's Draft Treaty owed its political impact to its favourable reception by President Mitterrand, who was at the time occupying the presidency of the European Council and who was partial to the general idea of European Union.

The concept of steps towards federal Union, promoted by federalists and supported by more specific interests, may be seen as a new federalism, more conscious than neofunctionalism of federalist motives and exogenous forces favouring movement towards Union, more explicit than classical federalists about the process that can lead up to acceptance of a federal constitution.

A new federalism

This new federalism[11] as it applies in Europe may now be summarized in ten propositions.

1. A federal system is designed to provide effective democratic governance in common for a group of states in fields where their interdependence substantially reduces their ability to do so separately, while they retain their own democratic governance in other fields. For European states, the principal fields of such interdependence are trade, money, cross-border environmental problems, and security.
2. The alternatives are attempts to reduce interdependence, which are generally harmful to the citizens' welfare, or governance by an intergovernmental system, less effective and more bureaucratic than federal democracy.
3. Movement towards federal democracy may be achieved

by placing successive building blocks on a pre-federal foundation, as in the development from the European Coal and Steel Community to the European Union of today.

4. The building blocks comprise federal elements in the Union's powers and institutions. By now the Union has such powers to deal with the problems of interdependence in the fields of internal and external trade, money, and the environment. It has a two-chamber legislature, in which the house of the citizens (European Parliament) shares power with the house of the states (Council) with respect to around half of the legislation and of the budget, and to the appointment and accountability of the executive (European Commission). The Parliament acts as a federal chamber where it shares power with the Council. The Council acts as a federal chamber when it votes under the procedure of (usually qualified) majority, by which it approves the budget and most of the legislation. The Commission acts as a federal executive, save that the Council retains detailed control over execution of law and policy in a number of fields. The Court of Justice is a federal judiciary responsible for ensuring the rule of Union law.
5. For foreign and security policy the Union does not have federal powers and its institutional arrangements are intergovernmental. Without integrated instruments of security policy responsible to federal institutions, the Union will not become a federal state.
6. If successfully accomplished, the installation of successive federal elements can make further movement towards a federal system more feasible in various ways. They can lend conviction to the idea that the Union's institutions may be entrusted with new tasks. They increase, as they accumulate, the potency of internal linkages, for example as the capital liberalization in the single market spurred the Emu project, which in turn raised the demand for more institutional reform. They reduce the number of further elements required to complete a federal system. But they can, to the contrary, evoke political and public resistance to the transfer of further powers to an increasingly powerful Union.

7. Nationalist statesmen and political forces, the inertia of existing states' structures, and protectionist economic interests have resisted movement towards a federal system. They have succeeded in maintaining the intergovernmental elements that remain in the institutions. But they have not prevented the attribution to the Union of the federal elements in the institutions and of most of the powers required to deal with the member states' interdependence in the economic and environmental fields.
8. Responding to the growth of interdependence, movement towards a federal system has been promoted by federalist statesmen and political forces. Particular moves have been supported by specific economic interests, including the more dynamic forces in the economy, and by political interests, including member states' need for stability within the European system and influence in the wider world.
9. Successive enlargements from the original six to the present fifteen member states have been accompanied by the introduction of some federal elements but also of some states that have resisted federal developments. Federalists fear, and nationalists hope, that further enlargement will weaken the Union if it is not accompanied by further federal reforms, in particular the general application of qualified majority voting in the Council and of co-decision with the Parliament for the approval of legislation and the budget, together with a progressive introduction of federal elements in the common foreign and security policy.
10. There can be no assurance that these reforms will be achieved. The forces of inertia, nationalism, and protectionism remain strong. But there are also powerful forces that favour such reforms, and thus the completion of a federal system of government to deal with the interdependence, at least with respect to the economy and the environment, among a large majority of European states.

The idea expressed in these propositions is in some respects a synthesis of the federalist and the neofunctionalist approaches. It offers a way to supplement federalist theory, which has tended to focus on the design of a constitution without considering the process of steps which may make that feasible; and it fills gaps in neofunctionalism caused by neglect of some essential political and economic forces and of constitutional questions. It is hoped, in these ways, to help understanding of the historic process of unification in Europe, and in particular to help understanding in Britain, where the case and prospects for a federal European Union have been underrated, owing partly to wartime experience, partly to a defensive mentality that followed the retreat from empire, and partly to a consequent provincialism. Along with this reluctance to contemplate a federal Union has gone a disinclination to think rigorously about the development of the Community's institutions, with the term *sui generis* often employed to avoid examining them in the light of constitutional principles. The conclusion of this book is that principles of federal government are relevant to consideration of the development of the European Union; and that, given the balance of forces in favour over against the contrary forces, a federal Community pillar is not unlikely to become a reality around the time of the first wave of enlargement. Steps towards it will certainly be proposed at the Intergovernmental Conference to be convened before that enlargement and at least some are likely to be taken, whether by all the member states or by a core group ready to proceed farther than the rest. The new federalism will thus be relevant, not only for the Union as it stands today but also for its extension to include most of Europe—and, perhaps, for eventual application in the wider world.

That is my view. I hope the book will have given readers the material on which they can form their own.

Notes

Chapter 1: Creating the Community and the Union

1. Statement by Robert Schuman, French foreign minister, 9 May 1950.
2. See Walter Lipgens (ed.), *Documents on the History of European Integration*, i. *Continental Plans for European Union 1939–1945*; ii. *Plans for European Union in Great Britain and in Exile 1939–1945* (Berlin and New York, 1985, 1986).
3. Alan S. Milward, *The Reconstruction of Western Europe 1945–51* (London, 1984), 310–11.
4. John Pinder, 'Federal Union 1939–41', in Lipgens (ed.), *Documents*, ii., 26–155; Richard Mayne and John Pinder, with John Roberts, *Federal Union: The Pioneers* (London, 1990).
5. Jean Monnet, *Les États-Unis d'Europe ont commencé: Discours et allocutions 1952–1954* (Paris, 1955), 51–60; Altiero Spinelli, *Diario europeo: 1948–1969*, ed. Edmondo Paolini (Bologna, 1989), 142.
6. Jean Monnet, *Memoirs*, trans. Richard Mayne (London, 1978), 343.
7. Luigi Vittorio Majocchi and Francesco Rossolillo, *Il Parlamento europeo* (Naples, 1979), 163–216, with introduction by Mario Albertini.
8. The principal neofunctionalist works were Ernst B. Haas, *The Uniting of Europe: Political, Social and Economical Forces 1950–1957* (London, 1958); Leon N. Lindberg, *The Political Dynamics of European Economic Integration* (Stanford, Calif., 1963); Leon N. Lindberg and Stuart A. Scheingold, *Europe's Would-Be Polity: Patterns of Change in the European Community* (Englewood Cliffs, NJ, 1970).
9. Press Conference, 15 May 1962.
10. For a full analysis of the Treaty on European Union and its implications, see Andrew Duff, Roy Pryce, and John Pinder (eds.), *Maastricht and Beyond: Building the European Union* (London and New York, 1994).
11. The Maastricht Treaty (TEU), while it establishes the CFSP and the cooperation in justice and home affairs, also comprises amendments to the existing treaties of the European Communities. The European Community Treaty (ECT) is the EEC Treaty as amended and renamed by the TEU.
12. 'Treaty on European Union: Final Draft by the Dutch Presidency as modified by the Maastricht Summit' (Article W.2; both the draft and the modification on which the British and Danes insisted are shown), Europe Documents, *Agence Europe*, No. 1750/1751, 13 Dec. 1991.
13. The Treaty of Amsterdam is reproduced and analysed in Andrew Duff, *The Treaty of Amsterdam: Text and Commentary* (London, 1997).

Chapter 2: Institutions or Constitution

1. Press Conference, 9 Sept. 1965.
2. See Altiero Spinelli, *The Eurocrats: Conflict and Crisis in the European Community* (Baltimore, 1966); David Coombes, *Politics and Bureaucracy in the European Community: A Portrait of the Commission of the E.E.C.* (London, 1970).
3. Commission of the EC, *Mémorandum sur la réforme de l'agriculture dans la Communauté Économique Européenne: Agriculture 1980*, COM (68) 1000 (Brussels, 21 Dec. 1968).
4. See Donald J. Puchala, 'Worm Cans and Worth Taxes: Fiscal Harmonization and the European Policy Process', in Helen Wallace, William Wallace, and Carole Webb (eds.), *Policy Making in the European Community* (Chichester, 1983; 1st edn. London, 1977).
5. T. C. Hartley, *The Foundations of European Community Law* (Oxford, 1994, 1st edn 1981), 55.
6. Jean Monnet, *Les État-Unis d'Europe ont commencé: Discours et allocutions 1952–1954* (Paris, 1955) 57; the French member of parliament was André Philip, see Étienne Hirsch, *Ainsi va la vie* (Lausanne, 1988), 107.
7. Jean Monnet, *Memoirs*, trans. Richard Mayne (London, 1978), 512–13.
8. Sir Michael Butler, *Europe: More than a Continent* (London, 1986), 158.
9. See Ch. 8, below, and Michael Shackleton, *Financing the European Community* (London, 1990), ch. 2.
10. B. M. Key, 'The Exercise by the European Parliament of its Power of Discharge', in R. Hrbek, J. Jamar, and W. Wessels (eds.), *The European Parliament on the Eve of the Second Direct Election: Balance Sheet and Prospects* (Bruges, 1984), 788.
11. Butler, *Europe*, 22.
12. For a full analysis of the Parliament's role following the Maastricht Treaty, see Richard Corbett, 'Representing the People', in Andrew Duff, Roy Pryce, and John Pinder (eds.), *Maastricht and Beyond: Building the European Union* (London and New York, 1994); for details on the Amsterdam Treaty and the Parliament, see Duff, 136-51.
13. Altiero Spinelli, *Towards the European Union*, Sixth Jean Monnet Lecture (European University Institute, Florence, 1984).
14. *Interim Report on the Intergovernmental Conference in the Context of Parliament's Strategy for European Union*, A3–47/90, approved by European Parliament, 14 Mar. 1990; European Parliament, Minutes of the sitting of 10 Feb. 1994, PE 179.622.
15. These concepts are summarized in Vernon Bogdanor (ed.), The Blackwell Encyclopaedia of Political Institutions (Oxford, 1987), 146–8, 532–4, 547–8.

16. Richard Corbett and Juliet Lodge, 'Progress and Prospects', in Juliet Lodge (ed.), *European Union: The European Community in Search of a Future* (London, 1986).

Chapter 3: From Six to Fifteen and More

1. Richard Mayne and John Pinder, with John Roberts, *Federal Union: The Pioneers* (London, 1990), 26–8.
2. Michael Charlton, *The Price of Victory* (London, 1983), 99, 102, 104, 106.
3. See Miriam Camps, *Britain and the European Community 1955–1963* (London, 1964), ch. 5.
4. Charlton, *The Price of Victory*, 304.
5. Camps, *Britain and the European Community*, 360; Charlton, *The Price of Victory*, 246.
6. Eric Roll, *Crowded Hours* (London, 1985), 115.
7. Marcus H. Miller, 'Estimates of the Static Balance-of-Payments and Welfare Costs Compared', in John Pinder (ed.), *The Economics of Europe: What the Common Market Means for Britain* (London, 1971), 147. For an account of the politics and diplomacy of British entry, see Uwe Kitzinger, *Diplomacy and Persuasion: How Britain Joined the Common Market* (London, 1973).
8. *The United Kingdom and the European Communities*, Cmnd 4715 (London, July 1971), 16.
9. Ibid. 25.
10. Ibid. 8.
11. See Michael Hodges and William Wallace (eds.), *Economic Divergence in the European Community* (London, 1981).
12. See Helen Wallace with Adam Ridley, *Europe: The Challenge of Diversity* (London, 1985).
13. See 'Europe Agreement establishing an Association between the European Communities and their Member States for the one part and the Republic of Poland for the other part', *Official Journal of the European Communities*, L348 vol. 36 (31 Dec. 1993).
14. 'Europe and the Challenge of Enlargement', report presented by the Commission to the Lisbon European Council held on 26 and 27 June 1992, *Bulletin of the European Communities*, Supplement 3/1992, 10.
15. 'Copenhagen European Council: Conclusions of the Presidency', *Bulletin of the European Communities*, 6/1993, 13.
16. 'Corfu European Council: Conclusions of the Presidency', *Bulletin of the European Union*, 6/1994, 14.
17. 'Report from the Council to the Essen European Council on a strategy to

prepare for the accession of the associated CCEE', Annex 4 to 'Essen European Council: Conclusions of the Presidency', *Bulletin of the European Union*, 12/1994, 20.

18. European Commission, *Study on alternative strategies for the development of relations in the field of agriculture between the EU and associated countries with a view to future accession of these countries: (Agriculture Strategy Paper)*, the Fischler Report, CSE (95) 607 (Brussels, Dec. 1995).
19. European Commission, 'Agenda 2000: For a stronger and wider Union', Document drawn up on the basis of COM(97)2000 final, *Bulletin of the European Union*, Supplement 5/1997.

Chapter 4: From Customs Union to Single Market

1. Comité Intergouvernemental créé par la Conférence de Messine, *Rapport des Chefs de Délégation aux Ministres des Affaires Étrangères*, the Spaak Report (Brussels, 21 Apr. 1956), 9–10. The economic arguments were later developed in Bela Balassa, *The Theory of Economic Integration* (London, 1961); Jacques Pelkmans, *Market Integration in the European Community* (The Hague, 1984); Paolo Cecchini with Michael Catinat and Alexis Jacquemin, *The European Challenge 1992: The Benefits of a Single Market* (Aldershot, 1988).
2. This 'acceleration' is analysed in Leon N. Lindberg, *The Political Dynamics of European Economic Integration* (Stanford Calif., 1963), ch.9.
3. For example, Commission of the EC, *The Competitiveness of the European Community Industry*, Document III/387/82 (Brussels, Mar. 1982); M. Albert and J. Ball, *Towards European Economic Recovery in the 1980s* (European Parliament, 31 Aug. 1983); Jacques Pelkmans, *Completing the Internal Market for Industrial Products* (Commission of the EC, Brussels, 1986).
4. Wisse Dekker, *Europe–1990* (Eindhoven, 1985); *Completing the Internal Market*, White Paper from the Commission to the European Council, June 1985.
5. *Completing the Internal Market*. The programme is analysed in Roland Bieber, Renaud Dehousse, John Pinder, and Joseph H. H. Weiler (eds.), *1992: One European Market? A Critical Analysis of the Commission's Internal Market Strategy* (Baden-Baden, 1988); Jacques Pelkmans and Alan Winters, *Europe's Domestic Market* (London, 1988); Cecchini, *European Challenge*.
6. Cecchini, *European Challenge*, 10–11.
7. Ibid., 27.

8. Ibid., 16; Pelkmans and Winters, *Europe's Domestic Market*, 32–4.
9. Richard H. Lauwaars, 'The "Model Directive" on Technical Harmonization', in Bieber, Dehousse, Pinder, and Weiler (eds.), *1992: One European Market?* 152–5. In the same book see also Christian Joerges, 'The New Approach to Technical Harmonization and the Interests of Consumers: Reflections on the Requirements and Difficulties of a Europeanization of Product Safety Policy', and Pieter VerLoren van Themaat, 'The Contributions to the Establishment of the Internal Market by the Case-Law of the Court of Justice of the European Communities', 154, 156–7.
10. See Lauwaars, 'Model Directive'.
11. Cecchini, *European Challenge*; the reports on which this summary book was based are explained and listed in it on 115–27.
12. J. Tinbergen, *International Economic Integration* (Amsterdam, 1954), 122.
13. John Pinder, 'Positive Integration and Negative Integration: Some Problems of Economic Union in the EEC', *The World Today* (Jan. 1968).

Chapter 5: Agricultural Policy

1. Miriam Camps, *European Unification in the Sixties: From the Veto to the Crisis* (New York, 1966), 15 ff.
2. Ibid., 40 ff.
3. Commission of the EC, *Mémorandum sur la réforme de l'agriculture dans la Communauté Économique Européenne: Agriculture 1980*, COM (68) 1000 (Brussels, 21 Dec. 1968). This episode is explained in Edmund Neville-Rolfe, *The Politics of Agriculture in the European Community* (London, 1984), which gives a detailed account of the development of the common agricultural policy up to 1983.
4. Glenda Goldstone Rosenthal, *The Men Behind the Decisions: Cases in European Policy-Making* (Lexington, Mass., 1975), ch. 6.
5. D. Biehl (chairman) and members of a study group of the Institut für Europäische Politik, *Common Agricultural Policy, European Integration and International Division of Labour* (Bonn, 1987), 8, 10, 20.
6. Commission of the EC, *Making a Success of the Single Act*, COM (87) 100, and *Report by the Commission to the Council and the Parliament on the Financing of the Community Budget*, COM (87) 101 (Brussels, 1987).
7. European Commission, *Study on alternative strategies for the development of relations in the field of agriculture* (Brussels, Dec. 1995); 'Agenda 2000: For a stronger and wider Union', *Bulletin of the European Union*, Supplement 5/1997, 26–33, 62–3.

Chapter 6: Industrial, Social, and Environmental Policy

1. See John Pinder (ed.), *National Industrial Strategies and the World Economy* (Totowa, NJ, 1982). See also the chapters by Christopher Wilkinson and Jean Waelbroeck in Alexis Jacquemin (ed.), *European Industry: Public Policy and Corporate Strategy* (Oxford, 1984).
2. The complexities of the steel industry in that region are discussed in Alan S. Milward, *The Reconstruction of Western Europe 1945–51* (London, 1984), ch. 12.
3. See Pinder (ed.), *National Industrial Strategies*, chs. 3 and 5.
4. Dennis Swann, *Competition and Industrial Policy in the European Community* (London, 1983), 92.
5. Ibid., 95.
6. See Emmanuel de Robien, 'The Role of European Industry in European Standardization: The Case of Information Technology', in Rita Beuter and Jacques Pelkmans (eds.), *Cementing the Internal Market* (Maastricht, 1986); and Margaret Sharp, 'The Community and New Technologies', in Juliet Lodge (ed.), *The European Community and the Challenge of the Future* (London, 1989), 207 ff.
7. Sharp, 'Community', 203.
8. See Ian Davidson, *Jobs and the Rhineland Model*, a Federal Trust report (London, 1998).
9. European Commission, *Growth, Competitiveness, Employment: The Challenges and Ways Forward into the 21st Century*, White Paper (Luxembourg, 1994).
10. Nigel Haigh and Konrad von Moltke, 'The European Community: An Environmental Force', *EPA Journal* (Washington, DC, July/Aug. 1990), 60.
11. Decision 93/389, *Official Journal of the European Communities*, L167, 9 July 1993. See also Nigel Haigh, 'Climate Change Policies and Politics in the European Community', in T. O'Riordan and J. Jäger (eds.), *Politics of Climate Change: A European Perspective* (London and New York, 1996), 166–8.

Chapter 7: From Monetary System to Single Currency

1. Tommaso Padoa-Schioppa, *Financial and Monetary Integration in Europe: 1990, 1992 and Beyond* (Group of Thirty, New York and London, 1990), 18.
2. Comité Intergouvernemental créé par la Conférence de Messine, *Rapport des Chefs de Délégation aux Ministres des Affaires Étrangères*, the Spaak Report (Brussels, 21 Apr. 1956), 74. For the part played by Triffin

and Uri, see Pierre Uri, 'Réflexion sur l'approche fonctionnaliste de Jean Monnet et suggestions pour l'avenir', in Giandomenico Majone, Emile Noël, and Peter Van den Bossche (eds.), *Jean Monnet et l'Europe d'aujourd'hui* (Baden-Baden, 1989), 76.

3. Robert Triffin, 'Note sur ma collaboration avec Jean Monnet', in *Témoignages à la mémoire de Jean Monnet* (Fondation Jean Monnet pour l'Europe and Centre de Recherches Européennes, Lausanne, 1989), 531.
4. For Triffin's proposals during that period on monetary reform, see his *Europe and the Money Muddle: From Bilateralism to Near-Convertibility, 1947–1956* (New Haven, Conn., 1957), 287–94; and his *Gold and the Dollar Crisis: The Future of Convertibility* (New Haven, Conn., 1961), 131–44.
5. *Action Committee for the United States of Europe: Statements and Declarations 1955–67* (London, 1969), 46, 60–2; and Triffin, 'Note', 531.
6. Robert Marjolin, *Le Travail d'une vie: Mémoires 1911–1986* (Paris, 1986), 312; Commission of the EEC, *Action Programme of the Community for the Second Stage* (Brussels, 1962). The development of monetary integration up to the mid-1970s is recounted in Loukas Tsoukalis, *The Politics and Economics of European Monetary Integration* (London, 1977).
7. See Triffin, *Gold and the Dollar Crisis*; Robert Mundell, 'A Theory of Optimum Currency Areas', *American Economic Review* (Sept. 1961); R. I. McKinnon, 'Optimum Currency Areas', American Economic Review (Sept. 1963).
8. Commission of the EEC, *Eighth General Report* (Brussels, 1965).
9. Tsoukalis, *Politics and Economics*, 72.
10. Jean Monnet, *Memoirs*, trans. Richard Mayne (London 1978), 194–5.
11. Tsoukalis, *Politics and Economics*, 88–9.
12. Herman Wortmann and Florent Bonn, 'Theorie und Praxis der Währungsunion in Europa', in R. Regul and H. Wolff (eds.), *Das Bankwesen im grösseren Europa* (Baden-Baden, 1963), cited in Tsoukalis, *Politics and Economics*, 36; Max Corden, 'The Adjustment Problem', in L. B. Krause and W. S. Salant (eds.), *European Monetary Unification and its Meaning for the United States* (Washington, DC, 1973); Giovanni Magnifico, *European Monetary Unification* (London, 1973); Peter Oppenheimer, 'The Problem of Monetary Union', in D. Evans (ed.) *Britain in the EEC* (London, 1973). Compare also with the literature on divergence, for example Michael Hodges and William Wallace (eds.), *Economic Divergence in the European Community* (London, 1981).
13. Giovanni Magnifico and John Williamson, *European Monetary Integration*, Federal Trust Study Group Report (London, 1972).
14. Commission of the EC, *Report on European Union*, Supplement to Bulletin of the European Communities, 5 (1975).

15. Commission of the EC, *Economic and Monetary Union: The Economic Rationale and Design of the System* (Brussels, 20 Mar. 1990), para. IV. 1. 3; speech by John Major, Chancellor of the Exchequer, 20 June 1990; Article 109f/117ECT.
16. Roy Jenkins, *European Diary: 1977–1981* (London, 1989), 22. For a complete account of the establishment of the EMS, see Peter Ludlow, *The Making of the European Monetary System* (London, 1982).
17. Jenkins, *European Diary*, 22–3.
18. Roy Jenkins, *Europe's Present Challenge and Future Opportunity*, First Jean Monnet Lecture (European University Institute, Florence, 1977), cited in Ludlow, *Making of the EMS*, 47–9.
19. Jenkins, *European Diary*, 197, 223–4.
20. Helmut Schmidt, Preface to Jean Monnet, *Erinnerungen eines Europäers* (Munich, 1978); Jenkins, *European Diary*, 286.
21. Ludlow, *Making of the EMS*, 76; Jenkins, *European Diary*, 137.
22. *The Times*, 11 July 1978, cited in Ludlow, *Making of the EMS*, 112–13.
23. Ludlow, *Making of the EMS*, 220.
24. Jenkins, *European Diary*, 353.
25. Commission of the EC, 'Benefits and Costs of Economic and Monetary Union', annex to Commission, *Economic and Monetary Union*; Michael J. Artis and Mark P. Taylor, 'Exchange Rates, Interest Rates, Capital Controls and the European Monetary System: Assessing the Track Record', in Francesco Giavazzi, Stefano Micossi, and Marcus Miller (eds.), *The European Monetary System* (Cambridge, 1988), 188, 202; and Emil-Maria Claasen and Eric Perée, 'Discussion' following Artis and Taylor, ibid., 209.
26. J. Godeaux, 'The Working of the EMS: A Personal Assessment', in Committee for the Study of Economic and Monetary Union, *Report on Economic and Monetary Union in the European Community*, the Delors report (Luxembourg, 1989), 192.
27. Case 203/80, Casati (1981) ECR 2595, cited in Pieter VerLoren van Themaat, 'The Contributions to the Establishment of the Internal Market by the Case-Law of the Court of Justice of the European Communities', 112, 121.
28. Paolo Cecchini with Michael Catinat and Alexis Jacquemin, *The European Challenge 1992: The Benefits of a Single Market* (Aldershot, 1988), 37–42, 84, 95.
29. Padoa-Schioppa, *Financial and Monetary Integration*, 19.
30. See n. 26 above.
31. Padoa-Schioppa, *Financial and Monetary Integration*, 22.
32. Commission, *Economic and Monetary Union*, para. II. 2.
33. Karl Otto Pöhl, 'The Further Development of the European Monetary

System', in Delors report (see n. 26 above), 129–55.

34. Maurice F. Doyle, 'Regional Policy and European Economic Integration', and J. Delors, 'Regional Implications of Economic and Monetary Integration', in Delors report, 61–79, 81–9.
35. Michael Emerson, Daniel Gros, Alexander Italiener, Jean Pisani-Ferry, Horst Reichenbach, *One Market, One Money: An Evaluation of the Potential Benefits and Costs of Forming an Economic and Monetary Union* (Oxford, 1992), 68.
36. 'Luxembourg European Council, Conclusions of the Presidency', *Bulletin of the European Union*, 12/1997.
37. Expositions of the two respective cases, as far as British participation is concerned, are to be found in Christopher Johnson, *In With the Euro, Out With the Pound: The Single Currency for Britain* (Harmondsworth, 1996), and John Redwood, *Our Currency, Our Country: The Dangers of Monetary Union* (Harmondsworth, 1997).

Chapter 8: European Budget and Public Finance Union

1. David Coombes with Ilka Wiebecke, *The Power of the Purse in the European Communities* (London, 1972), 10.
2. Jean Monnet, *Les États-Unis d'Europe ont commencé: Discours et allocutions 1952–1954* (Paris, 1955), 57–8.
3. Commission of the EC, *Report of the Study on the Role of Public Finance in European Integration*, the MacDougall report (Brussels, 1977), ii. 483; Dieter Biehl, 'A Federalist Budgetary Strategy for European Union', *Policy Studies* (Oct. 1985), 67; D. Biehl, 'The Public Finances of the Union', in Andrew Duff, Roy Price, and John Pinder (eds.), *Maastricht and Beyond: Building the European Union* (London and New York, 1994).
4. Miriam Camps, *European Unification in the Sixties: From the Veto to the Crisis* (New York, 1966), 38 ff.
5. See Coombes, *Power of the Purse*, and Helen Wallace, *Budgetary Politics: The Finances of the European Communities* (London, 1980).
6. Commission of the EC, *Rapport du groupe ad hoc pour l'examen du problème de l'accroissement des compétences du parlement européen*, the Vedel report (Brussels, 1972).
7. B. M. Key, 'The Exercise by the European Parliament of its Power of Discharge', in R. Hrbek, J. Jamar, and W. Wessels (eds.), *The European Parliament on the Eve of the Second Direct Election: Balance Sheet and Prospects* (Bruges, 1984), 788.
8. The MacDougall report (see n. 3) included two annexes in vol. ii on the

subject of fiscal federalism: Wallace E. Oates, 'Fiscal Federalism in Theory and Practice: Applications to the European Community'; Francesco Forte, 'Principles for the Assignment of Public Economic Functions in a Setting of Multilayer Government'..

9. MacDougall report, i. 16; Oates, 'Fiscal Federalism', 296.
10. MacDougall report, i. 20; Commission of the EC, 'Stable Money—Sound Finances: Community Public Finance in the Perspective of EMU', *European Economy*, 53 (Brussels, 1993), 6–7, 55.
11. MacDougall report, i. 17.
12. An economic analysis of the British budget question is given in Geoffrey Denton, *The British Budget Problem and the Future of the EEC Budget* (London, 1982). Accounts from participants include Sir Michael Butler, *Europe: More than a Continent* (London, 1986), ch. 7; Roy Jenkins, *European Diary: 1977–1981* (London, 1989), *passim.*
13. Marcus H. Miller, 'Estimates of the Static Balance-of-Payments and Welfare Costs Compared', and John Pinder 'What Membership Means for Britain', in John Pinder (ed.), *The Economics of Europe: What the Common Market Means for Britain* (London, 1971), 120, 147, 13.
14. *The United Kingdom and the European Communities*, Cmnd 4715 (London, July 1971), 25.
15. J. Ørstrøm Møller, 'Budgetary Imbalances', *Journal of European Integration*, 2–3 (1985), 128.
16. J. Delors, 'Regional Implications of Economic and Monetary Integration', in *Report on Economic and Monetary Union in the European Community*, the Delors report (Luxembourg, 1989), 88; Commission of the EC, *Report of the Study Group on the Role of Public Finance in European Integration*, the MacDougall report (Brussels, 1977), i. 32–3; Commission of the EC, 'Stable Money—Sound Finances'.
17. Commission of the EC, *Making a Success of the Single Act*, COM (87) 100, and *Report by the Commission to the Council and the Parliament on the Financing of the Community Budget*, COM (87) 101 (Brussels, 1987); Michael Shackleton, *Financing the European Community* (London, 1990), gives a full account of this decision and of subsequent events relating to the EC budget.
18. Commission, 'Stable Money—Sound Finances', 6–7, 55.
19. Shackleton, *Financing*, 30–1.
20. European Commission White Paper, *Growth, Competitiveness, Employment: The Challenges and the Ways Forward into the 21st Century* (Luxembourg, 1994), 33, 97.
21. European Commission, *From the Single Act to Maastricht and Beyond: The Means to Match our Ambitions*, COM (92) 2000 (Brussels, 11 Feb. 1992).

22. 'Edinburgh European Council 11–12 December 1992, Conclusions of the Presidency', *Bulletin of the European Communities*, 12/1992.
23. Commission of the EC, Communication from the Commission to the Council, *A Community Strategy to Limit Carbon Dioxide Emissions and to Improve Energy Efficiency*, SEC(91) 1744 final (Brussels, Oct. 1991).
24. Commission, 'Stable Money—Sound Finances'.
25. Ibid., 6–7, 55.
26. Delors, 'Regional Implications'.
27. *Report on Economic and Monetary Union in the European Community*, the Delors report (Luxembourg, 1989).
28. Commission, 'Stable Money—Sound Finances', 62–8.
29. M. Albert and J. Ball, *Towards European Economic Recovery in the 1980s* (European Parliament, 31 Aug 1983), ch. 5, para. 31.
30. Commission of the EC, *Economic and Monetary Union: The Economic Rationale and Design of the System* (Brussels, 20 Mar. 1990), para. IV. 2.2.
31. Commission, *Growth, Competitiveness, Employment* (see n. 20).
32. Biehl, 'A Federalist Budgetary Strategy', 71.
33. Commission of the EC, *Efficiency, Stability and Equity: A Strategy for the Evolution of the Economic System of the European Community*, the Padoa-Schioppa report (Brussels, 1987), 137–41.
34. European Commission, 'Agenda 2000: For a stronger and wider Union', Document drawn up on the basis of COM(97)2000 final, *Bulletin of the European Communities*, Supplement 9/97, 69.
35. Ibid., 61–76.
36. Ibid., 67.
37. Ibid.
38. Commission, 'Stable Money—Sound Finances', 115.
39. Biehl, 'A Federalist Budgetary Strategy', 66.

Chapter 9: From Common Tariff to Great Civilian Power

1. See John Pinder, 'Integrating Divergent Economies: The Extra-national Method', in Michael Hodges and William Wallace (eds.), *Economic Divergence in the European Community* (London, 1981), 194–5.
2. Miriam Camps, *Britain and the European Community 1955–1963* (London, 1964) 24, 32.
3. Comité Intergouvernemental créé par la Conférence de Messine, *Rapport des Chefs de Délégation aux Ministres des Affaires Étrangères*, the Spaak Report (Brussels, 21 Apr. 1956) 21–2, 30–1.
4. Cited in Murray Forsyth, *Unions of States: The Theory and Practice of Confederation* (Leicester, 1981), 162.

5. Bela Balassa, *The Theory of Economic Integration* (London, 1961), ch. 2. The original work on this subject was Jacob Viner, *The Customs Union Issue* (New York, 1950).
6. Michael Davenport, 'The Economic Impact of the EEC', in Andrea Boltho (ed.), *The European Economy: Growth and Crisis* (London, 1982), 227.
7. *Action Committee for the United States of Europe: Statements and Declarations 1955–67* (London, 1969), 62–5.
8. David Coombes, *Politics and Bureaucracy in the European Community: A Portrait of the Commission of the E.E.C.* (London, 1970), ch. 8.
9. Bela Balassa, *Trade Liberalization among Industrial Countries: Objectives and Alternatives* (New York, 1967), 122.
10. Lawrence B. Krause, *European Economic Integration and the United States* (Washington, DC, 1968), 224–5.
11. François Duchêne, 'Europe's Role in World Peace', in Richard Mayne (ed.), *Europe Tomorrow: Sixteen Europeans Look Ahead* (London, 1972), 43.
12. Gunnar Myrdal, *An International Economy: Problems and Prospects* (London, 1956), ch. 4.
13. Tommaso Padoa-Schioppa, *Financial and Monetary Integration in Europe: 1990, 1992 and Beyond* (Group of Thirty, New York and London, 1990), 28.
14. Camps, *Britain and the European Community*, 65.
15. Glenda Goldstone Rosenthal, *The Men Behind the Decisions: Cases in European Policy-Making* (Lexington, Mass., 1975), ch. 3.
16. Victoria Curzon, *The Essentials of Economic Integration: Lessons of EFTA Experience* (London, 1974), 303.
17. European Commission, 'Agenda 2000: For a stronger and wider Union', Document drawn up on the basis of COM(97)2000 final, *Bulletin of the European Union*, Supplement 9/97.
18. Jean Monnet, *Memoirs*, trans. Richard Mayne (London, 1978), 343.
19. 'Report of the Ministers of Foreign Affairs of the Member States on the Problems of Political Unification', the Davignon report, *Bulletin of the European Communities*, 11 (1970).
20. Wilhelm Späth, 'Die Arbeit des EPZ-Sekretariats: Eine Bilanz', *Europa-Archiv*, 6 (1990), 213–20.
21. Alfred Pijpers, Elfriede Regelsberger, and Wolfgang Wessels, 'A Common Foreign Policy for Western Europe?', in Pijpers, Regelsberger, and Wessels, with Geoffrey Edwards (eds.), *European Political Cooperation in the 1980s* (Dordrecht, 1988), 271–2.
22. *European Union*, Report by Mr Leo Tindemans to the European Council, *Supplement to Bulletin of the European Communities*, 1 (1976).

23. See Geoffrey Edwards and Simon Nuttall, 'Common Foreign and Security Policy', in Andrew Duff, John Pinder, and Roy Price (eds.), *Maastricht and Beyond: Building the European Union* (London, 1994), 84–103, and Andrew Duff, *The Treaty of Amsterdam: Text and Commentary* (London, 1997), 111–28.
24. Helmut Schmidt, 'Deutsch-französische Zusammenarbeit in der Sicherheitspolitik', *Europa-Archiv*, 11 (1987).
25. Jean Monnet, *Les États-Unis d'Europe ont commencé: Discours et allocutions 1952–1954* (Paris, 1955), 127–8.

Chapter 10: The Building of the Union

1. See Leon N. Lindberg and Stuart A. Scheingold, *Europe's Would-Be Polity: Patterns of Change in the European Community* (Englewood Cliffs, NJ, 1970), 7.
2. Ibid., ch. 9, citation from p. 285.
3. Press Conference, 15 May 1962.
4. Miriam Camps, *Britain and the European Community* 1955–1963 (London, 1964), 360.
5. *The United Kingdom and the Europe an Communities*, Cmnd 4715 (London, July 1971), 8.
6. Speech delivered in Bruges on 20 Sept. 1988.
7. John Major, 'Raise Your Eyes, There is a Land Beyond', *The Economist* (25 Sept. 1993), 27.
8. Robert O. Keohane and Joseph S. Nye, *Power and Interdependence: World Politics in Transition* (Boston, 1977), 240.
9. Stephen D. Krasner, 'Structural Causes and Regime Consequences: Regimes as Intervening Variables', in Krasner (ed.), *International Regimes* (Ithaca, 1983), 2.
10. Andrew Moravcsik, 'Preferences and Power in the European Community: A Liberal Intergovernmentalist Approach', *Journal of Common Market Studies* (Dec. 1993), 480, 507.
11. See John Pinder, 'European Community and Nation-State: A Case for a Neo-Federalism?', *International Affairs* (Jan. 1986) ; 'The New European Federalism: The Idea and the Achievements', in Michael Burgess and Alain-G. Gagnon (eds.), *Comparative Federalism and Federaton: Competing Traditions and Future Directions* (Hemel Hempstead, 1993).

Select Bibliography

The sources are listed in seven groups, corresponding to chapters in this book or to groups of chapters with related subjects: general and institutional (Chapters 1, 2, 10); enlargement and external relations (3, 9); single market, open frontiers (4); agriculture (5); employment, environmental, industrial, and social policies (6); money (7); budget (8).

General and institutional

Action Committee for the United States of Europe: Statements and Declarations 1955–67, Chatham House and PEP Joint European Series No. 9 (London, 1969).

Bieber, Roland, Jacqué, Jean-Paul, and Weiler, Joseph H. H. (eds.), *An Ever Closer Union: A Critical Analysis of the Draft Treaty Establishing the European Union*, The European Perspectives Series (Commission of the EC, Luxembourg, 1985).

Butler, Sir Michael, *Europe: More than a Continent* (London, 1986).

Camps, Miriam, *European Unification in the Sixties: From the Veto to the Crisis* (New York, 1966).

Charlton, Michael, *The Price of Victory* (London, 1983).

Coombes, David, *Politics and Bureaucracy in the European Community: A Portrait of the Commission of the E.E.C.* (London, 1970).

Corbett, Richard, Jacobs, Francis, and Shackleton, Michael, *The European Parliament*, 3rd edn. (London, 1995).

Dehousse, Renaud, *Europe: The Impossible Status Quo* (Basingstoke, 1997).

Duff, Andrew, *The Treaty of Amsterdam: Text and Commentary* (London, 1997).

—, Pinder, John, and Pryce, Roy (eds.), *Maastricht and Beyond: Building the European Union* (London, 1994).

Edwards, Geoffrey, and Spence, David, *The European Commission* (London, 1994).

Grant, Charles, *Delors: Inside the House that Jacques Built* (London, 1994).

Haas, Ernst B., *The Uniting of Europe: Political, Social and Economical Forces 1950–1957* (London, 1958).

Hartley, T. C., *The Foundations of European Community Law*, 3rd edn. (Oxford, 1994).

Hayes-Renshaw, Fiona, and Wallace, Helen, *The Council of Ministers* (Basingstoke, 1997).

Lindberg, Leon N., *The Political Dynamics of European Economic Integration* (Stanford, Calif., 1963).

—and Scheingold, Stuart A., *Europe's Would-be Polity: Patterns of Change in the European Community* (Englewood Cliffs, NJ, 1970).

Lodge, Juliet (ed.), *The European Community and the Challenge of the Future*, 2nd edn. (London, 1993).

Milward, Alan S., *The European Rescue of the Nation-State* (London, 1992).

Monnet, Jean, *Memoirs*, trans. Richard Mayne (London, 1978).

Moravcsik, Andrew, 'Preferences and Power in the European Community: A Liberal Intergovernmentalist Approach', *Journal of Common Market Studies* (Dec. 1993).

Padoa-Schioppa, Tommaso, *Efficiency, Stability, and Equity* (Oxford, 1987).

Nugent, Neill, *The Government and Politics of the European Union*, 3rd edn. (Basingstoke, 1994).

Pelkmans, Jacques, *European Integration: Methods and Economic Analysis* (Harlow, 1997).

Pinder, John, 'Positive Integration and Negative Integration: Some Problems of Economic Union in the EEC', *The World Today* (Jan. 1968).

—'European Community and Nation-State: A Case for a Neo-Federalism?', *International Affairs* (Jan. 1986).

Pryce, Roy (ed.), *The Dynamics of European Union* (Beckenham and New York, 1987).

Scharpf, F. W., 'The Joint-Decision Trap: Lessons from German Federalism and European Integration', *Public Administration* 66/3 (1988).

—*Negative and Positive Integration in the Political Economy of European Welfare States*, Jean Monnet Chair Papers, European University Institute (Florence, 1995).

Tsoukalis, Loukas, *The New European Economy Revisited*, 3rd edn. (Oxford, 1997).

Wallace, Helen, and Wallace, William, *Policy-Making in the European Union*, 3rd edn. (Oxford, 1996).

Weiler, J. H. H., 'The Transformation of Europe', *Yale Law Journal* (June 1991).

Westlake, Martin, *A Modern Guide to the European Parliament*, 3rd edn. (London, 1995).

Enlargement, external relations

Camps, Miriam, *Britain and the European Community 1955–1963* (London, 1964).

European Commission, *Preparation of the Associated Countries of Central and Eastern Europe for Integration into the Internal Market of the Union*, White Paper, COM (95) 163 (Brussels, May 1995).

—'Agenda 2000: For a stronger and wider Union', *Bulletin of the European Union*, Supplement 5/97, 1997.

Edwards, Geoffrey, and Nuttall, Simon, 'Common Foreign and Security Policy', in Duff, Andrew, Pinder, John, and Pryce, Roy (eds.), *Maastricht and Beyond: Building the European Union* (London, 1994).

Hine, R. C., *The Political Economy of European Trade: An Introduction to the Trade Policies of the EEC* (Brighton, 1985).

HMSO, White Paper, *The United Kingdom and the European Communities*, Cmnd 4715 (London, 1971).

Kitzinger, Uwe, *Diplomacy and Persuasion: How Britain Joined the Common Market* (London, 1973).

Nicholson, Francis, and East, Roger, *From the Six to the Twelve: The Enlargement of the European Communities* (Harlow, 1987).

Nuttall, Simon, *European Political Co-operation* (Oxford, 1992).

Pinder, John (ed.), *The Economics of Europe: What the Common Market Means for Britain* (London, 1971).

—*The European Community and Eastern Europe* (London, 1991).

Redmond, John (ed.), *Prospective Europeans: New Members for the European Union* (Hemel Hempstead, 1994).

Reinhardt Rummel (ed.), *Toward Political Union: Planning a Common Foreign and Security Policy in the European Community* (Boulder, 1992).

Tsoukalis, Loukas, *The European Community and its Mediterranean Enlargement* (London, 1981).

Wallace, Helen (ed.), *The Wider Western Europe: Reshaping the EC/EFTA Relationship* (London, 1991).

Single market, open frontiers

Bieber, Roland, Dehousse, Renaud, Pinder, John, and Weiler, Joseph H. H. (eds.), *1992: One European Market? A Critical Analysis of the Commission's Internal Market Strategy* (Baden-Baden, 1988).

Bieber, Roland, and Monar, Jörg (eds.), *Justice and Home Affairs in the European Union: The development of the Third Pillar* (Brussels, 1995).

Cecchini, Paolo, with Catinat, Michael, and Jacquemin, Alexis, *The*

European Challenge 1992: The Benefits of a Single Market (Aldershot, 1988).

Cockfield, Lord, *The European Union: Creating the Single Market* (Chichester, 1994).

Commission of the European Communities, *Completing the Internal Market*, White Paper from the Commission to the Council (Luxembourg, 1985).

Pelkmans, Jacques, *European Integration: Methods and Economic Analysis*, Part 2 (Harlow, 1997).

—, and Winters, Alan, *Europe's Domestic Market* (London, 1998).

Sutherland, Peter, et al., High Level Group on the Operation of the Internal Market, *The Internal Market after 1992: Meeting the Challenge* (Luxembourg, 1992).

Agriculture

Biehl, Dieter, et al., *Common Agricultural Policy, European Integration and International Division of Labour* (Bonn, 1987).

Butler, Fiona, 'The EC's Common Agricultural Policy', in Lodge (ed.), *European Community* (1993).

Commission of the European Communities, *Mémorandum sur la réforme de l'agriculture dans la Communauté Économique Européenne: Agriculture 1980*, COM (68) 1000 (Brussels, 21 Dec. 1968).

—*see also* European Commission.

Duchêne, François, Szczepanik, Edward, and Legg, Wilfred, *New Limits on Agriculture* (Beckenham, 1985).

European Commission, 'Agenda 2000: For a stronger and wider Union', *Bulletin of the European Union*, Supplement 5/97, 1997.

—*see also* Commission of the European Communities.

Franklin, Michael, *Rich Man's Farming: The Crisis in Agriculture* (London, 1988).

Neville-Rolfe, Edmund, *The Politics of Agriculture in the European Community* (London, 1984).

Ockenden, Jonathan, and Franklin, Michael, *European Agriculture: Making the CAP Fit the Future* (London, 1995).

Rieger, Elmar, 'The Common Agricultural Policy', in Wallace, Helen, and Wallace, William (eds.), *Policy-Making in the European Union*, 3rd edn. (Oxford, 1996).

Tracy, Michael, *Government and Agriculture in Western Europe 1880–1988* (London and New York, 1989).

—'Agricultural Policy and European Integration', in John Davis and Peter

Mathias (eds.), *The Nature of Industrialisation*, v (Oxford, 1990).

Employment, environmental, industrial, and social policies

Allen, David, 'Competition Policy', in Wallace, Helen, and Wallace, William, *Policy-Making in the European Union* (Oxford, 1996).

Bangemann, Martin, *Meeting the Global Challenge: Establishing a Successful European Industrial Policy* (London, 1992).

European Commission, *Growth, Competitiveness, Employment: The challenges and ways forward into the 21st century*, White Paper (Luxembourg, 1994).

Sharp, Margaret, 'The Community and New Technologies', in Lodge (ed.), *European Community* (1993).

Smith, Alasdair, and Tsoukalis, Loukas (eds.) *The Impact of Community Policies on Economic and Social Cohesion* (Bruges, 1997).

Swann, Dennis, *Competition and Industrial Policy in the European Community* (London, 1983).

Verhoeve, B., Bennett, G., and Wilkinson, D., *Maastricht and the Environment* (London, 1992).

Woolcock, Stephen, *The Single European Market: Centralization or Competition among National Rules?* (London, 1994).

Money

Commission of the European Communities, *One Market, One Money, European Economy*, No. 44, Sept. 1990. *See also* Emerson et al., below.

Committee for the Study of Economic and Monetary Union, *Report on Economic and Monetary Union in the European Community*, the Delors report (Luxembourg, 1989).

Delors report, *see preceding entry*.

De Grauwe, Paul, *The Economics of Monetary Integration* (Oxford, 1992).

Emerson, Michael, and Huhne, Christopher, *The Ecu Report* (London, 1991).

Emerson, Michael, et al., *One Market, One Money: An Evaluation of the Potential Benefits and Costs of Forming an Economic and Monetary Union* (Oxford, 1992). *See also* Commission of the EC, above.

European Commission, *Convergence Report 1998* (Brussels, 25 March 1998).

European Monetary Institute, *European Monetary Institute Report 1998* (Frankfurt, 25 March 1998).

Giavazzi, Francesco, Micossi, Stefano, and Miller, Marcus (eds.), *The European Monetary System* (Cambridge, 1988).

Gros, David, and Thygesen, Niels, *European Monetary Integration: From the European Monetary System to European Monetary Union* (London, 1992).

Johnson, Christopher, *In With the Euro, Out With the Pound: The Single Currency for Britain* (Harmondsworth, 1996).

Kenen, Peter B., *Economic and Monetary Union in Europe: Moving Beyond Maastricht* (Cambridge, 1995).

Ludlow, Peter, *The Making of the European Monetary System* (London, 1982).

Magnifico, Giovanni, *European Monetary Unification* (London, 1973).

Padoa-Schioppa, Tommaso, *Financial and Monetary Integration in Europe: 1990, 1992 and Beyond* (Group of Thirty, New York and London, 1990).

—*The Road to Monetary Union in Europe: The Emperor, the King, and the Genies* (Oxford, 1994).

Redwood, John, *Our Currency, Our Country: The Dangers of Monetary Union* (Harmondsworth, 1997).

Werner report, *Report to the Council and the Commission on the Realisation by Stages of Economic and Monetary Union in the Community*, Supplement to Bulletin of the European Communities 11 (1970).

Budget

Iain Begg, *Financing the European Union* (Sheffield, 1998).

Biehl, Dieter, 'The Public Finances of the Union', in Duff, Andrew, Pinder, John, and Pryce, Roy, *Maastricht and Beyond: Building the European Union* (London, 1994).

Commission of the European Communities, *Report of the Study Group on the Role of Public Finance in European Integration*, the MacDougall report (Brussels, 1977).

—*Making a Success of the Single Act: A New Frontier for Europe*, COM (87) 100 (Brussels, 1987).

—*Report to the Council and Parliament on the Financing of the Community Budget*, COM (87) 101 (Brussels, 1987).

—*From the Single Act to Maastricht and Beyond: The Means to Match our Ambitions*, COM (92) 2000 (Brussels, 1992).

—'Stable Money—Sound Finances: Community Public Finance in the Perspective of EMU', *European Economy*, 53 (Brussels, 1993).

—*see also* European Commission.

Coombes, David, with Wiebecke, Ilke, *The Power of the Purse in the European Communities* (London, 1972).
Denton, Geoffrey, *The British Budget Problem and the Future of the EEC Budget* (London, 1982).
European Commission, 'Agenda 2000: For a stronger and wider Union', *Bulletin of the European Union*, Supplement 5/97, 1997.
Laffan, Brigid, and Shackleton, Michael, 'The Budget', in Wallace, Helen, and Wallace, William (eds.), *Policy-Making in the European Union* (Oxford, 1996).
MacDougall report, *see* Commission of the EC (1977), *above*.
Shackleton, Michael, *Financing the European Community* (London, 1990).
Wallace, Helen, *Budgetary Politics: The Finances of the European Communities* (London, 1980).

Index

A Very Short Introduction

CLASSICS

Mary Beard and John Henderson

This *Very Short Introduction* to Classics links a haunting temple on a lonely mountainside to the glory of ancient Greece and the grandeur of Rome, and to Classics within modern culture—from Jefferson and Byron to Asterix and Ben-Hur.

'This little book should be in the hands of every student, and every tourist to the lands of the ancient world . . . a splendid piece of work'
Peter Wiseman
Author of *Talking to Virgil*

'an eminently readable and useful guide to many of the modern debates enlivening the field . . . the most up-to-date and accessible introduction available'
Edith Hall
Author of *Inventing the Barbarian*

'lively and up-to-date . . . it shows classics as a living enterprise, not a warehouse of relics'
New Statesman and Society

'nobody could fail to be informed and entertained—the accent of the book is provocative and stimulating'
Times Literary Supplement

A Very Short Introduction

POLITICS

Kenneth Minogue

Since politics is both complex and controversial it is easy to miss the wood for the trees. In this Very Short Introduction Kenneth Minogue has brought the many dimensions of politics into a single focus: he discusses both the everyday grind of democracy and the attraction of grand ideals such as freedom and justice.

'Kenneth Minogue is a very lively stylist who does not distort difficult ideas.'
Maurice Cranston

'a dazzling but unpretentious display of great scholarship and humane reflection'
Professor Neil O'Sullivan, University of Hull

'Minogue is an admirable choice for showing us the nuts and bolts of the subject.'
Nicholas Lezard, *Guardian*

'This is a fascinating book which sketches, in a very short space, one view of the nature of politics . . . the reader is challenged, provoked and stimulated by Minogue's trenchant views.'
Talking Politics

A Very Short Introduction

ARCHAEOLOGY

Paul Bahn

'Archaeology starts, really, at the point when the first recognizable 'artefacts' appear—on current evidence, that was in East Africa about 2.5 million years ago—and stretches right up to the present day. What you threw in the garbage yesterday, no matter how useless, disgusting, or potentially embarrassing, has now become part of the recent archaeological record.'

This Very Short Introduction reflects the enduring popularity of archaeology—a subject which appeals as a pastime, career, and academic discipline, encompasses the whole globe, and surveys 2.5 million years. From deserts to jungles, from deep caves to mountain-tops, from pebble tools to satellite photographs, from excavation to abstract theory, archaeology interacts with nearly every other discipline in its attempts to reconstruct the past.

'very lively indeed and remarkably perceptive . . . a quite brilliant and level-headed look at the curious world of archaeology'
Professor Barry Cunliffe,
University of Oxford

A Very Short Introduction

BUDDHISM

Damien Keown

'Karma can be either good or bad. Buddhists speak of good karma as "merit", and much effort is expended in acquiring it. Some picture it as a kind of spiritual capital—like money in a bank account—whereby credit is built up as the deposit on a heavenly rebirth.'

This Very Short Introduction introduces the reader both to the teachings of the Buddha and to the integration of Buddhism into daily life. What are the distinctive features of Buddhism? Who was the Buddha, and what are his teachings? How has Buddhist thought developed over the centuries, and how can contemporary dilemmas be faced from a Buddhist perspective?

'Damien Keown's book is a readable and wonderfully lucid introduction to one of mankind's most beautiful, profound, and compelling systems of wisdom. The rise of the East makes understanding and learning from Buddhism, a living doctrine, more urgent than ever before. Keown's impressive powers of explanation help us to come to terms with a vital contemporary reality.'
Bryan Appleyard

A Very Short Introduction

JUDAISM

Norman Solomon

'Norman Solomon has achieved the near impossible with his enlightened very short introduction to Judaism. Since it is well known that Judaism is almost impossible to summarize, and that there are as many different opinions about Jewish matters as there are Jews, this is a small masterpiece in its success in representing various shades of Jewish opinion, often mutually contradictory. Solomon also manages to keep the reader engaged, never patronizes, assumes little knowledge but a keen mind, and takes us through Jewish life and history with such gusto that one feels enlivened, rather than exhausted, at the end.'
Rabbi Julia Neuberger

'This book will serve a very useful purpose indeed. I'll use it myself to discuss, to teach, agree with, and disagree with, in the Jewish manner!'
Rabbi Lionel Blue

'A magnificent achievement. Dr Solomon's treatment, fresh, very readable, witty and stimulating, will delight everyone interested in religion in the modern world.'
Dr Louis Jacobs, University of Lancaster

THE OXFORD AUTHORS

General Editor: Frank Kermode

THE OXFORD AUTHORS is a series of authoritative editions of major English writers. Aimed at both students and general readers, each volume contains a generous selection of the best writings—poetry, prose, and letters—to give the essence of a writer's work and thinking. All the texts are complemented by essential notes, an introduction, chronology, and suggestions for further reading.

Matthew Arnold
William Blake
Lord Byron
John Clare
Samuel Taylor Coleridge
John Donne
John Dryden
Ralph Waldo Emerson
Thomas Hardy
George Herbert and Henry Vaughan
Gerard Manley Hopkins
Samuel Johnson
Ben Jonson
John Keats
Andrew Marvell
John Milton
Alexander Pope
Sir Philip Sidney
Oscar Wilde
William Wordsworth

THE OXFORD AUTHORS

SAMUEL TAYLOR COLERIDGE

Edited by H. J. Jackson

Samuel Taylor Coleridge, poet, critic, and radical thinker, exerted an enormous influence over contemporaries as different as Wordsworth, Southey, and Lamb. He was also a dedicated reformer, and set out to use his reputation as a public speaker and literary philosopher to change the course of English thought.

This collection represents the best of Coleridge's poetry from every period of his life, particularly his prolific early years, which produced *The Rime of the Ancient Mariner*, *Christabel*, and *Kubla Khan*. The central section of the book is devoted to his most significant critical work, *Biographia Literaria*, and reproduces it in full. It provides a vital background for both the poetry section which precedes it and for the shorter prose works which follow.

THE OXFORD AUTHORS

JOHN DRYDEN

Edited by Keith Walker

Keith Walker's selection from the extensive works of Dryden admirably supports the perception that he was the leading writer of his day. In his brisk, illuminating introduction, Dr Walker draws attention to the links between the cultural and political context in which Dryden was writing and the works he produced.

The major poetry and prose works appear in full, and special emphasis has been placed on Dryden's classical translations, his safest means of expression as a Catholic in the London of William of Orange. His versions of Homer, Horace, and Ovid are reproduced in full. There are also substantial selections from his Virgil, Juvenal, and other classical writers.

THE OXFORD AUTHORS

SAMUEL JOHNSON

Edited by Donald Greene

Samuel Johnson the 'personality' is well known to most readers—perhaps too well known, for, as Edmund Wilson wrote, 'That Johnson really was one of the best English writers of his time, that he deserved his great reputation, is a fact that we are likely to lose sight of.' This volume tries to correct this state of affairs by providing a selection from Johnson's manifold writings that includes not only his more familiar pieces, but a substantial sampling of less well-known prose dealing with political, historical, legal, theological, even bibliographical matters, and of his shorter poetry, letters and journals. In it the reader will find not only a superb mastery of the English language, but, as Johnson said of Bacon, 'the observations of a strong mind operating on life'.

THE OXFORD AUTHORS

JOHN KEATS

Edited by Elizabeth Cook

This volume contains a full selection of Keats's poetry and prose works including *Endymion* in its entirety, the Odes, 'Lamia', and both versions of 'Hyperion'. The poetry is presented in order of composition illustrating the staggering speed with which Keats's work matured. Further valuable insight into his creative process is given by reproducing, in their original form, a number of poems that were not published in his lifetime. A large proportion of the prose section is devoted to Keats's letters, considered among the most remarkable ever written. They provide not only the best biographical detail available, but are also invaluable in shedding light on his poetry.

THE OXFORD AUTHORS

JOHN MILTON

Edited by Stephen Orgel and Jonathan Goldberg

Milton's influence on English poetry and criticism has been incalculable, and his best-known works, *Paradise Lost, Paradise Regained*, and *Samson Agonistes* form a natural mainstay for this freshly edited and modernized selection of his writings. All the English and Italian verse, and most of the Latin and Greek, is included, as is a generous selection of his major prose works. The poems are arranged in order of publication, essential in enabling the reader to understand the progress of Milton's career in relation to the political and religious upheavals of his time.